D1625255

MAR 2 2 2005

**Carnegie
Library of
Pittsburgh**

**Main**

WITHDRAWN
FROM THE COLLECTION
CARNEGIE LIBRARY OF PITTSBURGH

| CLP-Main | |

# That Toddlin' Town

Music in American Life

*A list of books in the series appears at the end of this book.*

ML3518.S46 2004
Sengstock, Charles A.
That toddlin' town :
Chicago's white dance bands
and orchestras, 1900-1950
Urbana : University of
Illinois Press, c2004.

# THAT TODDLIN' TOWN

Chicago's White Dance Bands
and Orchestras, 1900–1950

**Charles A. Sengstock Jr.**

University of Illinois Press
Urbana and Chicago

© 2004 by the Board of Trustees
of the University of Illinois
All rights reserved
Manufactured in the United States of America
C 5 4 3 2 1

♾ This book is printed on acid-free paper.

Library of Congress Cataloging-in-Publication Data
Sengstock, Charles A.
That toddlin' town : Chicago's white dance bands and
orchestras, 1900–1950 / Charles A. Sengstock Jr.
p.   cm.
Includes bibliographical references (p. ) and index.
ISBN 0–252–02954–2 (cloth : alk. paper)
1. Big bands—Illinois—Chicago.
2. Chicago (Ill.)—Social life and customs—20th century.
I. Title.
ML3518.S46     2004
784.4'8'097731109041—dc22     2004009184

*For Norma, Laura, and Chuck*

*In memory of John F. Steiner,*
*my friend and mentor*
*for over forty years*

# Contents

*Illustrations follow page 96*

# Preface

THIS book was never intended to be a book at all.

I had an intense interest in music as a youngster and led a small dance combo around Chicago in the late 1940s and early 1950s. Dance bands were still big during that time and I made many visits to the Melody Mill, Oh Henry, and Paradise Ballrooms and to that Mount Olympus of all grand ballrooms, the Aragon. By 1948, however, my focus changed to the traditional jazz music then making a big comeback. Following my university graduation I began working in commercial broadcasting, first at WSOY in Decatur, Illinois, where I had a half-hour Dixieland jazz show, and later at the venerable and powerful WGN in Chicago, which by then also operated WGN television.

The veteran WGN radio announcer Pierre Andre, so closely identified with the station's early remote broadcasts of band performances and such network programs as *Little Orphan Annie,* was still a member of the staff and used to intrigue me with tales about the many bands he announced for at the Blackhawk, the Congress Hotel, and dozens of other Chicago locations. That again sparked my interest in the dance bands, but I wasn't quite ready to give up my jazz focus. It was then that the noted Chicago jazz historian, record collector, and producer Dr. John F. Steiner invited me to join him in reviewing the microfilm files of the *Chicago Defender* to identify and record events surrounding the development of early jazz music on the city's South Side.

The *Chicago Defender* was one of the earliest (it began publishing in 1905) and most influential newspapers serving the black population not only in Chicago but also in many other parts of the country. Its coverage of news on the South Side bore witness to the beginnings of jazz in the city between 1910 and 1930. I quickly noticed the close relationship between the jazz bands and the many commercial dance bands, both black and white, a connection that was also identified by some of the early jazz chroniclers in the late 1930s. Many jazz musicians had to work in the commercial bands to make ends meet, which resulted in a dramatic cross-fertilization of influences and ideas.

At the time of our research I was employed by the Armour Research Foundation (a part of Illinois Institute of Technology), which conveniently had offices at Thirty-fifth and South State Streets, one of the two or three most famous street intersections in early Chicago jazz history. When Steiner and I were not interviewing some of the old jazz musicians, I spent my spare time photographing those buildings still standing from the jazz years.

By the time Steiner and I completed our survey I had become more intrigued with the dance bands, particularly Chicago's white dance bands, than I was with the developing jazz scene on the South Side. The idea of exploring the white Chicago bands in more detail intrigued me. Steiner was a walking encyclopedia of information on this topic so he was able to mentor me in that area of my musical education. I sensed that Chicago bands had played a significant role in the development of the whole dance band industry in the late twenties and during the next two decades, and I wanted to learn more. This I was able to do, ironically, during a five-year residency in Arizona. I soon discovered that several veteran Chicago dance-band leaders and musicians were then living there in retirement. Over time I became acquainted with some of them and began to interview them and develop files on the early Chicago bands and how they were interrelated.

Upon my return to Chicago in 1973 I continued to build my contacts with many of the city's dance-band leaders and musicians who had worked in the bands of the 1920s through the 1950s. My files grew thicker with each interview and conversation and eventually formed the heart of this book. Steiner shared with me additional interviews with white bandleaders and musicians he had conducted and provided me with his insights and with information from his vast and overflowing files. With a growing understanding of this information, I began writing articles on both jazz and the Chicago dance bands for various local and special-interest publications.

Unlike jazz music, which has been chronicled and carefully analyzed by numerous authors beginning in the late 1930s, dance bands didn't become the sole focus of books until the late 1960s, nearly forty years after the era began. The dance bands didn't seem to draw that much attention. The first book was Leo Walker's *Great Dance Bands* (1962). That was followed by George T. Simon's *The Big Bands* (1967). Simon had been the editor-in-chief of *Metronome* magazine and, in a later book, *Simon Says* (1971), he drew heavily on his own writing from the magazine in the thirties and forties.

Other authors followed with books in the 1970s but most of these looked at dance bands in general, with little emphasis on the white Chicago bands specifically other than some of the well-known bands of the 1920s, such as Isham Jones and the Benson Orchestra of Chicago. Some interesting and fresh insights into the Chicago dance band scene were presented, ironically, in two books on the development of jazz music. William Howland Kenney's

*Chicago Jazz: A Cultural History, 1904–1930* (1993) in little more than a score of pages distilled the essence of Chicago's 1920s dance halls and dance bands as they related to jazz music. Richard Sudhalter's extensive study *Lost Chords: White Musicians and Their Contribution to Jazz, 1915–1945* (1999) discussed many white Chicago dance band musicians and leaders with some attention to the dance venues in connection with his main thesis.

Two other books of significance, Dan E. Moldea's *Dark Victory* (1986) and Dennis McDougal's *The Last Mogul: Wasserman, MCA, and the Hidden History of Hollywood* (1998), detailed the history of MCA, the entertainment behemoth. Also of some interest is an incomplete, unpublished manuscript on the early days of MCA by the late Karl Kramer, a retired MCA vice president, which is part of the John Steiner Collection at the University of Chicago Library. The bibliography of the present book lists these works as well as a number of fine biographical and autobiographical books and articles on several bandleaders and musicians.

A word about the terminology I use in this book is in order. For variety, I use the words "orchestra" and "band" interchangeably, although technically they are different. An orchestra generally is a musical organization containing largely string instruments as well as woodwinds, some percussion, and occasionally some brass. A band most often is a musical organization made up of brass , saxophones and other reed instruments, and percussion instruments, but no strings. To confuse things further, many dance bands had strings, and many dance bands without strings called themselves dance orchestras. The line between the terms became blurred over time from improper usage not only by observers of the musical scene but by those working in the business.

Much of the information appearing in the following pages comes from many personal interviews with musicians and leaders, my review of contemporary publications, and my own experience as a musician and an observer of the musical scene in Chicago. I have chosen to organize the information in a straightforward manner. For example, the chapters on the venues that feature dance bands are organized by type of establishment, that is, ballrooms, hotels, cabarets and nightclubs, and theaters. Maps showing the location of the most important dance venues appear in appendix A. Appendix B is a listing of the important Chicago dance venues and many of the dance bands that played in them.

Readers will find that a few of the citations in the endnotes and bibliography lack page numbers. These occasional omissions resulted from some early research (primarily in the *Chicago Defender,* a few early Chicago dailies, and *Down Beat*) not originally intended for publication in book form. Also, some of the *Chicago Tribune* citations show only the date of an article; page numbers were often not included in the clippings in the *Chicago Tribune* archives, which I had access to more than twenty years ago as a former employee.

My focus on the white Chicago dance bands, where they played, and the entrepreneurs who helped create and shape the new dance band industry is somewhat new among observers of that scene. I hope the information in this book will serve as a basis for further research and will stimulate others to explore more deeply the social and cultural history of this rich field.

# Acknowledgments

WITHOUT the help and assistance of many people, this book would not have been possible. Several people in particular were encouraging and helpful in this effort: Dr. John Steiner; Joseph L. Kayser; Don Roth; Ruth Marion Tobias and her husband, Burt Tobias; and Charles Walton. Sadly, Dr. Steiner, Joe Kayser, Don Roth, and Burt Tobias did not live to see this book published.

John Steiner, a friend and collaborator for more than forty years and also a widely recognized jazz and Chicago music history expert, was a guide through the shoals of interpreting history. He graciously shared with me his thoughts and much information from his files on the Chicago music scene and made many helpful suggestions.

Joe Kayser was a fount of information on Chicago popular music between 1923 and the 1960s. As a popular Chicago bandleader in the twenties and, later, a successful booking agent, he had a nearly photographic memory for dates and places that was incredibly helpful. His son, Joseph R. Kayser, another friend and supporter, also grew up in the dance band business as a band manager. He was also helpful in providing photos and information.

Burt and Ruth Tobias shared their encyclopedic knowledge of the Chicago jobbing bands. Ruth, a vocalist and bass player, worked with Lew Diamond, Bud Dinwiddie, Joe Vera, Don McGrane, Benny Strong, and scores more. She is a board member of the Chicago Federation of Musicians. Burt, a teacher and one of the finest trumpet players in town, played in several road bands, had lengthy engagements in the Oriental Theater orchestra and at the Chez Paree, and later spent eighteen years with Lou Breese.

Don Roth, who later owned and managed the Blackhawk Restaurant his father opened in 1920, was extremely generous with his time and offered important insight into what became a Chicago institution. In addition, Joan Zimmermann of the Don Roth Restaurants, Inc., took an early interest in this project and has generously assisted me.

I am grateful also to Charles Walton, a retired musician, teacher, bandmaster, board member of the Chicago Federation of Musicians, and historian, who kindly guided me through the South Side musical scene of the 1940s and

1950s. He is chronicling through personal interviews the history leading up to the merger of the two Chicago music union locals in 1966.

I thank all of these individuals and the scores of others who so generously gave of their time and information during the preparation of this book. In particular, I owe gratitude to Andrew Karzas, the former owner of the Aragon Ballroom, and the bandleaders Dick Sarlo, Ray Pearl, and H. T. Lega, the latter of whom led the Teddy Lee band for more than thirty years. I received invaluable help from the late Jules Herbuveaux, a popular 1920s bandleader, radio producer, and finally vice president–Midwest for NBC, who largely influenced the creation of the so-called "Chicago School of television" and whose family has graciously given me permission to use several photos and much information.

Personnel at several libraries and local historical societies should be recognized for their enormous help in gathering materials, many of them scarce. Thanks to the now-retired Elaine Stenzel and her excellent staff of reference librarians at the Northbrook Public Library, in Northbrook, Illinois, for acquiring books and articles from practically all points of the compass; to Judy Hughes of the Northbrook Historical Society; and to Fred Huscher of the Morton Grove Historical Society. I am grateful too for assistance from Chicago-area community historical societies in Glenview, Homewood, and Niles, and to Deborah Gust, researcher at the Curt Teich Archives of the Lake County (Illinois) Discovery Museum.

Deborah Gillaspie, curator of the John Steiner Collection, Chicago Jazz Archive, at the University of Chicago Library, deserves a nod of thanks, too, for making available resources from that wonderful collection. Two people at the Music Research Information Center, Harold Washington Library in Chicago, have been helpful and supportive through the years: Richard Schwegel, now retired head of the center, and his successor, Christopher Popa. Also my gratitude goes to Tim Samuelson, Cultural Historian for the City of Chicago Department of Cultural Affairs, who can answer almost any questions on the city's history.

Special acknowledgements go to Larry Gushee and George O'Hare. Gushee, a retired professor of music at the University of Illinois and a jazz historian, provided information on the bandleader Bert Kelly, which he acquired with the assistance of Jean-Christopher Averty and Albert R. Kelly Jr. He also has been a constant source of information on people and places. George O'Hare, a retired retailing executive and successful motivational speaker, kindly provided information on his uncle, the bandleader Anderson "Husk" O'Hare.

To many musicians, bandleaders, and others who assisted me, I extend my gratitude for their time and information. Many of my meetings with these individuals have evolved into friendships, which I cherish. Thanks go to Charlie Agnew, Robert Baird, Ardeth Maupin Ball, Eddie Ballantine, Nanette Herbuveaux Barber, Tony Barron, Memo Bernabei, Gay Claridge, Gary Cohen, Harry Cool, Harvey Crawford, Paul Crum, Joe Cupita, Fred Edmiston, Charles Elgar, Larry Faith, Ted FioRito, Tom Fitzsimmons, Chuck Foster, Larry Fotine, Jan Garber, Lon Gault, Don Glasser, Conrad Good, Charles A. Guse, Norbert "Louie" and Dorothy Henderson, Ray Herbeck, Tom Hilliard, Phil Holdman, Jeanne Carlsen Hrico, Ione Kassel, Joseph R. Kayser, Warren Ketter, Warren Kime, Bob Kirk, Norm Krone, Billy Leach, Ray Lee, Clarence Lejcar, Andy and Phil Lincoln, Guy Lombardo, Freddy Martin, Frankie Masters, Dick Parker, Dick Polk, Andy Powell, Don Ragon, George Rank, Bill and Ruth Reinhardt, Ray Robbins, Larry Rodger, Ernie Rudy, Carl Schreiber, Buddy Shiffman, Koby Sirinski, Fred C. Smith, Bill Snyder, Al Trace, Orrin Tucker, Art VanDamme, Rudy and Eddie Verderbar, Bruce Vermazen, Tom Weiss, Ed Ward, Patricia Verderbar Williams, Richard Williams, George Winslow, and Frank York. My thanks too to the staffs of WBBM and WGN.

Finally, my gratitude goes to Judith McCulloh, executive editor and assistant director of the University of Illinois Press; to Carol Bolton Betts, my editor; and to all the staff at the Press for their patience, understanding, and support during our journey to publication.

## Special Photograph Credits

I thank the following people who provided photos that appear in this book and who, in the interest of brevity, could not be credited in the captions. The copy of the original photo of Jules Herbuveaux and the NBC Orchestra is from Mrs. Thomas Barber, Mr. Herbuveaux's daughter. The copy of the original photo of the exterior of Rainbo Garden is from the John Steiner Collection, Chicago Jazz Archive, University of Chicago Library. The copy of the original photograph of the Ben Bernie Orchestra is from Conrad Good. A special thank-you to David R. Phillips, Chicago Architectural Photographing Company, for his assistance.

That Toddlin' Town

# Introduction

ON an October weekend in 1952, staff members at the popular Blackhawk Restaurant in Chicago's Loop removed the bandstand and dance floor, ending the restaurant's reign as one of the nation's premier bastions of big band music. It was a painful moment for the owner, Don Roth, whose father, Otto, had hired the restaurant's first regular dance band—the Coon-Sanders Nighthawks—in 1926, but the dance band era had ended and Roth knew it. The following Monday when he reopened the restaurant, food once again was the centerpiece, as it had been when the Blackhawk first opened its doors in 1920, only this time it was served from giant silver beef trolleys and spinning salad bowls.

The path of the Blackhawk in many ways symbolized the era of dance bands in Chicago. It began its dancing policy in September 1926, about six years after the dance bands began attracting attention, and brought it to a quiet close about the time many bands were calling it quits.[1] In the intervening years, dance bands had become the glamorous vanguard of the popular music business in Chicago and the nation, a business that embraced nightclub show bands, theater pit and stage bands, ballroom bands, and those musical organizations playing in the city's numerous radio and, later, television studios. The love affair that Chicago—and America—had with dance bands lasted only a little over thirty-five years, the blink of an eye in history, but nationally the bands became a $145 million–plus enterprise and provided work for thousands of musicians.[2] The bands also provided a measure of fascination and delight in the lives of millions of dancers, spectators, and radio listeners.

This book is about the white Chicago dance bands, the venues they played, and their important early role in the business of big bands. It is also about the entrepreneurs, innovators, and leaders who created and shaped the development of the dance band business. The story of Chicago's black commercial dance bands and the interrelationships between them and the jazz musicians from New Orleans and elsewhere is an exciting one but it is not reprised here. It has been recounted numerous times by many excellent jazz scholars and authors who have comprehensively documented the bands' personnel, chronologies, and elements of style. Any further discussion would be redundant.

Until recently the history of the white Chicago dance bands has been largely left untold. Although much has been written about U.S. dance bands in general, there has been little concentration on the commercial white dance orchestras in Chicago beyond the Benson Orchestra of Chicago, Isham Jones, the Coon-Sanders Nighthawks, and a few others. That is ironic because many of the 1920s white Chicago dance bands became the nationally popular bands of the 1930s and, to a lesser degree, of the 1940s. Recently, however, quite a few recordings of 1920s white Chicago dance bands have been reissued, many of which contain superb liner notes. As I noted in the preface, several fine books have been published in the past decade or two that have begun to shine a welcome spotlight on the white Chicago bands.

The modern dance bands in Chicago first appeared on the scene after 1900 but their roots probably go back to the pianists and small groups that accompanied dancers in the rough taverns and early concert saloons of the late 1800s. These rustic dance venues, according to social historians, gave rise to the modern dance halls that began springing up in Chicago in the early 1910s.[3] By the 1920s, more-refined social dancing had become extremely popular in public and socially respectable venues like hotels and restaurants. In fact it became a fad.

Vernon and Irene Castle, Maurice and Walton, and a few other popular touring dance teams heightened America's growing interest in ballroom-style dancing as they whirled and stepped their way across U.S. and European stages and dance floors. The Castles were especially popular in the United States between 1913 and 1915.[4] Their elegance of motion and rhythm opened up a new world to an American public for whom dancing mostly had been a stiff, overly formal, and sometimes awkward social experience or a series of ritualistic ethnic folk dances. Irene Castle's costumes alone set the fashion for women in the United States and on the Continent.

The Castles' smart new dance steps opened up the possibilities of dancing to popular music of the day. On a whirlwind tour of the United States in 1914 with a stop in Chicago, the duo traveled with two excellent black musical orchestras, one led by Ford Dabney and the other by James Reese Europe. Europe later led the famous U.S. Army Hell Fighters military band during World War I.[5] Maurice and Walton and other dance teams also appeared on Chicago stages and in cabarets about this time, further sparking interest in ballroom dancing. It became a social pastime open to everyone, not just high society. After that, dancing no longer was limited to traditional waltzes or the two-step.

In Chicago several early dance halls were prospering in the pre–World

War I period and many new cabarets joined the dancing party. New dance orchestras were formed as proprietors scrambled to meet the growing demand for public dancing, but the development of social dancing in Chicago was not a smooth process. For years prior to the 1910s, much of the so-called social dancing had been in less-than-wholesome settings, often those where liquor was either served or available.[6] Many of these rough dance halls were hangouts for prostitutes. There followed years of reform efforts by courageous men and women who worked through social-improvement associations and organizations and collaborated with municipal authorities. By 1920, they succeeded in cleaning up a large part of what had become a pox on the community's morality.

The city during the 1910s and 1920s had become a thriving regional center for music publishing firms, record companies, and vaudeville booking agencies and the home of what later became a major symphony orchestra. Most of the downtown legitimate theaters had pit orchestras. Some large movie houses began combining variety acts with films, requiring pit orchestras to accompany the performers and to play for the silent films. The mid-1910s also was the time the cabaret movement hit Chicago. Social dancing was an integral part of the cabaret experience, and orchestras were employed to accompany the acts and, between shows, to play for the dancers. The cabaret idea spread rapidly in town and by 1920 there were several very large cabarets featuring elaborate floor shows and orchestras of up to ten or more pieces.

The roadhouse, often described as a cabaret in the suburbs or countryside, was an interesting outgrowth of the urban cabaret. Roadhouses had been around for years but became especially popular in the 1920s during Prohibition, when the sale and consumption of alcoholic beverages was illegal. Getting a drink of illicit booze was considerably easier at some roadhouses because their remote locations made them harder to police. At the same time, increased automobile ownership and the rapid construction of all-weather hard roads gave city residents greater mobility, and driving into the countryside in the summer to get an illegal drink became a popular pastime for many. Not all roadhouses sold illegal alcoholic beverages. Many establishments, especially the larger ones, enticed patrons with floor shows, popular dance bands, and occasionally some gambling.

Early radio probably was the biggest booster of dance bands. By late 1922, Chicago's early stations were putting dance bands on the air from several dance halls, restaurants, hotels, and cabarets. The publicity and promotional benefits the bands received through these early remote broadcasts made them celebrities. It was a two-way street, however, because the bands provided the stations with cheap program fare in the form of organized music during the formative years of radio. Station operators quickly learned to present more sophisticated programming, however, and by 1926 they began recruiting some of the city's dance bands to staff their studios and play for sponsored programs.

With this new demand for dance music, supplying musicians and dance bands became a thriving business. Thousands of musicians were employed by the end of the 1920s to play for Chicago dancers; another two thousand musicians played only in the city's theaters.[7] Hundreds more accompanied entertainers and played for dancing in clubs and hotel dining rooms. Contrast this to the musical scene prior to 1900. The few dance bands playing regularly in the 1890s and earlier catered mostly to the society crowd. But there were other audiences to be served. By the early 1900s Henry Erlinger, a pioneer Chicago bandleader, was one of the leaders hired for several of the infamous First Ward balls sponsored by the political bosses Michael "Hinky-Dink" Kenna and John "Bathhouse" Coughlin at the giant Coliseum on South Wabash.[8] Eli Courlander, another early dance-band leader in this period, headed the orchestra playing at the White City dance hall in 1906, one of the earliest in Chicago.[9]

Johnny Hand was the best known of the early Chicago orchestra leaders; he and his orchestra were favorites of local society by 1886. A German immigrant, Hand arrived in Chicago in 1851 and organized his first orchestra in 1869.[10] He quickly obtained jobs playing for prominent Chicagoans. His orchestra played at the elaborate seventeenth-birthday party for Marshall Field and in 1909 for a charity ball sponsored by Mrs. Potter Palmer, who was said to be one of Hand's biggest boosters.[11] Because of his prominence as society's favorite bandleader and because he was revered as a musical "Dutch uncle" to early Chicagoans, Hand developed quite a bit of clout with the movers and shakers of the city and state, who did him favors from time to time. When he died in 1916 he was accorded a lavish funeral with socially prominent admirers and musicians participating in the cortege to Graceland Cemetery.[12]

Hand's group was not the only musical organization that played for Chicago's moneyed class in the late nineteenth century. Billy Henderson, a black musician and bandleader, often furnished dance music for the Pullman and Armour families, both then living on Chicago's Near South Side.[13] There were other bands and orchestras at the time, but little is recorded about them in contemporary publications.

In the overall scheme of show business, the dance bands did not gain a respected role until the early twenties. Before that, bands and orchestras had played for dancing and had accompanied performers in the vaudeville, legitimate, and burlesque theaters and in the cabarets and cafés but were considered part of the background. Even worse, in those few early hotels that provided music for diners, the orchestras—usually string ensembles—often were hidden behind screens. It was a world where musicians entered by the back door and sometimes played behind potted palms. Unlike small children, they were to be heard but not seen.

Chicago was the stage upon which an entrepreneurial drama played out during the 1920s, which ultimately gave birth to the modern dance-band business. Edgar Benson, who was Chicago's leading provider of bands, orchestras, and floor-show acts until the early 1920s, had controlled the local popular music scene since 1900. He was overtaken and supplanted by Jules Stein and his new organization, known as the Music Corporation of America (MCA). Within four years Stein changed the balance of power in the Chicago music booking business through new thinking and ideas and aggressive marketing techniques that capitalized on the power of radio to promote the bands. MCA ultimately became one of the largest entertainment talent and production combines in the world, with receipts of $224 million a year by 1975.[14] Almost single-handedly it reinvented the band booking business and turned it into a major industry.

James C. Petrillo, president of Local 10 of the American Federation of Musicians, was a third important Chicago personality who played a pivotal role in the development of the modern dance band industry during the 1920s. A forceful and, when necessary, confrontational labor leader, Petrillo always tried to obtain the most work, the best working conditions, and the highest pay for his musicians, and he generally succeeded. His efforts on behalf of his union members helped shape the dance band business.

There were many influential early Chicago entrepreneurs who owned or operated the hotels, cabarets, dance halls, and theaters in which the bands and orchestras played. Many now unrecognized names such as Paddy Harmon, J. Louis Guyon, the Karzas brothers, Otto Roth, Al Tierney, Fred Mann, the Chamales brothers, Sam Hare, and Jack Huff played important roles in the development of the dance band business. They created the venues in which the bands played and helped shape both bands and their establishments into key entertainment attractions. A. J. Balaban showcased his movie-theater pit orchestras by putting them on the stage. In so doing he made stars out of nearly anonymous pit bandleaders. Paul Ash, his most famous celebrity-bandleader, quickly became a major show business phenomenon in 1920s Chicago.

While the Blackhawk Restaurant became one of the most sought-after venues in the nation among bandleaders, there were three other important Chicago entertainment spots that could propel a band to fame: the Aragon and Trianon ballrooms and the College Inn of the Sherman Hotel. The secret ingredient in the formula was the radio remote broadcast. The early Chicago cabarets and major downtown hotels such as the Palmer House, the Stevens, and the Morrison also had radio wires but they never developed a track record as hit-makers for dance bands as had the Blackhawk, Aragon, Trianon, and College Inn. Radio station WGN should share some of the credit for the success of the Blackhawk, Aragon, and Trianon as band builders. The remote broadcasts from those three establishments were piped through WGN, which literally blanketed the Midwest and more with its powerful clear-channel signal.[15] For building a dance band's reputation it was the best station in the nation. Coincidentally, the opening of the Trianon Ballroom on the South Side, the first of the modern ballrooms, and the first radio broadcasts in Chicago both occurred in 1922.

As the bands gained popularity in the ballrooms, hotel dining rooms, and on radio, they also were attractions on the vaudeville stage. Thus, Guy Lombardo in the late 1920s could move to the stage of the Palace Theater in Chicago's Loop based on his radio-generated popularity at the Granada Café and earn four thousand dollars a week.[16] The bands also were featured stage acts, not theater bands per se, and they were paid big money for those years. Stage appearances, especially in the late 1930s and early 1940s, often were tied to one or more of the bands' hit recordings.

The Hollywood movie studios looked with interest at the dance bands, their leaders, and their vocalists as potential movie stars by the early 1930s. Dorothy Lamour, then a Chicago vocalist, is perhaps the best example of a band vocalist in the city who succeeded in Hollywood. Many of the better-known bands associated with Chicago appeared in movies, including those of Ted FioRito and Guy Lombardo as well as Ben Bernie and Jan Garber. It was a glamorous time and dance bands had become a big business.

Ballrooms, cabarets, hotels, theaters, and radio stations all influenced the dance bands in some way. The string ensembles and other purveyors of dinner music in hotel dining rooms and restaurants learned the art of providing steady and proper dance tempos to an increasingly sophisticated dancing public. In the cabarets and hotel show rooms, dance bands acquired the skills of accompanying variety acts, a talent previously claimed mostly by the vaudeville and music-theater pit musicians. The dance-band leaders and musicians learned the secrets of showmanship and presentation from their stage band counterparts in the major downtown movie palaces, which added polish to the dance bands. The dance-band leaders, who formerly were unanimated in front of the bands, now understood the importance of being a lively personality and master of ceremonies. Radio taught musicians and leaders alike the discipline of playing against the clock and adapting to the quick changes in cues often necessary in commercial broadcasts in studio settings.

A key thrust of this book is to examine dance bands as a business. It is easy to dismiss dancing and dance music along with most areas of show business as being just entertainment. Audiences saw only the leaders, musicians, and vocalists; but behind all that talent were large, moneymaking enterprises that employed thousands of people and in turn gave business to other highly specialized support companies. The dance band business in its day was a giant economic system.

# 1 Edgar Benson and the Early Chicago Booking Agents

CHICAGO'S white dance bands rose to popularity on the wings of the social dancing craze of the 1910s and early 1920s. A decade later, they were in the vanguard of a growing nationwide business. Dance bands soon were the darlings of the entertainment world and by 1940 became a multimillion-dollar industry. Although organized into a viable and profitable Chicago business by 1920, the bands quickly were propelled to fame in the next five years by an infant technology called radio broadcasting. Radio and the dance bands became inseparable partners over the next twenty years in a relationship from which both profited handsomely. It probably would not have happened, however, without a set of circumstances and conditions that were unique to Chicago.

By the 1920s the city boasted a well-established and organized group of excellent dance bands, innumerable cabarets and dance halls in which to play, several strong musicians' unions, and a young but innovative broadcast industry.[1] Perhaps most important of all the circumstances that ensured Chicago's place as the cradle of the dance band business was the presence during the 1920s of three dynamic and competitive men. Two were inventive and enterprising booking entrepreneurs, Edgar Benson and Jules Stein. The third was James C. Petrillo, head of the Chicago Federation of Musicians, the local affiliate of the American Federation of Musicians and the largest of several musicians unions in the city.

Edgar Benson founded the Benson Organization, a pioneer booking agency, around the turn of the twentieth century and by 1910 had gained control of most of the dance band business in the city. By 1920 he was firmly entrenched as the largest booker of dance bands in Chicago, and he claimed his was the largest organization of its kind in the United States.[2] All his musical groups were known as "Benson Organizations"; to Benson the name of the group or the leader was secondary.

He was challenged in the 1920s by a forward-looking marketing wizard, Jules Stein, who had not only a clear vision of where the future of the business lay (he named his company Music Corporation of America) but the ability to make that vision a reality. Under Benson the dance band business had become static, but Stein reinvented it by using marketing and merchandising techniques and by recognizing the "brand value" of a bandleader's name and the promotional power of radio. He established a new and modern business model and changed significantly the landscape of the band booking business within a few years. In the process he completed the commercialization of the dance bands that had begun under Benson and set in motion the dynamics for a vibrant new industry.

## Edgar Benson, Chicago's First Dance Band Impresario

Playing dance music in Chicago at the beginning of the twentieth century was a cottage industry. Those musicians lucky enough to be employed in the pit bands of local vaudeville or legitimate theaters might find their work seasonal at best. Even classical musicians working in the Chicago Symphony at that time were not employed year round. For most musicians music was a sideline. They had commonplace day jobs and played in small musical groups at night. Many of the nighttime musical engagements were in the city's myriad tawdry, often disreputable taverns or early dance halls. There were few organized bands or orchestras of any size playing for dancing on a regular basis. Chicago's high society provided most of the dance work that was available for the larger orchestras. Because there wasn't an abundance of dance engagements, band leaders such as Johnny Hand, Billy Henderson, Henry Erlinger, and others who played for the city's socially elite probably handled their own bookings. With the exception of Hand, none would have had enough dance jobs to attract the attention of a vaudeville or legitimate theater booking agency. By then Hand had been a popular director for nearly half a century and had sewed up most of the city's society business.[3]

In the late 1890s, however, there came on the Chicago scene an ambitious young cellist from Missouri named Edgar Benson.[4] His small but popular dance combo eventually was offered more engagements around town than it could handle, so Benson began booking other orchestras and combos to fill them. To manage the increased business, he formed a small company, the Benson Organization, around 1897.

Benson astutely noted the new cabaret movement taking shape in town by the mid-1910s and the growing interest in public dancing. He moved quickly to provide talent for the floor shows and dance music in the downtown hotels and fine dining establishments. By 1922 he claimed to have "twenty of the very best vaudeville acts" and "all kinds of dancing acts" under his management.[5] With a growing catalog of both musical and variety-show talent, Benson over time worked out a clever business proposition to which the hotel and restaurant managers readily subscribed. He agreed to furnish music for dancing and talent for floor shows in return for the cover charges conventionally added to customers' tabs.[6]

Benson's complete music service saved those places that hired bands and acts the headache of dealing with two or more talent agencies. Best of all, the cost of talent didn't cut into the venues' normal profits. Using this formula Benson eventually was able to sign many of the large downtown hotels, cabarets, and restaurants to contracts for his services. Presenting floor shows in exchange for the cover charges became a standard practice in Chicago and elsewhere and was adopted by most talent bookers and show producers.[7]

Benson developed significant buying power in the cabaret-talent department by booking entire shows for his growing number of hotel and restaurant clients. His reach in procuring acts extended to all parts of the country. One of his biggest productions each year was the show he presented at the Marigold Gardens, on Chicago's North Side, in the late 1910s and early 1920s. The Marigold shows were among the county's top cabaret productions and were regularly reviewed by the entertainment trade press.

An advertisement in the 1922 program entitled *Marigold Gardens Benson Revue* boasted that the Benson organization had booked "five symphony orchestras, nine brass bands, thirty dance orchestras, six jazz bands, ten novelty orchestras," and "scores of instrumental soloists and vocalists." For the time it was quite an impressive array of musical attractions. Benson provided one-stop shopping for many convention managers and party planners of the day.

The following year Benson published a catalog that contained photographs of seventeen bands and orchestras in addition to the Benson Entertainers, listed about thirty-five leaders, and declared that he had a stable of five hundred musicians.[8] (See a partial listing of Benson bands and orchestras in appendix C.) The catalog went on to announce boldly, "The Benson musical units comprise the largest aggregation of musicians under one management in the world." This probably wasn't true because about this time the Meyer Davis organization, based in Washington, D.C., boasted of having 120 dance bands working at locations up and down the East Coast, from Maine to North Carolina; but who was checking?[9]

On any given night, Benson may have had at least twenty musical or entertainment groups engaged at regular venues around town and another thirty units playing for casual engagements or at private parties. On weekends, most of his five hundred musicians and entertainers probably were working. His insight and business acumen changed the way musical talent and bands were hired and booked. This new professional approach not only resulted in a lucrative business for Benson but also commercialized the dance bands. Benson provided steady, sometimes full-time work for a host of leaders and musicians for whom music previously had been a sideline. By 1915, he had cornered a large share of the dance band and cabaret business in downtown Chicago's most popular hotels, restaurants, and leading clubs and a big chunk of the society and casual engagements around town. By 1920 Benson dominated the popular music business in Chicago.

The Benson Orchestra of Chicago (BOC) was the agency's flagship musical organization and included nine of Benson's top musicians. The BOC was nationally known through popular early Victor recordings, made in the Camden, New Jersey, studios in 1920. Personnel on the earliest Benson recordings were Rick Adkins, trumpet; Guy Carey, trombone; Matty Amaturo, sax; Tommy Thatcher, sax; Joe Baum, violin; Joe Miller, banjo; Bill Foeste, string bass; Art Layfield, drums; and Roy Bargy, piano and director.

Over the next six years, the orchestra recorded more than one hundred sides for Victor, a large output for one musical organization. Roy Bargy and then Don Bestor were directors of the Benson Orchestra from 1920 to 1925. However, other Benson leaders such as Paul Biese, Ralph Williams, Frank Westphal, Walter Ford, and George Mallen are thought to have been directors on some of the Victor recording sessions. All together about thirty Benson musicians—always key men in his organization—participated during six years of Victor recordings.

The popular BOC records generated several key summer-long engagements for the orchestra at East Coast locations such as the Million-Dollar Pier in Atlantic City. Directing Benson's other popular Chicago orchestras in the late teens through the mid-twenties were Paul Biese, Isham Jones, Frank Westphal, Ralph Williams, Jack Chapman, and Charlie Straight. Bargy and Bestor also led other Benson units during this period. All these orchestras were additionally known as "Benson Organizations" even though Biese, Bargy, and Jones were in the prime of their careers by then and had achieved some independent stature among dancers and venue operators. Isham Jones was especially popular because of the many hit songs he composed and his popular Brunswick recordings.

Some of Benson's numerous other groups are practically unknown today except to record collectors and music historians, but they held some important Chicago location engagements in the 1910s and 1920s. Al Copeland and George Mallen led orchestras at the Arcadia Ballroom on the North Side; Irving Margraf for years led a string quintet in the main dining room of the Blackstone Hotel; and Walter Ford headed the show band at the Tent, an early North Side Chicago cabaret. Benson surprisingly also booked the talented black violinist Clarence Black and his orchestra on casual engagements.

Benson operated his organization as what today would be called a temporary employment agency, furnishing day labor or short-term help to clients. In Benson's case, it was *night* labor and the clients were hotels, cabarets, large downtown restaurants, and ballrooms where he might provide a band or entertainers for several weeks or for a whole season. He also supplied musical groups for companies and conventions or to private parties for casual or single performances.

Benson musicians received their weekly assignments every Monday morning in room 515 at the firm's twelfth-floor offices in the Garrick Theater building, 64 West Randoph Street. Here they would be given a job slip containing the date, time, mode of dress, and pay for each job assignment that week. Independent bandleaders had a similar though less formal ritual at the musicians union hall, located at 175 West Washington Street, where on Mondays they would pick musicians from those present for upcoming engagements. During the 1930s and early 1940s, a more informal version of that practice moved to the sidewalk at the corner of Randolph and Dearborn Streets.

Benson ran a fairly sophisticated business for the 1920s but it operated on 1910s technology. Telephones were just coming into fairly wide business use in that decade so most of his business probably was done by mail, via telegraph, and in person at his office. Benson could assemble on demand musical groups ranging from small combos to large concert orchestras from his stable of five hundred musicians. He paid all his musicians directly on a per-job basis, with the exception of a few key men and leaders who had performance contracts that assured them an agreed-upon income.

According to one bandleader and agent, Joe Kayser, Benson had a well-run, no-nonsense operation. Kayser had come to Chicago in 1912 with the St. Louis pianist Gene Rodemich. Rodemich played piano in the Walter Blaufus orchestra at the College Inn of the Sherman Hotel, and Kayser worked on casual engagements for the Benson Organization.[10] Tommy Thatcher, Benson's right-hand man, along with Ike Goldsmith and Lew Diamond—all musicians themselves—handled day-to-day booking and office operations. Kayser reported that George Hillman booked acts for the Benson office. But whether it was a band or an act, it remained a "Benson Organization."

Although the listings of bands and orchestras shown in the Benson Marigold program for 1922 and in the 1923 catalog were extensive and impressive, the same musicians might play in several different groups, depending on what jobs were available; only the name of the unit and the leader changed. Headliner bands such as the BOC and the orchestras of Isham Jones, Ralph Williams, Roy Bargy, Charlie Straight, and Paul Biese were exceptions and usually had steady personnel. But Benson was said to have made personnel changes even in some of these bands if he felt a particular group might be attracting unwelcome attention that would detract from its being a "Benson Organization."[11]

Because Benson had the most work and the best jobs in town, he also had the best musicians, according to Kayser. But if a Benson musician accepted other employment without permission, he was stricken from the roster and could find it difficult getting hired elsewhere. In the teens and early twenties, Benson was the booking czar of Chicago music. Following his example, most jobbing bands had a core group of "first call" musicians who were expected to be available for the leader's or booker's jobs. These musicians weren't free to accept other jobs unless their primary leader or booker didn't have work for them.

By 1925 Benson owned half interest in and was vice president of the Hearst Music Company. Thomas Quigley, formerly the company's U.S. general manager, was president of the firm.[12] Both Quigley and Jerome Levey owned interest in the other half of the company, and one of Benson's bandleaders, Ralph A. Foote, was secretary-treasurer of Hearst. The original Hearst firm, owned by Joseph X. Hearst, had gone bankrupt and Quigley gained title to the defunct firm's American property rights for ten thousand dollars in 1924.

Benson was criticized in the trade press for double dipping, or using his recording orchestras to play music published by his publishing firm. As a businessman, however, Benson probably was just hedging his bets, like many other publishers. It was not uncommon at that time for publishers to give gratuities or payoffs to important vaudeville performers or orchestra leaders to play and promote their songs.[13] Although not an admired practice, it was part of the business culture of the time and not unlike the so-called payola schemes used in later years. Some bandleaders, Isham Jones being one of the most prominent, also had interests in publishing firms. Jones owned an interest in Weil Publishing but also placed songs he wrote with other publishers. Many leaders in the late 1930s and 1940s owned their own publishing companies and shamelessly promoted their own tunes on their radio broadcasts.[14] The radio networks finally tried to put a stop to it.

Other Chicago bandleaders booked many of their own jobs. Al Turk's band for years was the regular attraction at the Princess Ballroom on Chicago's West Side but often played casual dates around the city and out of town. The black bandleaders Elgar, Oliver, and Cooke limited their bookings mostly to the city's South and West Sides in the 1920s, although Oliver did make at least two road trips in the Midwest booked by others and Elgar played long engagements in Milwaukee.

The bandleader Dave Peyton, a pillar of the South Side black music community, began booking bands out of his music store at 3109 South State Street as early as 1914.[15] By 1919, he had established a downtown office at 145 North Clark Street, where he continued to book band engagements, but he also began writing arrangements and special material for vaudeville performers Al Jolson, Eva Tanguay, and Joe Howard.

Booking bands and cabaret and vaudeville acts out of music stores was rather common in the teens and early 1920s.[16] Music publishers also functioned as informal booking offices because various bands and vaudeville singers often promoted the songs they published or sold. Joe Kayser said it was common practice in the teens and earlier for musicians and performers not aligned with a booking office to pick up casual jobs this way. As a young man passing through Chicago in 1906 or 1907, Kayser was booked as a soprano for the Haymarket Theater through the Will Rossiter Publishing Company in the Loop.[17]

There were other dance-band booking agencies in Chicago in the 1910s and 1920s, although none was as big or commanding as the Benson Organization. But the public's increased interest in ballroom-style dancing was providing more and more work for the city's budding dance bands. C. Cope Harvey operated one of them. Harvey is best known as the leader of dance bands at the White City Amusement Park, located at Sixty-third Street and South Parkway, and at the Merry Garden Ballroom on the South Side. Harvey's band became a mainstay at the White City's Casino between 1914 and the early twenties. Beginning in 1912 he also booked other bands on the South Side, which made him the city's second oldest (after Benson) orchestra-booking office.[18] Harvey entered the U.S. Army in 1917, during World War I. Because of his musical and administrative skills, he was given a commission and named officer-in-charge of the 132nd U.S. Army Division Infantry Band, which won numerous awards for its playing in Europe.

Harvey plunged back into the music business upon his release from the army in 1919 and significantly expanded his market. He began booking the bands of Al Lehmas, Barney Richards (later president of Chicago's Local 10 of the American Federation of Musicians), Chris Meldgard, Cal Callner, and others as well as several local concert groups. With this increased inventory of musical groups he proceeded to book engagements at downtown Chicago venues such as the Bismarck and Stevens hotels.

Bert Kelly was another early 1910s bandleader and booker in Chicago. A small operator by Benson's standards, Kelly booked several jazz-oriented dance combos of three to six pieces in downtown hotels such as the Congress, the Grand-Pacific, and the Fort Dearborn;[19] at the South Side's White City Casino; at Al Tierney's Auto Inn; and at the Green Mill Gardens at Lawrence and Broadway Avenues.[20]

Kelly had arrived in town in 1914 from San Francisco to accept a daytime promotion and publicity job but he soon found nighttime employment playing banjo in several clubs, including the Green Mill Gardens, then newly opened on the North Side. Before long he was leading his own quartet at the College Inn, playing for dancing between floor shows.[21]

Although Kelly's playing and booking career lasted only a few years, his College Inn group was credited in a trade publication article with introducing the jazz orchestra to Chicago.[22] Kelly's College Inn quartet began playing several months prior to the arrival in Chicago of Tom Brown's band, the first documented white group from New Orleans playing an early form of jazz.

Kelly also managed the House That Jack Built, near present-day Glenview, one of the earliest and biggest of the rural Cook County roadhouses.[23] It later became Villa Venice. In 1919 Kelly began operating the former Casino Gardens on North Clark Street, just north of the Chicago River, and changed the name to the Red Lantern. A few years earlier, the club had featured the Original Dixieland Jazz Band, which had gone on to fame in New York City. Kelly opened his namesake club, Bert Kelly's Stables, in 1921 on North Rush Street, also just north of the river, which quickly became a popular watering hole.[24] As he spent more time managing his business he became less active in booking bands. But Kelly left to the Chicago dance band business a double legacy, as an important booker and as a leader who was among the first to recognize the public's taste for jazz music.

Arnold Johnson was a Chicago-born piano accompanist for vaudeville acts, but by 1917 he was leading a band at the Green Mill Gardens. He recorded with Paul Biese and His Novelty Orchestra—Johnson, the saxophonist Paul Biese, and the banjoist Ralph Williams—for Columbia in New York in 1919 and was a member of the Frisco Jazz Band.[25] About this time Johnson also established a small booking agency with offices at 20 East Jackson Boulevard in downtown Chicago, from which he later booked bands for, among others, Green Mill Gardens and the Playdium (the former Driscoll's Danceland Ballroom) on the West Side.

During the 1920s Johnson took his band to Hollywood, Florida, for several winter seasons during the land boom there, always returning to Chicago in the spring.[26] He and his band again toured several vaudeville circuits in that decade. By the early 1930s Johnson left Chicago to settle in New York, where he had several bands working in such venues as the Park Lane and Paramount hotels. Johnson was never a major force in Chicago's band booking business, but his was one among many small-sized agencies on the music scene by the 1920s.

One of the most ambitious of the early Chicago bookers was a young promoter with the unusual name of "Husk" O'Hare. An alumnus of Austin High School on Chicago's West Side, O'Hare—whose given name was Anderson—had the drive and flair of a super salesman and promoter combined. He is said to have taken his membership examination for the musicians union playing the cymbals. This may be an apocryphal story, but it offers insight into his chutzpah.

O'Hare, who may have secretly wanted to emulate Edgar Benson and his enormous success in Chicago, began leading and booking bands by the late 1910s and had an office at 202 South State Street. Following service in World War I, he opened a new booking business with a partner, Sol Weisner, and moved into another office in the mid-1920s.[27] At one time or another in the twenties, the agency was said to have been booking more than twenty bands simultaneously (some say as many as forty-two during the summer season). O'Hare made his name known all over the city by numerous promotional schemes. His success was possibly helped along by the large flashing sign he rented atop the building in which he and Weisner had their offices, on Monroe Street near Wabash Avenue.

In addition to placing bands in many season-long summer resorts in Illinois and neighboring states, he also booked his groups into some of the city's neighborhood ballrooms. Husk O'Hare and His Own Band, led by O'Hare himself, enjoyed stays of up to three years at the LaSalle and Stevens (later Conrad Hilton) hotels. For a time, his was the house band at radio station WBBM. On his many radio remotes, his call was "Husk O'Hare, the Genial Gentleman of the Air."

With the exception of the hotel and radio studio jobs, O'Hare geared his music and musical aggregations to a young audience. Most of his musicians were themselves young (in their twenties) as opposed to the players in Benson's organization, who were thirty and older. Apparently using the Benson model, most of O'Hare's bands carried his name in some fashion (for example, Husk O'Hare's Campus Serenaders, Husk O'Hare's Footwarmers, and Husk O'Hare and His Greatest Band). Like Benson, O'Hare had his own stable of musicians, whom he would put together in varying combinations for any given job. Again like Benson's organization, his "A-list" musicians got the best jobs or played on extended engagements.

Husk O'Hare's Own Band, or simply Husk O'Hare and His Band, most frequently included Roy Weaver, William Linay, Carroll Webster, Cecil Reader, Art Groah, James Kirkwood, Ellis Bennett, Elsworth Garman, Don Gersman, and Ray Davis.[28] During the summers his many resort bands often were led by Hep Polson, Harry Miller, Elsworth Garman, or any number of his other musicians.

O'Hare was no stranger to the new music called jazz. He is said to have promoted the Friar's Society Orchestra's first recording date, at the Gennett Records studio in Richmond, Indiana, in 1921.[29] It was through that session that O'Hare reportedly incurred the enmity of the band members because he was credited as leader of the band on the first few records, which of course he was not. O'Hare in reality had only booked the sessions. The musicians, as a result, were said to have severed their connection with O'Hare immediately and changed the name of the band to the New Orleans Rhythm Kings (now sometimes referred to as NORK) on their remaining recordings.

Because of this incident, O'Hare later came to be seen by some Chicago jazz musicians as a self-serving hustler or promoter. He was called a "small-time booker" in one article describing the recording incident.[30] It was an inaccurate characterization, although it probably reflected the bias against him among some of the jazz fraternity of the 1920s and 1930s and their early chroniclers. As a leader and booker of very commercial bands, O'Hare naturally would have been the target of some scorn from the jazzmen as well as other side-men. It was the nature of the business. O'Hare had a fairly sizable booking office, working with more than twenty bands at the time MCA came on the scene. However, with the exception of WBBM, the LaSalle Hotel, and, later, the Stevens Hotel, where Husk's main band played, many of the jobs for his other bands were in second-tier venues in town and at summer locations in the Midwest.

O'Hare's brother George ran a club called the Castle Gardens in the Loop, an upstairs place just off State Street on Quincy during the 1920s, and Husk's band played there. For a time in about 1924, the pianist and jazz pioneer Jelly Roll Morton had a band there that played several nights a week, alternating with O'Hare's Four Aces.[31] It could have been one of Morton's road bands just prior to or following a tour, of which he did several a year between 1924 and 1928. O'Hare also may have been a link between the Gennett studios and Morton's recording session there in 1923, although it seems more likely that Melrose Brothers, Morton's Chicago publisher, was the catalyst to Morton's recording in Richmond.[32] Joseph "King" Oliver's jazz band, so popular on the city's South Side at Lincoln Gardens in 1922 and 1923, had a second job on Friday afternoons at Castle Gardens.[33] O'Hare is said to have been the person bringing the Oliver band to the attention of Gennett Records, which recorded the band in Richmond in early 1923. Husk and his brother George also ran another downtown club, the Bali, and for a time operated Husk O'Hare's Coconut Grove, a large roadhouse in north suburban Morton Grove. There is some irony in the fact that, while O'Hare's bands were mostly commercial, his recordings are listed not in the dance band discographies but in the jazz discographies.

Among all of the major vaudeville booking offices in Chicago during the 1920s, only Ernie Young and a group known as the Society Entertainers seemed to see any future in booking dance bands, even though the bands were beginning to assume a bigger role in cabarets and hotels. Even Young's interest in bands was secondary to his main interest in producing and mounting shows. One can only assume the vaudeville agencies were busy enough booking their acts into the numerous theaters through the Midwest and/or saw the band business as no more than a local enterprise.

Failing to recognize a budding business or trend, let alone a new industry, is a common oversight by many firms well established in their own businesses. The case history files of the country's graduate business schools are filled with such examples. Edgar Benson did the reverse; he began booking vaudeville acts after he had established his band booking business, recognizing the opportunity for providing complete floor shows to hotels and upscale restaurants.

Benson was an astute businessman for the time, creating from literally nothing a thriving dance-band booking business. He invented the business model that led to the commercialization of dance bands in Chicago and throughout the United States. At first he simply booked organized dance combos to fill jobs he had procured, but soon he put together a roster of competent musicians of known ability whom he could assemble in various combinations to meet a customer's need. His organization office became a shopping center for music and variety acts of all kinds, from dance halls and hotel dine-and-dance venues to conventions to private parties. Over the years he also assembled a cadre of capable administrators, many of whom were musicians by night, to help run his business during the day. It was a well-oiled machine.

Benson recognized rather early the importance of recordings especially to his flagship group, the Benson Orchestra of Chicago. The BOC Victor records became his best advertising vehicle and spread his name to all areas of the country, particularly the East Coast, which resulted in numerous out-of-town engagements for the orchestra. He intuitively knew the value of what marketers later called backward integration, which he tried to implement through his connection with the Hearst Music Company by using his record company connections to sell tunes in the Hearst catalog, as the previously noted trade publication articles suggested.

Although Benson seemed to understand the promotional value of recordings, he appeared to overlook the potential of radio broadcasting, especially where a few of his bandleaders—Isham Jones, Roy Bargy, and Paul Biese— were concerned. This may have been an issue in the series of disputes that occurred later between Benson and his leaders. Much of the later trouble also may have stemmed from Benson's autocratic management style. His style may have been a key to his original success, but it became a liability as the environment changed.

The 1920s was a decade of startling changes: new prosperity, new technologies, new music, and a new social awareness especially among young people. It would take a totally new mind-set and a sharpened sense of the changing world to appreciate where the dance band business was headed, and two men who had those qualities—Jules C. Stein and James C. Petrillo—emerged on the Chicago dance band scene. They would not only challenge Edgar Benson but also reinvent the dance band business.

# 2 Jules Stein and James Petrillo

TWO of the most powerful men in the music business, Jules Caesar Stein and James Caesar Petrillo, emerged from rough-and-tumble 1920s Chicago. They both were tough minded and they both wielded enormous power in their lifetimes, but they presented themselves in totally different ways. Jules Stein was a medical doctor who was quiet, reserved, dignified, and diplomatic. The company he founded became the largest entertainment conglomerate in the country. James Petrillo, a man of little formal education, was brash, outspoken, and often confrontational. He ultimately became president of the American Federation of Musicians (AFM). Though remarkably different personalities and with different agendas, the two worked tirelessly to represent their respective constituencies and in so doing helped to turn a budding dance business into a giant and lucrative industry.

Jules Stein was the genius behind the Music Corporation of America (MCA), which redefined the dance-band booking business. He literally transformed what had been a mostly local type of business providing a variety of musical groups for hire by the night or the week into a nationwide, later international industry. Stein above all was a creative and strategic thinker. He quickly recognized the value of the bandleader's name as a brand name and the promotional power of the new medium called radio broadcasting. He used radio along with modern marketing, merchandising, and promotional techniques to sell the bands' services, which was a dramatic new approach. This was the "push" in the MCA-conceived marketing cycle; to establish the "pull," Stein sought out and signed up hotels, ballrooms, and other locations throughout the Midwest and beyond that hired dance bands, in the process becoming their exclusive band provider. Very soon he had under contract some of the most important ballroom and hotel owners and managers, who were buying his dance bands.

Stein not only broke Edgar Benson's domination of the local Chicago dance band and music market in the process; he also outwitted Benson and other smaller, local band bookers who were still doing business on the old 1910s model, and he eventually drove Benson out of town. While accomplishing all this, Stein brought a refined and tempered style of doing business to an industry more associated with hyperbole and drum-beating exploitation.[1]

Jules Stein was a young Chicago ophthalmologist, but he couldn't make up his mind whether he wanted to be an eye doctor or run a promising band-booking agency. As a student at the University of Chicago and Rush Medical College, he had played saxophone and violin in small orchestras during the 1910s.[2] After college he also began booking small groups around town and quickly discovered that it paid better than playing his instruments.

The bulk of Stein's early business was arranging engagements for several small bands in the territory around Chicago and as far east as Pennsylvania to play at summer resorts, small out-of-town hotels, and other venues. Around Chicago he booked local groups to play casual engagements at weddings, private parties, school dances, and, occasionally, a few small restaurants. But seldom could he book one of his bands into a major downtown Chicago venue because of Benson's hold on that business.[3]

About 1920, Stein partnered with the colorful vaudeville agent Ernie Young, who had built a successful firm under his name that booked mostly variety acts and revues for such venues as the Marigold Gardens, Rainbo Garden, and the Morrison Hotel's Terrace Gardens.[4] A third partner was Fred Hamm, a former Benson sideman and leader who then was leading Young's show band. Hamm later was co-writer of "Bye Bye Blues" with Burt Lown, Chauncey Gray, and Dave Bennett. In 1924 at the age of twenty-nine, Stein bought out his two partners and opened a two-room office at 159 North State Street with a secretary and one employee.[5] He continued to call his business Music Corporation of America, a very pretentious name for such a small enterprise. It must have brought snickers from the Benson office, assuming the people there noticed at all.[6]

Although he continued to practice medicine, Stein did well with his small string of orchestras. He claimed he invented the one-nighter tour for dance bands, although the bandleader and booker Meyer Davis, based in Washington, D.C., and Philadelphia, and the Jan Garber–Milton Davis dance band had been doing the same thing in the eastern and southeastern states as early as 1918–20.[7] Joe Kayser, a Meyer Davis alumnus who later was based in Rockford, Illinois, toured the northern Illinois territory on the same basis by 1921. Stein's main contribution to the art of one-night booking was the application of modern marketing and promotion methods to promote his established list of name bands and the establishment of contractual relationships with dance venues to supply work for his bands.

MCA booked a few early Chicago bands on out-of-town tours, one of which, Joseph "King" Oliver's group, already had achieved some recognition through his Okeh, Paramount, and Gennett recordings.[8] Roy Bargy, a Benson bandleader, also was booked for road engagements by Stein. But if Stein hoped to book anything more substantial than one-night and short-term engagements in the Midwest territory, especially in Chicago, he needed a substantial local name band that could be the agency's headliner.

By June 1924, Stein had identified his potential headliner. Paul Biese, an early Chicago saxophone virtuoso and a long-term Benson leader, broke with Benson and let MCA handle all his bookings.[9] Biese led one of the most popular dance bands in the city before 1921. His band had played at the Edgewater Beach and Sherman hotels and drew big crowds to the Pantheon Theater, on the North Side. He also had made some early Brunswick, Victor, and Columbia records. In the early 1920s, Biese's band, in a contest, bested seventeen other groups and became known as "Paul Biese and His Champion Band." Stein's invasion of Benson's precincts to sign Biese was a coup for MCA.

With a long-term Biese contract in his pocket, Stein now had a popular Chicago band he hoped he could book into a downtown venue, but he knew it would be tough because of Benson. To bide his time, Stein placed the Biese band in short-term engagements in St. Paul, St. Louis, and Cincinnati. Between these location bookings, Stein also sent the Biese band on one-nighter tours through Nebraska, Iowa, Indiana, Ohio, and Michigan, guided by Stein's tour manager, Hank Linder.[10]

About the time Stein was sewing up the Biese contract, he began talking to another band, the Coon-Sanders Kansas City Nighthawks, led by Carlton Coon and Joe Sanders. The popular Kansas City dance band was then playing a summer-long engagement at the Lincoln Tavern, a north-suburban Chicago roadhouse. The Nighthawks eventually would prove to be a gold mine for Stein and for MCA.

The Coon-Sanders Kansas City Nighthawks had become very popular with early 1920s crystal-set owners in the Midwest through the band's late-night broadcasts from Kansas City's Muehlbach Hotel via the pioneer radio station WDAF. Because of this the Nighthawks received many offers for engagements in other cities, Chicago among them. For example, the Coon-Sanders authority Fred W. Edmiston revealed in his detailed history of the band, *The Coon-Sanders Nighthawks: "The Band That Made Radio Famous"* (2003), that Fred Mann's North Side Rainbo Garden made an offer to the band at that time.[11]

Based on the band's popularity, Jack Huff, the operator of Lincoln Tavern, a plush roadhouse in north suburban Morton Grove, hopped a train to Kansas City in 1924 and booked the band directly with the Nighthawks' co-leaders for an all-summer booking at his establishment.[12] The ever-observant Jules Stein, cognizant of the large listening audience the Nighthawks had cultivated, went to visit the Nighthawks several times at the Morton Grove roadhouse. He could see the promotional possibilities of radio and what it had done for the group. He also clearly saw the Nighthawks as a potential client he could book through the Midwest, capitalizing on its broadcast reputation. (While at the Lincoln Tavern, the Nighthawks broadcast regularly over KYW, then a Chicago station.)

Stein presented his plan to both Joe and "Coonie" between sets, explaining how financially lucrative a road trip could be for them following their stay at the Tavern. The idea was simple but powerful: leverage the band's radio popularity into a series of personal appearances across the Midwest. Joe and Coonie eventually consented to the road trip if Stein could come up with some guarantee money ahead of time.

The five-week tour through Indiana, Illinois, Iowa, and Wisconsin began at the conclusion of the Nighthawks' engagement at Lincoln Tavern and ended before the band moved into Chicago's upscale Congress Hotel to play a previously booked season-long engagement beginning that October. Both the summer tour and the Congress engagement were smashing successes. At the conclusion of the engagement in the spring of 1925 there followed another tour of one-nighters, from which Stein, Coon, and Sanders profited handsomely.[13]

About this time Stein hired Billy Goodheart, a young college graduate who was said to be as success-driven as Stein. Goodheart was a good salesman and did much of the early fieldwork for MCA, identifying and contracting with ballrooms and hotels in the Midwest and South to hire MCA bands. Stein took things a step further by announcing that he planned to open a Chicago booking department. At this point it was rumored that Benson had contacted Stein, without success, to establish a working agreement between the two firms.[14] At first glance, this seems unlikely since Benson, from all outside appearances, was at the peak of his power in 1925. However, Benson may have recognized Stein's skill at booking one-nighters in the territory and reasoned that the two agencies together would make an unbeatable combination: Benson for the Chicago market and Stein for the Midwest and beyond. But that is only speculation.

To make his point more emphatically with the Chicago musical fraternity and to attract some more dance bands to the fold, Stein placed a full-page ad in the September 1925 issue of *Intermezzo,* the monthly magazine of Local 10, Chicago Federation of Musicians, which is affiliated with the American Federation of Musicians.[15] The ad copy said that, in addition to the Coon-Sanders Original Nighthawks, MCA now had Paul Biese under "exclusive management." Stein's ad concluded by announcing the rather stunning news that Isham Jones and his Brunswick Recording Orchestra were now being managed by MCA for out-of-town engagements only. Both Biese and Jones had for years been key attractions in the Benson stable of bands.

The ad proclaimed that MCA was the creator of the "circuit of orchestras," referring to the agency's growing one-nighter business and its newfound ability to move its numerous bands in and out of its client's venues for short engagements. Clearly, an increasingly confident Stein was announcing to the Benson Organization that he was going to take on Benson in his own backyard. Ironically, Stein's old partner, Ernie Young, was not completely out of the MCA picture. At the bottom of the *Intermezzo* ad was a note: "The Ernie Young Music Corporation is a branch of the M-C-A." An August 1921 trade journal advertisement for Young's previous agency had trumpeted it as "The largest independent vaudeville agency in the world."[16]

Young was busier than ever with revues at five major Chicago show rooms. The revues ranged in size from ten principal entertainers, twenty chorus girls, and a band at Pershing Palace and Marigold Gardens to smaller, more intimate shows at the Moulin Rouge, Ike Bloom's Deauville, and George Liederman's Rendezvous. Young also had shows playing in hotel show rooms in New Orleans, Baltimore, and Kansas City and even took a small revue to the Hollywood, Florida, Country Club.[17]

A month after the *Intermezzo* ad appeared, Stein suffered what appeared to be a major setback: Paul Biese, his local name bandleader and the man he had hoped would carry the MCA banner into a downtown Chicago location, died suddenly on October 26, after surgery following a Stein-booked engagement in Cincinnati.[18] It was clearly a blow to the plans of the new company. The best-known band Stein now had in his fold was the Coon-Sanders Nighthawks but the band was playing its second season (1925–26) at the ritzy downtown Congress Hotel, an engagement MCA had not even booked. The Nighthawks had joined the Chicago Federation of Musicians (CFM) in the fall of 1924 upon returning from their first triumphant road tour for Stein and prior to going into the Congress.[19] This was an important step for the band because Chicago's Local 10 had a ruling that no booker could "import" an out-of-town band to play in Chicago.[20] Now Stein could book the Nighthawks as a local Chicago band, so he began selling Otto Roth, owner of the Blackhawk Restaurant at Randolph and Wabash, on the idea of installing one of MCA's name dance bands in Roth's fine-dining establishment. Stein and Roth knew each other because Stein often ate there.

The dance-and-dine policy was growing popular among the major Chicago hotel dining rooms, cabarets, and a few stylish restaurants in the twenties. Stein decided that the Coon-Sanders Nighthawks, flush with the success of their summer and spring tours, would be a perfect choice to play in the Blackhawk's main dining room for the 1926–27 season if he could convince Roth. Roth eventually saw the potential of such a major policy change at his restaurant and accepted Stein's proposition to install Coon-Sanders for the 1926–27 season. Stein now had achieved his goal of procuring a major, season-long booking in the Chicago Loop, heretofore hallowed Benson territory. He had broken additional new ground by selling a band to a restaurant that had earlier hired such Benson stalwarts as Paul Biese, Ralph Williams, and Frank Westphal for special occasions. Benson now must have gotten the message, if he was paying attention.

Because the Nighthawks were still traveling on their 1926 MCA-booked summer road tour, Stein chose Charlie Straight's band to fill in from September eleventh until the twenty-fifth, the Nighthawks' scheduled opening.[21] Straight was a natural. He was a veteran Chicago leader known for his long engagements at the Lincoln Tavern during the summers and at the North Side's Rendezvous Café in the winters. Along with Isham Jones and Paul Biese, he had headed one of Chicago's top dance organizations in the early twenties. Straight's group was now an MCA traveling band and was appearing at the Plantation Room of the Muehlbach Hotel in Kansas City.

The Nighthawks opened their first season at the Blackhawk on September 25, as planned. The band was a big success, according to Don Roth, the son of the Blackhawk's founder.[22] Aided by a remote line first from Chicago radio station WBBM and later from WGN, both the Blackhawk and the Nighthawks prospered, as did Stein. It shouldn't have required a hard sell to persuade the radio stations to install a line at the Blackhawk for the Coon-Sanders band. The ensemble was famous in the Midwest through its WDAF broadcasts from Kansas City and had been heard in Chicago the summer of 1924 from the Lincoln Tavern and, more recently, from the Congress Hotel over KYW. Once the band switched to WGN, the signal of which was (and still is) widely received throughout America's heartland, it began building an even larger potential audience. Stein exploited this by booking another long midwestern tour for the Nighthawks at the end of the 1926–27 Blackhawk season.[23]

With the commissions Stein was receiving from the numerous bands he was booking (between 10 percent and 15 percent of their gross) he now began devoting full time to MCA and hired more employees for his growing business. About this time MCA moved to a larger office in the recently completed Masonic Building at 32 West Randolph Street. What had been a lucrative sideline for Stein suddenly blossomed into a promising business. Signing up more Chicago and Midwest bands became a priority for Stein and company by 1925. As MCA cast its net around Chicago, many of the earliest local bands it landed were Benson bands and could be booked at first only for out-of-town engagements. The previously mentioned Charlie Straight, Eddie Neibauer's Seattle Harmony Kings, Don Bestor, Earl Hoffman, Vic Meyers, Isham Jones, Art Kassel, and Bobby Meeker also eventually signed with MCA.

These Chicago bands formed the backbone of the early MCA catalog, filling engagements in the large number of hotels, ballrooms, and other locations in MCA's growing Midwest circuit. Some of the major location bookings for the bands besides Chicago's Blackhawk were the Muehlbach Hotel in Kansas City, the Schroeder Hotel in Milwaukee, the Brown in Louisville, and the Hotel Jefferson in St. Louis. Cincinnati's Gibson Hotel and Castle Farm, the William Penn in Pittsburgh, and the Sherman Hotel in Chicago also were early subscribers to MCA. Having missed out on a commission for Coon-Sanders's two season-long engagements at the Congress Hotel in Chicago (the jobs were booked directly with the band), MCA also contracted to provide bands for that hotel.

Meanwhile, with MCA's assistance, Don Bestor, who had left the Benson Organization, took over the Glen Wortendike band, from Hamilton, Ohio. With his new band, Bestor played an engagement at the Muehlbach Hotel and then moved to Dallas where he and the band played for the grand opening of the new Baker Hotel in 1926. With that engagement MCA added the Baker to its growing list of hotels and locations hiring its bands exclusively.

Stein's idea for the circuit of orchestras, which provided a series of new bands every few weeks or months to his growing number of contract dance venues, attracted the attention of other entrepreneurs. One group of bandleaders, bookers, and ballroom operators in the East formed an organization called National Attractions, Inc., in late 1924 through which they hoped to replicate Stein's idea by providing musical groups to ballrooms in twenty-six midwestern and eastern cities every week.[24] In another twenty cities the bands would play for only three days each week. The ambitious plan called for leasing, operating, or even building new venues. For whatever reason, however, the organization did not last long.

It was while MCA scouts were trolling for more new bands in Ohio that they stumbled on one of their biggest finds, Guy Lombardo and the Royal Canadians. Originally from London, Ontario, but then playing in Cleveland, Lombardo became Stein's second big success in Chicago. In September 1927, MCA was able to bring the Lombardo band into Al Quodbach's Granada Café on the South Side surreptitiously by having Quodbach hire the band directly. This circumvented the union ruling against agency-imported bands. According to Lombardo, the politically connected Al Quodbach took care of the union matter with Petrillo, with whom he was said to be friendly.[25] What is known is that the following March the Lombardo band joined Local 10 of the musicians union as a group.[26] It certainly would have been in both Stein's and Lombardo's best interests for the band to be members of the Chicago local just as it had been for the Coon-Sanders band three years earlier. Once enrolled, Guy, Carmen, and Lebert Lombardo, along with two other musicians in the original band, maintained their Chicago membership through the years.

Not long afterward, the musicians union rescinded the nettlesome rule and allowed bookers to import out-of-town bands to play in Chicago. But the bands had to pay the local union a 30 percent tax. On September 15, 1934, the American Federation of Musicians finally reduced the traveling tax to 10 percent.[27]

With help again from a WBBM radio line, the Lombardo band's popularity soared and Stein sent the Royal Canadians on lucrative one-nighter tours during the summers. Things were going well for Stein at this point, with Coon-Sanders at the Blackhawk, Lombardo's orchestra at the Granada, and more and more good local units like Art Kassel and Wayne King joining the MCA bandwagon. There was no looking back for Stein. Coincidental with Lombardo's success, Stein opened MCA's first permanent office in New York City in 1928 although he had had a small office in Times Square since 1926 and had put Billy Goodheart in charge.[28] In the few short years since he went on his own, Stein had attracted most of Benson's best bands and continued to recruit many others from the great midwestern territory.

Stein now used his New York office to begin recruiting East Coast dance bands for his inventory and lining up more venues in which his expanding list of bands could play. By the mid-1930s, MCA became the leading dance band agency in the United States. The dramatic growth of MCA from a two-room booking office to a colossus of the entertainment industry three decades later is a story that has been told many times in detail and there is no need to recite it here again. Suffice it to say, the MCA-inspired approach used with Coon-Sanders and Guy Lombardo became the foolproof formula for building bands: get them plenty of broadcast time for engagements at specific locations and then exploit the radio coverage with lucrative tours throughout the listening area.

Jules Stein was not alone in discovering the power of dance band remotes, but he creatively put together the concept of rotating bands, broadcasting their music, and arranging well-planned, well-promoted one-nighter tours, which was certainly a paradigm shift for that time. It is ironic that few of the major vaudeville booking agencies then based in Chicago seem to have recognized the potential of the dance band market early in the game, even though MCA (and, later, other agencies) was using vaudeville and circus exploitation techniques. As mentioned earlier, Ernie Young and another agency called Society Entertainers seemed to be the two exceptions in Chicago. Young booked Fred Hamm's and Dave Peyton's bands in the 1920s but mostly in conjunction with his floor shows. The New York–based William Morris Agency, one of the biggest vaudeville bookers, belatedly set up a band department in 1939 but pulled the plug just six years later.[29] It was too late; William Morris clearly was no match for MCA.

MCA, on the other hand, employing a new business model, did in the 1930s and 1940s what the vaudeville agencies should have done in the 1920s. It expanded its horizon in the greater entertainment field, moving into other, related areas of show business: movie and radio talent, production, music publishing, recording, and, for a time, supplying liquor, party supplies, and other needs of the ballroom and hotel operators.[30]

## Benson's Fall from Grace

The balance of power and influence in the Chicago dance band business shifted dramatically from the Benson Organization to Stein's Music Corporation of America in the three years between 1925 and 1928. MCA was aggressively moving forward on its campaign to sign up Chicago and midwestern dance bands and dance venues while the Benson Organization began to lose ground to its competitor. Nineteen twenty-six was the watershed year because that is when MCA successfully broke into Benson's hallowed downtown Chicago area with the booking of the Coon-Sanders Nighthawks into the Blackhawk. It was a slap in the face for Benson because he had booked several casual engagements at the Blackhawk in the early 1920s for Paul Biese, Ralph Williams, and Frank Westphal, three of his top bands. But Stein was instrumental in turning the restaurant into the first-class dine-and-dance venue it later became.

Benson was losing some of his key downtown locations at this time as well. In addition, there apparently was dissension between Benson and some of his key bandleaders. William Howland Kenney, in his book *Chicago Jazz: A Cultural History — 1904–1930* (1993), noted that Isham Jones, Paul Biese, and Roy Bargy were seeking independence from Benson's iron-fisted management.[31] The public seemed unaware of this drama's being played out in the city but the trade press paid close attention. Several articles mentioning Benson's reputed troubles appeared between late January and early July 1925 in *Variety,* one of the two most important weekly trade papers in the entertainment industry.[32] Three articles reported that Benson had lost thirteen or more major hotel and cabaret locations where he had long-term contract bands. The other articles either addressed dissension in the Benson ranks or criticized some personnel actions Benson had taken with his musicians.

While the articles appear to be based on bandstand or union-hall gossip, there apparently was some truth to the reports of friction between Benson and Isham Jones, Roy Bargy, and, to a certain extent, Don Bestor. All three leaders had developed some celebrity either through the Benson Orchestra of Chicago or, in the case of Jones, through his own song-writing and recording successes. It's easy to see how this celebrity would conflict with Benson's rather generic approach to the business. Benson's leaders were expected only to direct Benson musical organizations. Jones, Bargy, and Bestor seem to have been caught between their popularity on the one hand and Benson's desire to maintain the status quo on the other. Benson apparently neither understood nor accepted the public's admiration of or increasing demand for celebrity bandleaders.

Benson and Bargy had had an earlier falling out around 1922 when Bargy was director of the Benson Orchestra of Chicago. In fact, Bargy left Benson briefly at the end of 1922 and took a band into the new Trianon Ballroom, an engagement arranged by Ernie Young.[33] Bargy later returned to the Benson fold, fronting an orchestra at the Morrison beginning in 1924, but a month later Bargy departed and moved to the Isham Jones band as pianist and arranger, where he remained for nearly two years.[34] Nearly eighty years later, it is hard to discern all the reasons for these changes. If the articles critical of Benson are to be believed, it can be assumed he was again orchestrating personnel moves to suit his own agenda.

For the most part, Isham Jones, under a Benson contract, appears to have put up with his boss's controlling ways; he was, after all, becoming wealthy through his song-writing royalties. But by spring 1925, Benson lost the prized contract for the College Inn. That meant Jones lost his high-visibility job there.

So Jones took his band to New York at that time and, to let everyone know he was there, placed a number of ads in the trade paper *Variety*.[35] Meanwhile, MCA continued to enlist Benson orchestras. Isham Jones, who by now was a national name, was signed by MCA late that summer for one-nighters only, but he still had a contractual relationship with Benson for local engagements.

Things continued to unravel for Benson and by 1928 most of his best bands had moved to MCA or other agencies. As reported earlier, Paul Biese had left Benson in 1924 and signed up with MCA to book all his engagements. Don Bestor surrendered leadership of the Benson Orchestra of Chicago in 1925 and formed a band of his own and began touring for MCA.[36] Fred Hamm, whom Benson coaxed back into the fold, replaced Bestor. Clearly there was trouble in paradise. Benson's rigid management style and his ignoring the changing market and musical environment may have brought on some of his woes.

Key Benson office people like George Hillman, Gus C. Edwards (a shrewd businessman as well as an entertainer–bandleader–talent scout), Tommy Thatcher, and Lew Diamond also left the agency. According to Joe Kayser, they joined a small company called Kennaway, Inc., started by John Key to design, produce, and sell dance programs for proms and programs for conventions.[37] With the new, experienced management talent on board, Kennaway soon began booking acts and bands. In 1936 Charlie Green of Consolidated Radio Artists bought out the three surviving partners of Kennaway: Tommy Thatcher, Gus C. Edwards, and George Hillman. Two years later Edwards went to New York to head the entire company, which now included Mills Artists, Inc.

Benson's fall from grace in the Chicago marketplace was as swift as MCA's aggressive rise to power following its breakthroughs with Coon-Sanders in 1926 and Guy Lombardo in 1927 and the opening of its New York office. By 1930, with little business left, Benson moved to New York where he again became an agent and manager for bands and orchestras. He continued in business through the mid-1940s, but it must have been difficult for him to observe from the sidelines MCA's spectacular rise to national success in a business he once controlled in Chicago. Benson died in 1946.[38]

The three major radio networks—the Columbia Broadcasting System (CBS), the National Broadcasting Company (NBC), and Mutual—realized by the early 1930s that they controlled the airtime over which the dance bands were playing, and they decided to flex their muscles and start their own booking organizations. In this way they could assure booking their bands at prime locations by offering network airtime as an inducement. Joe Kayser gave up his orchestra in the spring of 1935 to head the Midwest office of the NBC

Artists Bureau. MCA and the musicians union saw this as unfair competition and a monopolistic practice and urged the U.S. Department of Justice to investigate.[39]

The Federal Communications Commission put pressure on the networks to divest their artists' bureaus, an act that James Petrillo and the musicians union supported. To sweeten the pot, MCA offered to buy the CBS band-booking arm for $50,000 per year.[40] CBS agreed to the deal in 1941 and, in addition, gave MCA eighteen hours of sustaining (unsponsored) radio time each week to broadcast its dance bands. MCA then made a similar offer to NBC but it was refused. Petrillo later pulled the networks' licenses, leaving MCA as the only major booker controlling a block of radio time. MCA gained an enormous competitive advantage by being able to offer CBS network airtime in its client hotels and ballrooms.

MCA became the Goliath in the business, but many other large and influential agencies grew up in the 1930s, including General Amusement Corporation (GAC, formerly Rockwell-O'Keefe), Frederick Brothers (begun in Oklahoma), Amusement Service Corporation, Associated Booking Corporation, and Willard Alexander (an MCA alum). The giant William Morris agency (mentioned earlier), a major force in managing and booking vaudeville talent, didn't enter the dance band market until 1939, but it had booked bands as theater stage acts as far back as the 1920s. Thanks to MCA, the band business became so big that there seemed to be room for many.

The mid-1920s was a time of dramatic economic, technologic, and social change. It also was a period of dynamic expansion and upheaval in the Chicago dance-band booking business. The post–World War I economic boom occurred just as commercial radio broadcasting was emerging. Phonograph records still were enormously popular although sales had peaked in the later 1910s.[41] Adding to the welter of changes taking place was the sudden and explosive growth in automobile ownership, which gave new freedom to a population that rapidly was becoming socially emancipated. It was especially liberating to individuals in their late teens and early twenties.

How did all these factors affect the dance band business? The economic boom and supercharged fervor of the 1920s intensified the public's hunger for entertainment in general and for social dancing in particular. The automobile allowed people to travel farther to outlying ballrooms and roadhouses, many of which began employing bands and cabaret entertainers. And radio made the bands more popular then ever. These developments helped create new booking opportunities for MCA, O'Hare, and a few other agencies in the city that were alert to the new trends. If Benson noticed this market at all, he probably was too busy trying to shore up his collapsing business to do anything about it.

Benson, however, did attempt to organize his own circuit about 1925. With few exceptions, though, the Benson circuit offerings were his regular Chicago-based bands and they were mostly available for summer-long engagements. For Benson, it was too little, too late.

Even the Benson Orchestra of Chicago, which had developed regional and national celebrity through its much-admired early 1920s Victor recordings, lost favor. The orchestra's style, with a few exceptions, seemed anachronistic compared to that of other orchestras of the period, including several of Benson's own units, such as that of Isham Jones. By 1923 or 1924 the Benson Orchestra of Chicago was musically over the hill although it continued to record until 1925 but with changing personnel, once again reflecting Benson's loss of key men.

In the final analysis Benson probably was done in by his own belief that his reign over the Chicago band market could not or would not be challenged and that things would continue the same way indefinitely. By the mid-1920s, dance bands were evolving into commodities. Benson had filled his clients' dance and music needs by sending out his standing groups, where possible. For many casual engagements, however, Benson would put together a custom group of almost any size from his roster of five hundred musicians and leaders, all of whom worked directly for him.

MCA simplified Benson's formula by booking only organized dance bands operating under their leaders' names, which MCA sold as commodities. The agency hired no musicians or leaders directly, except on rare occasions. Benson charged for his musical groups what the traffic would bear or took the cover charges. After paying his musicians and leaders, the remainder was his. MCA, on the other hand, kept only a percentage of the total charge for the band as commission, usually 10 to 15 percent. But MCA made its money on volume; it simply booked more bands.

The Husk O'Hare–Sol Weisner agency may have had as many bands as MCA in 1925, but it never seemed to grow beyond the greater Chicago market even though Husk's own band did play out-of-town engagements in New York and elsewhere. But only the band fronted by O'Hare himself developed any name recognition. O'Hare had established a relatively solid business by 1925, booking second-tier bands and orchestras into neighborhood ballrooms, summer resorts, and an occasional downtown location. A born marketer, O'Hare readily grasped the significance of recordings and then radio broadcasting as a way of promoting his own and other groups handled by his agency. But following the more restrictive Benson model, O'Hare's groups were always further identified as Husk O'Hare bands. By the late 1920s, O'Hare and his bands, too, had lost out to MCA. Ironically, MCA began booking Husk's own band by 1930.

MCA had taken over the Chicago market between 1925 and 1928 in a sudden shift in power. Over the next decade it would rapidly become a major, national economic force in the entertainment business. It grew into a large, successful talent agency and production company that responded deftly to the changing trends in the market. It ultimately became so large and influential that the U.S. government filed a civil antitrust suit against it in the early 1960s. The corporation was charged with acting as a production agency (MCA by then had acquired Decca Records, Universal Pictures, a bank, and Revue Productions, a producer of television shows) at the same time it operated a talent agency representing many movie stars and performers.[42]

In 1962, MCA signed a consent decree to end the government action, agreeing to dissolve its talent agency business.[43] In 1990 the Matsushita Electric Industrial Company of Japan acquired MCA. Five years later Matsushita sold 80 percent of MCA to Seagram, the large Canadian distillery, which was diversifying into the entertainment industry.[44] Today, the surviving company operates under the name Universal. The MCA name was retired in 1996.

## James C. Petrillo and the Musicians Union

By the early 1920s Chicago musicians had four unions in a town known for its strong labor organizations. If you didn't belong to one, you likely didn't work. By the late 1920s one of the competing organizations, the Chicago Federation of Musicians, emerged as the strongest and most influential. It also played a key role in the establishment of the early dance-band business in Chicago.

Joseph F. Winkler and James C. Petrillo, two 1920s CFM union leaders, also played key roles in the drama that unfolded in the mid-twenties as the Benson Organization competed with the Music Corporation of America. Petrillo, who succeeded Winkler, was a forceful and dynamic leader who was both street-wise and politically astute. He worked hard to maximize the amount of work for his musicians and secure for them the best economic and working conditions. In his zeal he employed such strategies as the use of standby musicians, who were paid to wait in the wings, usually at radio stations, while unpaid musicians, usually in ballrooms or hotel orchestras doing remote broadcasts, performed a given engagement or program.

Another Petrillo strategy was to establish minimum numbers of musicians who could play in the theaters, large hotel rooms, radio stations, convention sites, and other locations that employed musicians.[45] This guaranteed that such employers used an adequate number of musicians for a given performance. It also created more work by forcing these venues to use the established minimum numbers of musicians instead of trying to get by with just a few.

Of the four main competing musicians' labor organizations in Chicago early in the twentieth century, three were for white musicians and a fourth was for black musicians. The American Musicians Union (AMU) challenged the Chicago Federation of Musicians, Local 10, for power in the city until 1937. The AMU was founded in 1900, a year earlier than CFM, and had about 2,500 members. But by the mid-1930s, it was losing ground to the more powerful CFM led by James C. Petrillo. In 1937 Petrillo made an overture to the AMU members; they could join the CFM and pay no initiation fee, which at that time was one hundred dollars.[46] Most of the AMU members couldn't afford to pass up such an offer and made the switch, considerably strengthening the CFM's position. Members of the smaller Polish-American Musicians Union were given a similar offer the same year and joined the CFM.

A factor in Edgar Benson's organizational demise, according to Joe Kayser, may have been his close relationship with Joseph F. Winkler, the former Local 10 president.[47] Winkler was unseated in a contentious 1922 election by Petrillo, the local's vice president. To make matters worse, according to Kayser, Benson's relationship with Petrillo was thought to be rocky at best. Jules Stein, on the other hand, also a CFM member, seemed to get along very well with Petrillo. While some of this is speculation, these types of relationships or friendships in business often are the keys to success or failure.

There was a second local of the American Federation of Musicians in Chicago, Local 208, which represented the black musicians on the city's South Side. Until the 1950s the white local had jurisdiction in the area generally north of Eighteenth Street and south of Fifty-first Street. The black local's jurisdiction was the area between those boundaries. In an agreement between the two locals, black musicians could play in the white jurisdiction but had to be paid Local 10 union wages, which were higher than those of Local 208.[48] But the local black musicians still faced a number of difficulties working within the white local's jurisdiction and it wasn't until the merger that conditions began to improve.

Within the greater fold of the much larger white Local 10, members often formed cliques based on what kinds of jobs they played most frequently. Further stratification of white union members came through various nationality or ethnic groups, which formed clubs that met and sponsored social affairs periodically. These clubs—the Czechoslovak, German, Jewish, Italian, Polish, and others at the height of their activity in the 1930s and 1940s—were especially active politically in union affairs and elections. The Polish American club originally was the Polish-American Musicians Union and, as mentioned earlier, was absorbed by the CFM in 1937. There were similar clubs within the black union local. The union local, however, was the overall unifying force.

In 1966, following many years of discussion and negotiation, locals 10 and 208 finally merged and became Local 10-208 of the American Federation of Musicians, which embraced blacks and whites. Local 10-208 is a much smaller organization today than it was at its peaks in the mid-1920s and again just after World War II. With the exception of the musicians playing in the Chicago Symphony, the Lyric Opera, and the Grant Park orchestra; those doing some limited studio work; or those playing in the few legitimate theaters today, jobbing bands and rock groups provide the bulk of available employment for today's musicians.

The musicians union has met technological change through the years with courage and usually with great success. Even in those cases where the technology was a definite threat to employment, union leaders generally found a way to assert the need for fair wages and working conditions. One of the earliest of those technological threats, radio broadcasting, posed a significant challenge to James Petrillo. He and the union went toe-to-toe with both the government and broadcast-industry executives many times to arrive finally at accommodations for musicians.

The Chicago Federation of Musicians and, later, the American Federation of Musicians under Petrillo's leadership helped pave the way for an enormous and thriving dance band business, which was at its height during the thirties and forties. As if a reminder to all who listened, the Petrillo imprimatur was officially stamped on all band remotes by the 1950s. At the end of each broadcast, the announcer would remind listeners that the broadcast was being brought to them through the cooperation of whatever station or network "and the American Federation of Musicians, James C. Petrillo, president."

Two people could not have been more unlike one another in personality or in the way they did things, yet no two people could have been more in tune with one another than MCA's Jules Stein and James Petrillo. They had many differences along the way, some of them serious clashes, but they never let those disagreements or conflicts deflect them from their responsibilities or dedication to their respective organizations. Both can be criticized for pushing their own beliefs and self-interests a bit too aggressively at times, but without them the music business would not have been the same.

❖ ❖ ❖

Four major forces combined to shape the early dance band business in 1920s Chicago: the booking agents led by Edgar Benson and by Jules Stein's MCA; the musicians union; the entrepreneurs who operated the dance venues; and the early radio stations. The dance bands wouldn't become a major industry per se until the early 1930s, but these influences set the process in motion a decade earlier. In the public's mind, however, it was radio broadcasting that brought the dance bands into their homes and made them an exciting part of their world, especially during the economic depression of the 1930s. And it was radio that continued to find innovative ways to give voice to the dance bands until the 1950s.

# 3 How Radio Made Stars of the Dance Bands

RADIO broadcasting and dance bands seemed made for each other in the 1920s and 1930s. Radio could propel a band to fame, and dance band music was great late-night program fare for the budding radio stations. That became clear soon after the first dance band broadcasts were heard on primitive crystal radios in the early 1920s. Jules Stein took notice of radio's promotional power for dance bands and turned the medium into a gold mine.

America's interest in radio grew quickly because it offered a totally new form of entertainment. As a result, radio stations, and later, networks, evolved rapidly into a big business. In 1923 there were 190,000 radio receivers in use nationwide.[1] A few years later about 15,000,000 homes had radios. In 1925 people in Chicago led the nation in seeking radio station licenses, with 136 applications.[2] Companies quickly bought time on the stations to capitalize on radio's formidable power as an advertising medium for their products. Some companies started their own stations.

Since most dance bands sounded alike in those days, the challenge for an orchestra broadcasting frequently from one dance venue or other was to develop a special sound that would quickly identify it to listeners. Bands introduced theme songs and tag lines such as "The Musical Gems of Ray Pearl" or "Art Kassel and his Kassels in the Air." But more than that, they hired arrangers to give their music a distinctive sound, which often resulted in music with more style than substance.

Toward the end of the 1920s, even though dance bands were still popular late-at-night listening entertainment, the radio stations and new networks began hiring their own musicians and leaders to furnish music for the growing number of sponsored variety and musical shows heard during the early evening. This move , combined with the sizable layoffs of local theater musicians in the wake of the introduction of talking movies in 1927, and the forcible closings of numerous cabarets for Prohibition violations accounted for perhaps the largest shift in musical talent ever to take place in Chicago. Two thousand musicians played in Chicago theaters in 1926; seven years later there were only 125.[3]

The Guyon's Paradise Orchestra, directed by the saxophonist Jules Herbuveaux, was the first dance band to broadcast in Chicago. On the evening of January 2, 1922, the orchestra played a selection of dance tunes in the KYW studio on the nineteenth floor of the Commonwealth Edison Building. The studio was heavily draped to absorb sound. This was the second official night of broadcasting for Chicago's first radio station, according to Herbuveaux, and the listening audience would have been small.[4] The station had first gone on the air for one evening the previous November with a concert from the Auditorium Theater featuring the Civic Opera Company, whose director was the former diva Mary Garden.

Herbuveaux said his group was selected to debut on KYW because he played the saxophone. "The saxophone was a big deal at that time, so they wanted to exhibit the fact that they [KYW] had gotten away from the old-fashioned 'professor-string-type waltz music' and got a guy up in front with a saxophone," he recalled. The band played at KYW only one night, without pay, according to Herbuveaux. Jack Chapman's orchestra, playing in the main dining room of the Drake Hotel that summer, probably made the first true remote broadcast in Chicago via WDAP (a predecessor of WGN), then broadcasting from atop the Drake.[5]

The musicians playing in the early bands and orchestras at clubs and ballrooms at first paid little heed to the crude and clumsy-looking microphones during the remotes. They looked upon them simply as a means for outsiders to eavesdrop on the proceedings. As the musicians saw it, their role was to play for the live audience and satisfy their dancing needs, even when they knew they were on the air. Little did they realize that those early rudimentary broadcasts would later help propel dance bands to untold success in the entertainment world.

Early broadcasts often began while the dance band was in the middle of a number, usually with a brief announcement such as, "We now join a dance program already in progress from the main dining room of the Stevens Hotel." The program might go on for an hour or more because there were no real time limits in the early days. When the band stopped for a break, the station might turn to an organist, who was told to keep playing. Very soon, however, station managers and the bandleaders began to understand the need for more orderly presentations of the remote broadcasts. Radio was now formulating program standards that would prevail for decades.

As mentioned earlier, some bandleaders hired arrangers to provide that extra little bit of individuality they were all seeking. Before the advent of broadcasting, most dance bands played the same stock arrangements provided by the music publishers, which the musicians often "doctored," or customized, by adding, subtracting, or rearranging the elements and/or solos.[6] Only the better-established orchestras or those well known through their recordings used specially written arrangements, which, while expensive, helped to set them apart in the way they sounded.

Announcers began to provide continuity rather than just announcing song titles. Many announcers outdid themselves with the word pictures they created to describe the venues from which the dance music emanated. While this purple prose attracted a lot of listeners to the broadcast locations, many of the places did not live up to the on-air buildups.

More important, both stations and bands began adhering to rather strict time constraints as the broadcast schedule was divided into quarter-, half-, and full-hour program segments.

By 1924 there were many Chicago bands on the air late at night. Some of the better-known musical groups even had sponsored programs by the mid-1920s, most but not all of them coming from the stations' studios. On a given night you could hear the Isham Jones orchestra appearing at the College Inn of the Sherman Hotel (WLS), the Oriole Terrace Orchestra from the Edgewater Beach Hotel (WIBO), or Joe Kayser's Orchestra from the Arcadia (WLIB-Elgin, another predecessor of WGN). Clarence M. Jones broadcast from the downtown Moulin Rouge on Wabash (KYW); Sammy Stewart and his Knights of Syncopation (KYW) and the Trianon Orchestra under the baton of Dell Lampe played via the Trianon Ballroom's own station WMBB (for World's Most Beautiful Ballroom). The Ralph Williams orchestra was a regular late-night radio attraction over WQJ from the North Side's Rainbo Garden where the station, owned by the Calumet Baking Powder Company, also had its studios.

Jules Herbuveaux's orchestra later was broadcast regularly over WTAS, based in Elgin.[7] Other bands were frequently heard over the same station in the early 1920s, occasionally playing at the Purple Grackle roadhouse nearby. However, WTAS and WLIB, another early station, didn't survive the 1920s.[8]

These broadcasts became launching pads for performers as well as for bands. Nick Lucas, a singer and guitar player with the Oriole Terrace Orchestra, built a reputation on his energetic vocalizing of "Toot Toot Tootsie," "No, No, Nora," and "Charlie My Boy," all compositions by the orchestra co-leader Ted FioRito. On that basis, Lucas left the band for a vaudeville career that lasted thirty years or more. His successor, Mark Fisher from Pittsburgh, also became a well-known celebrity on subsequent broadcasts and later was a bandleader and theater master of ceremonies par excellence. FioRito and the Oriole Terrace Orchestra co-leader Dan Russo, seeing the possibilities of radio, in 1925 established WIBO in partnership with the Nelson Brothers, and their band would frequently be heard on this station.

Of all the 1920s Chicago leaders, Guy Lombardo knew best how to play to the radio audience, and he demonstrated it to perfection over the WBBM line that was installed in November 1927, about a month after Lombardo opened at Al Quodbach's Granada Café at Sixty-eighth and Cottage Grove.[9] After Lombardo was on the air for a few weeks, the crowds were lined up at the door of the café every night.

Lombardo also is credited with slowing down the dance tempos from the fast Chicago 1920s one-step to the slow fox-trot. His orchestra's sound was unlike anything most Chicago musicians and listeners had ever heard before. The long-time bandleader Joe Kayser, who often went to the Granada to hear Lombardo, called the band's distinctive sound the nanny-goat sound, referring to the wide vibrato of the sax section led by Guy's brother Carmen.

It must have been maddening for the Granada's clientele during the band broadcasts because, in those days before public-address systems, they couldn't hear Carmen or the trio sing, or hear the little unamplified guitar fills; everything was directed to the broadcast microphone. Kayser said the Lombardo band "was so smart when they were on the air, they played to the air," not to the audience in the room. Also, Kayser pointed out, electric-powered radios using alternating current had just come on the market and the new receivers with orthophonic speakers added much depth of sound to the broadcasts of Lombardo's orchestra and other bands.[10]

The Coon-Sanders and Lombardo bands by 1927 were the two most popular in the city. Isham Jones, another favorite, had broken up his band the year before, following a long tour. A large measure of these bands' popularity stemmed from their remote broadcasts. Fan mail, telegrams, and telephone calls were the informal rating services of the day. Jack Chapman's first WGN broadcast from the Drake drew six hundred letters.[11] The grand champions at drawing listener interest, however, were the Coon-Sanders Nighthawks. Within a few years of their debut at the Blackhawk, the Nighthawks were receiving so many telegrams during their remotes, especially the special Monday late-night show, that Western Union put a teletype machine right on the bandstand. This allowed Joe and "Coonie" to respond immediately to the greetings and requests over the air. Over five hundred telegrams were received in a two-hour period during one broadcast.[12]

Radio stations in other U.S. cities were among the first to beam their broadcasts of a few early dance bands into the night air. One of the earliest (in 1920) was Cleveland's WTAM, which broadcast the Emerson Gill orchestra from the Bamboo Inn. Paul Specht, another pioneer in adopting the new medium of radio, was heard via Detroit's WWM about the same time.

By the early to mid-1920s, with nearly half the American households having radios, Chicago bands could be heard all over the radio dial at night. Broadcasting dance bands was a cheap and convenient way for the early stations to fill air time, especially during the late evening hours in which advertisers had little interest. Managers of ballrooms, restaurants, and hotels most often paid the charges for the telephone line that carried the broadcast to the studio and they usually gave a small fee to the station to cover costs of the program engineer and an announcer. Without spending much more than street-car fare for the two-man broadcast crew, the station or network got free music programming and maybe made a few extra bucks after all the costs were tabulated. The economics of the remote broadcasts remained the same through much of the 1930s.

As president of the Chicago Federation of Musicians, James C. Petrillo railed at the local stations for not paying musicians and performers appearing on the air waves. By the mid-twenties he had won his point, and musicians playing at radio studios were compensated. He was still uneasy, however, about all the local dance bands playing on remote broadcasts from ballrooms, clubs, and cabarets with no additional compensation. The bands were paid by their ballroom or club employers but they still were giving their talent free for the late-at-night broadcasts.

It was to rectify this point that Petrillo insisted that stations provide an equal number of standby musicians to wait in the wings at the studio while dance bands or otherwise unpaid musicians played on the air.[13] The stations eventually agreed to abide by this arrangement. Petrillo's resolution of this dilemma was brilliant because it not only provided additional employment for musicians for the duration of the agreement but, above all, it permitted dance bands to continue doing remotes, which gave them invaluable broadcast exposure. The practice was later outlawed by the passage of the Lea Act in 1946, which made it illegal for stations to pay for services that were either unneeded or unperformed.[14] Petrillo again challenged the radio stations, this time over their using phonograph records instead of employing live musicians. One solution was for the stations to hire musicians as record spinners.

The hotel, cabaret, and ballroom proprietors quickly saw the advantage of paying the telephone line charges. The paying customers who came in after hearing the radio broadcasts were more than welcome. Attracting business was the name of the game for the proprietors. These shrewd businessmen also quickly saw the remote line as bait they could dangle when negotiating bookings for dance bands. Later MCA and the network band-booking agencies gained access to blocks of radio time that they, in turn, used to gain hotel customers for their bands. Bandleaders most often were willing to accept a lower fee—sometimes union scale wages, even when a hefty payroll meant taking a loss—to play a location with a good radio wire. The broadcast buildup would enable them to collect big fees on the subsequent lucrative one-nighter tours. MCA, of course, had clearly understood the potential of linking radio exposure and one-nighter tours. It was one of its basic building blocks for promoting bands.

As broadcasts came to have greater significance for the dance bands, leaders and musicians alike would mentally prepare themselves to put forth their very best efforts. Often they were so psyched up when they were on the air that they outdid themselves, rendering performances they could not later duplicate. The bands often used their best arrangements for the broadcasts. Some second- or third-tier bands continued playing mostly stock arrangements or doctored stocks on the job into the 1930s but used special arrangements while on the air. This often resulted in a special "broadcast persona," an image or distinctive sound that was not always evident when the bands played their usual ballroom or dining-room sets for dancers.

Bandleaders who were especially gregarious occasionally felt obliged to act as hosts or they arranged brief speaking roles during the remotes. By the early 1940s some Chicago stations, however, forbade leaders to say anything during remote broadcasts, believing that announcers were meant to talk and leaders to direct their orchestras. Chuck Foster, a California bandleader who made Chicago his headquarters in the 1950s and early 1960s, said he had always cohosted his remotes at the Peacock Court of the Mark Hopkins Hotel in San Francisco and the Biltmore Bowl in Los Angeles.[15] In California Foster had been using rhyming song introductions during medleys as the band played a two- to four-bar segue from one tune to another. When he played at Chicago's Stevens Hotel for the first time, in early 1941, he briefed the WGN announcer before the broadcast about his planned routine. Then came the surprise as the announcer told Foster in no uncertain terms that nobody but the announcer introduced the tunes during WGN remotes. Foster assured him it wasn't a problem, that he would take full responsibility.

Frank Schreiber, WGN's general manager, was listening to Foster's first broadcast that night and immediately called the hotel manager and made clear his concerns. The hotel manager, Schreiber, and Foster met the following morning in the hotel office and it was agreed, presumably under threat of the station's pulling the remote line, that Foster would no longer have a speaking role in the broadcasts.

For a time, the musicians union also prohibited bandleaders from speaking or making special appearances unless they were paid, but that rule was eased in later years as radio grew more informal. If they spoke at all, leaders most often were called in at the beginning of the broadcast to greet the radio audience and again at the end to say "thank you for listening." But some leaders insisted on introducing the tunes and painting word pictures about the medleys or songs they were about to play. Glenn Miller had his "something old, something new, something borrowed, something blue" medley. Sammy Kaye had tunes from the "dusty manuscripts," and Art Kassel called out "Kassels in the Air" between every other tune. A number of other leaders used clichés to announce "songs from the memory book."

By the 1930s and 1940s, most big Chicago network stations staked out certain remote locations as their own. No one station could cover them all, but some of the more important venues had the luxury of several stations' doing remotes from their locations. The WGN/Mutual Network did regular band broadcasts from the Aragon and Trianon, the Blackhawk, the Palmer House and Bismarck hotels, and occasionally the Melody Mill and Oh Henry ballrooms. The WBBM/CBS Network had its microphones located at the Ambassador East, the Drake and LaSalle hotels, the Latin Quarter, the Band Box, and, in later years, the London House.[16] The WMAQ/NBC-Red Network had the Sherman, Congress, Morrison, and Edgewater Beach hotels, the Grand Terrace and, later, the Blue Note jazz club as their semipermanent remote locations.

The Stevens, the Bismarck, and occasionally the Sherman and Edgewater Beach hotels were mostly WENR/NBC-Blue Network sites (NBC then operated the Red and the Blue networks), along with the Chez Paree. All four radio networks did remote pickups from the Aragon and Trianon, Melody Mill, and Oh Henry ballrooms over the years. Independent station WIND had a line into the Paradise Ballroom on Chicago's West Side. WLS, the purveyor of dance-band music on its airwaves in the early and mid-1920s from the Sherman Hotel, was not an active player after 1928 when the station was sold by Sears Roebuck and Company to *Prairie Farmer,* the midwestern agricultural publication.[17] The station became a hillbilly/country-and-western mecca for the next thirty years with its parade of programs like the *National Barn Dance.*

Some stations developed reputations as "makers of bands" because of their coverage and the prestige of the remote sites from which they broadcast. WGN in Chicago had that reputation, and the best-known bandleaders readily admitted that WGN broadcasts gave them a boost toward success.[18] The 50,000-watt clear-channel voice of WGN was heard from Minnesota to central Texas, and from western Pennsylvania to Utah, providing dance-band music in the late-night and early morning hours. The station's remote locations also benefited greatly by this exposure.

In a large market like Chicago, the clearance of tunes before broadcast became a ritual because of the licensing requirements of the American Society of Composers, Authors, and Publishers (ASCAP); Broadcast Music Inc. (BMI); and the Society for European Stage Authors and Composers (SESAC). This was especially true in the late thirties and forties. All leaders were expected to submit their "play lists" to the stations one or two days in advance, especially if they were network pickups. The standard form listed title of music, composer, author, publisher, and licensor. In this way the licensing organizations were able to ascertain what tunes were being played and how many times. Through these calculations they paid appropriate royalties to their member composers, authors, and publishers.

## Commercially Sponsored Broadcasts

Quick to realize how the frequency and reach of regular radio broadcasts could build a band's following, MCA advanced its band broadcast strategy one step further. It began promoting its bands for sponsored broadcasts so it could present its stable of musical organizations in regularly assigned, weekly prime listening slots rather than just late at night. This, of course, also brought in additional commissions to MCA. In this earlier evening time period, the bands would gain support from more than just the dial-hopping night owls. In addition, the popularity of dance bands made them a relatively easy sale to potential sponsors anxious to advertise their products.

Local Chicago radio stations were the first outlets Stein approached, which resulted in a string of sponsored evening programs. Later, because Chicago was a key originating point for the networks, CBS, NBC, and Mutual began picking up and feeding some of the broadcasts to their affiliates across the country. Often these early programs featured a vaudeville comedian or show business celebrity. The *Fibber McGee and Molly* radio show, which began in Chicago's NBC studios, featured the Ted Weems orchestra. When the show moved to the West Coast, the former Chicago NBC conductor Billy Mills became the bandleader.

The Chicago bands, MCA's earliest clients, got a lion's share of the radio feature spots during the late twenties and early thirties. Although most of these bands are still remembered today, some of the shows' sponsors are no longer in business. Charlie Agnew played on *The Yeastfoam Hour,* on a program sponsored by Armin Face Cream, and on the better-known *Lucky Strike Magic Carpet Show.* Ben Bernie, then very popular and working at the College Inn and at the Century of Progress World's Fair, was sponsored by Pabst Blue Ribbon malt mixes for the home brewer (Prohibition was still in force). Both Herbie Kaye and the Coon-Sanders Nighthawks were sponsored at different times during the late twenties and early thirties by Florsheim Shoes. The Nighthawks also had Maytag Washers for a sponsor via NBC. Wayne King was just becoming known as "the waltz king" and was heard on his well-known *Lady Esther Serenade,* sponsored by a cosmetics company, on NBC. King also worked on sponsored shows for Pure Oil, Standard Oil, Armour Packing Company, and Sanatron radio tubes. The list of shows booked by MCA for its roster of bands included programs with Ted FioRito and his orchestra for Frigidaire and Skelly Oil.

Some radio shows featured unusual matchups of talent. One of the unlikeliest pairings was Frankie Masters and his orchestra with the poet Edgar Guest. Another unusual booking occurred when Tiny Hill and his orchestra, especially hot in the late thirties because of their success at the Melody Mill Ballroom and their hit record of "Angry," made weekly appearances on the well-known *Your Hit Parade* program. The Hill band, a distinctly laid-back, down-home type of organization, contrasted with the more sophisticated *Your Hit Parade* presentation in New York. Perhaps the outstanding example of an early sponsored dance-band show developed by MCA and broadcast from Chicago was Kay Kyser's *Kollege of Musical Knowledge,* heard in the mid-1930s.[19] More about the Kay Kyser radio show appears in chapter 8, in a discussion about the Blackhawk Restaurant.

The commercial broadcasts brought in revenue for the stations and networks, not the sustaining dance-band remotes. MCA's Stein saw that clearly as he promoted more and more sponsored broadcasts featuring his bands. The local Chicago stations, budding networks, and advertising agencies aggressively created new programs to sell to a growing list of sponsors with products to market. Many of these new programs required music, which meant *live music* provided by union musicians. So the stations and Chicago-based network affiliates began actively recruiting musicians, leaders, and, in some cases, whole orchestras by the late 1920s.

It began as a trickle at first. Henry Selinger, concert master of the Chicago Symphony, and a few of his colleagues joined the staff of WGN en masse in 1924 as the Drake Concert Ensemble. It was a part-time assignment since they worked evenings for the Benson Organization in the Drake Hotel's main dining room. Selinger shortly became the station's musical director. Two years later he conducted WGN's fifteen-piece Tribune Philharmonic orchestra, and eventually he became program manager.[20] The number of Chicago-originated commercial programs grew rapidly and the demand for theater and show conductors grew with it.

Coincidentally, the introduction of talking pictures in 1927 put many theater musicians and conductors out of work. The federal government forcibly closed a number of cabarets in 1928 when patrons were found to be carrying alcoholic beverages. The economic depression beginning in 1930 pushed more musicians onto the street. Some owners themselves closed the doors of their clubs as the crowds thinned, and a few ballrooms went on reduced dancing schedules due to lack of business. This put many more musicians and conductors in the unemployment lines.

The conductors Harry Kogen, Al Short, and Walter Blaufus moved to NBC. Al Morey, a former Aragon dance band and theater stage bandleader, joined WBBM; the former RCA Victor recording director Roy Shield was recruited by NBC-Chicago along with Joe Gallicchio, who had been conductor of the concert sessions at the Edgewater Beach Hotel. These leaders, along with Henry Selinger, led the way into radio.

During the late 1920s and into the early 1930s many more musicians and leaders entered the radio studios. The Chicago network stations, which were key originating points, needed the musical and show business expertise that many of these Chicago leaders possessed. Jules Herbuveaux joined KYW and later went to NBC. Rex Maupin, who had been a trumpet player in and arranger for the Herbuveaux KYW orchestra, became a conductor with that group and later followed Herbuveaux to NBC. The prominent violinist and arranger Victor Young, who had played with the FioRito-Russo orchestra and in the theaters, went to WGN with the Jean Goldkette Chicago unit and, of course, later moved to Hollywood, where he received numerous Academy Award nominations for his movie scores.

Some musicians joined radio station staffs as producers and directors and in other production capacities as Chicago developed into a major production center for network programs in the thirties. In this decade all three major Chicago network-affiliated stations had staff orchestras and many of the smaller stations had several staff musicians, if not small orchestras. By 1931, James C. Petrillo had worked out contractual agreements with the key local stations on how many musicians they would hire. In Chicago that year, pay for studio musicians ranged from $120 to $150 per week, more than musicians in New York received, which was a sign of the midwestern city's musical preeminence.[21]

At WMAQ, Jules Herbuveaux became director of the staff orchestra in 1928. He was succeeded two years later by Paul Whiteman, who, with his band, tarried in Chicago until 1932. Whiteman and company alternated between the NBC studios, where they played for local and network shows, and the Edgewater Beach Hotel, where they were the house orchestra.[22] Whiteman also supervised the network's musical activities for the Midwest region. When the Whiteman entourage moved to New York, WMAQ and NBC brought in Roy Shield, formerly recording director for Victor, from the West Coast to be music director.

The 1930s were a golden period for music shows emanating from Chicago on the three major networks. Roy Shield was conductor of *The Carnation Contented Hour* and was later succeeded on that show by Josef Pasternack (not the Hollywood director), who had been a top conductor with Victor Red Seal records and helped develop Enrico Caruso as a top Victor artist. Two other very popular NBC network shows of the period were *The Sinclair Minstrels* and *The Lady Esther Serenade* with Wayne King and, later, Freddy Martin. Jules Herbuveaux, who had moved into production (and later became program manager), was the director for all three of these shows.

*The Breakfast Club,* starring Don McNeil, began at WMAQ in 1932 as a seemingly insignificant show. It later was heard on the NBC-Blue and then the ABC networks for more than thirty-seven years, making it one of the longest-running radio variety shows in history. Walter Blaufus, Harry Kogen, Rex Maupin, and Eddie Ballantine were the orchestra conductors, with Ballantine working the longest—twenty-five years, until the show went off the air in 1969.

As the geographical focus of network broadcasting gradually shifted from Chicago to New York in the late thirties, the MCA New York booking office began to take the initiative for booking some of these broadcasts. Guy Lombardo (sponsored by Robert Burns Panatellas and Esso Oil) and Don Bestor (General Tire, Jack Benny for Jello) had some of the earliest MCA-booked radio shows emanating from New York. By the late 1930s, MCA's Los Angeles office also initiated network shows for Ted FioRito (*The Lady Esther Serenade* and *Hollywood Hotel,* with Dick Powell). Guy Lombardo's orchestra, meanwhile, became ubiquitous on the airwaves and the band became a national icon, especially in connection with the country's New Year's Eve celebration.

There is no better illustration of MCA's negotiation of lucrative radio contracts for its bands than the deals it sealed for the popular Lombardo band in 1931.[23] In exchange for its appearance on fifty-two broadcasts of the *Robert Burns Hour,* the group was paid $100,000. Next MCA procured for the band a thirty-week contract to play on a CBS show called *Radio Follies* for $50,000, not an insignificant amount of money for a Depression year. These contracts demonstrate not only the growing popularity of dance bands in general and Lombardo's in particular, but also the skill of MCA at exploiting this marriage of bands and radio broadcasting. Always exploring new sources of income, MCA began competing with advertising agencies in the late thirties by producing entire radio programs to present to the networks. This further increased its leverage with both the bands and with the networks for which the bands had become very popular programming fare.[24]

The Chicago station WBBM was acquired by CBS in 1931 and hired several conductors. Billy Mills and Howard Neumiller were the staff leaders in the early thirties.[25] By 1935, Clarence Wheeler was music director at WBBM. Caesar Petrillo, James Petrillo's younger brother and a staff trombonist, succeeded Wheeler in that post in 1938 and remained until 1963. In addition to many dramatic shows, Caesar Petrillo and his staff of conductors supported a host of music shows, some of them sponsored by Wrigley gum. Coincidentally, the WBBM studios were located in the Wrigley Building until 1954.

Ben Bernie, "the old maestro," popular so long from his College Inn days, settled in Chicago and hosted several CBS shows emanating from the WBBM studios during the late thirties and early forties. The shows featured fine musicians such as the guitarist Les Paul, among others. Bernie retired to the West Coast early in 1943, only to die shortly thereafter.[26]

Jimmy Hilliard, a staff musician and arranger, later served as a conductor of WBBM's dance orchestra from the late 1930s to the mid-1940s. He departed to join the fledgling Mercury Record Company as artists-and-repertoire head, which was the beginning of an admirable career in this industry.[27] He left Mercury shortly thereafter for Decca in New York, then went to Victor, and finally settled at Warner Brothers, where he was largely responsible for putting comedians such as Redd Foxx, Bob Newhart, and Allan Sherman on vinyl, starting a whole trend in comedy records.

WGN, the third major network station in Chicago and owned by the *Chicago Tribune,* hired the aforementioned Henry Selinger as its music director in the mid-twenties. Ernest Peachin, a trumpet virtuoso and brass-band director, joined Selinger in 1930, first as an assistant conductor and then as general musical director until 1934. About this time Harold Stokes briefly joined the staff at WGN with the Jean Goldkette orchestra he was leading. Stokes later returned as a staff conductor. The young Chicago Civic Opera director Henry Weber, a gifted and classically trained conductor, was brought in to reorganize the station's concert orchestra in 1934 and remained as conductor. He used his vast knowledge of opera and operettas to launch in 1941 the famous WGN program *Chicago Theater of the Air,* on which condensed versions of various operettas and operatic works were broadcast each Saturday evening.

The talented radio arranger Robert Trendler came on staff as Weber's assistant conductor in 1941 to direct the chorus and to lead the station's dance band. He later succeeded Weber as director of music and remained until 1975 when the station discontinued its staff orchestra, the last in Chicago. Until 1986 only a trio of musicians remained at WGN-TV to accompany the *Bozo's Circus* television show.

In 1941, the U.S. government forced NBC to dispose of either its Red or Blue network.[28] NBC chose to sell the Blue network, which under new ownership became the American Broadcasting Company (ABC). Now there were four radio networks. All the announcers, musicians, technicians, and writers from the Blue Network went to work for ABC. WENR in Chicago, which had been owned by the NBC Blue Network, became ABC's Chicago outlet. Harold Stokes moved from WGN to WENR that year and soon became program director for the station and head of programming for ABC's Midwest region. As such, he helped create a number of new shows for the fledgling radio network as well as the later television network.

By the 1950s remote band broadcasts from ballrooms, hotel dining rooms, and nightclubs had become anachronisms. Modern listeners had moved beyond the level of some of the old-style programming still being offered by amplitude modulation (AM) stations. New frequency modulated (FM) radio stations went on the air in the late 1940s and provided technically superior, static-free broadcasts that enhanced music programming. They quickly leveraged this capability to steal away AM listening audiences.

Television began to replace nighttime radio as a preferred home entertainment medium by the late 1940s and further changed the broadcast landscape. Advertisers poured more and more of their promotional dollars into the new lively visual medium to sponsor variety shows and dramas. Radio—AM radio especially—was struggling to survive. It offered little or no live music and changed mostly to a recorded music, news, and sports format.

Changing public tastes in music following World War II, a shift in entertainment preferences, and the increasing popularity of television were all factors in the demise of radio remotes. People no longer danced as much, but it was more than that. Young couples, buying homes and raising young families, didn't have the money to go out on the town except on special occasions, and they preferred to stay at home watching television. Fewer and fewer people cared about listening to dance bands either in person or on the radio.

The dance bands themselves may have been accessories in killing the golden goose of radio remotes by clinging rigidly to an outdated format, but the radio stations and networks must bear part of the blame.[29] The late-evening broadcasts were in a backwater of the daily radio schedule and they were unsponsored. Nobody seemed to pay any attention. The music changed but the stylized routine of the shows did not. Sweet bands, swing bands; it didn't matter. Listening today to a recorded remote band broadcast from the 1940s or from the early 1950s demonstrates how little things had changed since the early 1930s.

WBBM and WGN, which pioneered and perfected the remote concept, seemed reluctant to give up remote broadcasts of the bands and continued to carry a few as late as the 1960s. WGN was still doing a regular pickup from the Chez Paree nightclub (Ted FioRito's orchestra) in 1957 and 1958, complete with an on-site announcer. In 1964, WGN broadcast one hour of Wayne King's final appearance at the Aragon, and three years later the station broadcast an hour of Guy Lombardo's music from the Empire Room of the Palmer House Hotel. WBBM continued to carry a nightly fifteen-minute remote from Al Hausberg's Milford "Over Thirty" Ballroom on the Northwest Side until 1965, when the station moved to an all-talk format. Today band remotes have become popular listening fare on nostalgia broadcasts and old-time radio programs.

The active period for broadcast bands and orchestras lasted a little over fifty years. It started tentatively in the mid- to late 1920s as early stations hired small bands and it intensified from the 1930s to the late 1940s. As radio began losing out to television, some orchestras moved to television with the advent of big productions in the 1950s only to sputter in the late sixties under the enormous weight of production costs and come to a quiet end in 1975.

It had been a wild and exciting ride for the leaders, musicians, and arrangers during that half century, resulting in many thousands of hours of fine music and entertainment. Dance bands had created a lucrative business not only for broadcasters but also for large advertising agencies and, of course, for MCA. Radio and dance bands had truly formed an association made in music heaven. The pairing resulted not only in a successful and mutually productive partnership but also in the emergence of two giant industries: dance bands and commercial broadcasting.

# 4 Ice Rinks, Beer Gardens, and Other Early Chicago Dance Halls

A writer for *Variety* credited Chicago with having "started the metropolitan dancing craze" that became a popular social pastime in the early twentieth century.[1] The large dance halls had the biggest number of dancers and were among the biggest employers of the early dance bands.

Chicago's modern ballrooms grew out of the large dance halls that opened shortly after 1900. There was no single standard for dance halls at that time either in their design and construction or in the way they were operated. Most of the city's early dance halls, as a result, were located in buildings or facilities converted from other uses. It would take another two decades for the concept of the modern ballroom to develop fully.

The dancing business matured by the 1920s when the early dance halls were joined by newer, modern, and often palatial facilities. The Depression years of the early and mid-1930s, however, did not generally treat ballrooms kindly and several of the early, by now tired, grande dames fell by the wayside. For the others, World War II and the 1940s were the last hurrah. It was all downhill from there. A dramatic decline in dancing combined with the demise of the dance bands brought an end to the era by the early fifties. Only a few, mostly neighborhood or suburban ballrooms survived into the 1960s, the suburban venues supported mostly by a population shift away from the city.

The first decade of the ballroom era was not a comfortable one for the operators of these dance palaces, many of whom were new to the emerging business of dance hall management. The lack of uniformity of dance halls only complicated matters. One early dance hall opened in a former West Side ice skating rink. Several large but seasonal dance halls were built just after 1900 at the city's two large amusement parks. Others emerged from early beer gardens.

The larger dance halls became well managed and profitable within a decade. By 1922 dance halls had become a big business. *Variety* that year estimated that approximately fifteen thousand people danced each week night in the city's ten biggest dance halls and more than forty-five thousand per night showed up on weekends.[2] Admissions per couple ran from twenty-five cents to two dollars. The article attributed a five-month drop in ticket sales at downtown theaters to the increasing popularity of dance halls.

Both young and old dancers patronizing the larger establishments could expect to dance to a large orchestra in clean, decent surroundings among well-behaved crowds. It hadn't always been like that, but the entrepreneurs learned quickly. The learning experience included a good deal of pressure from both the City of Chicago and social reform agencies.

One of the first problems the ballroom operators had to resolve was how to change the public's perception of their enterprises as dance halls. The term "dance hall" itself dated back to the early 1800s and smacked of the wild mining and cow towns on the western frontier; it had negative connotations. In the 1890s and the early twentieth century, large numbers of smaller dance halls in Chicago still operated in connection with or adjacent to taverns, concert halls, or other establishments serving liquor. In some cases, they were near or connected with brothels.[3] Many other dance halls were little more than sleazy dumps in rough parts of town where the combination of alcohol and dancing frequently resulted in lewd and obscene behavior, especially among young people.

Even as late as 1931, the trade publication *Orchestra World* urged business people operating establishments used only for social dancing to think of new names that were synonymous with "ballroom" and evoked a less sleazy image.[4] This may account for the earlier and frequent use of the name "gardens" even when there was no garden present.

The concern that the combination of liquor and social dancing might influence the behavior of ballroom dancers, especially the younger people, was one reason the Juvenile Protective Association (JPA) was organized. Formed in Chicago just after the turn of the twentieth century, the social reform group sought to respond to a long list of social, moral, and health risks faced by children and young people in the teeming West Side neighborhoods where many of the city's immigrant families had recently settled. The growing number of early ballrooms quickly attracted the JPA's attention.[5] When surveying dance halls, JPA representatives examined issues such as whether liquor was sold on the premises or nearby, what the prevailing dress habits were, how well the premises were supervised, what kind of music was being played and at what tempos, and, most important of all, the dancers' conduct.

The JPA, which was closely allied with Jane Addams's Hull-House, began

working with ballroom managers to eliminate suggestive or indecent dancing styles or crude behavior on the dance floor.[6] JPA investigators policed the
ballrooms and other dance venues around Chicago, even the outlying Cook
County roadhouses, and issued periodic reports. The reports not only make
interesting reading but illuminate the risky social behavior that often resulted
from the combination of alcoholic beverages and dancing.[7] It didn't take long
for the ballroom operators to realize that the JPA was a fact of life and could
adversely affect their business, so they came to an accommodation with the
organization's leaders.

Another JPA concern was that the slow dance tempos used by the orchestras in most ballrooms encouraged indecent dancing, which was most often
defined as dancing too closely combined with abundant pelvic movement and
other suggestive gestures. This concern ultimately was resolved by increasing
considerably the tempo of the dance music. The faster dance tempos became
unique to Chicago in the early and mid-1920s.[8] In fact, the Chicago bandleader
Isham Jones encountered difficulty with New York dancers in 1925 because
of his fast dance tempo.

The JPA's diligent pursuit of socially acceptable dancing conditions and
improved etiquette of the dancers in the early years of the twentieth century
greatly influenced the way ballrooms were managed and how they were per-
ceived by the public for the next three decades. In essence, the JPA helped the
dance hall operators to redefine and reshape—if not reform—their business.

Three of the earliest major dance venues in Chicago began in European-style outdoor gardens and two more were connected with huge outdoor
amusement parks. The idea of al fresco drinking, summer dining, and entertainment in Chicago may hark back to the traditions of the city's large German
population, which was estimated in 1890 to be more than 150,000.[9] By 1900
Bismarck Gardens on the North Side and Sans Souci and Edelweiss Gardens
on the South Side were already established as major venues. Most of them
installed dance floors early in their operations. The city's two large amusement
parks—White City and Riverview—each had one or more indoor ballrooms
equipped with numerous windows and doors that could be opened to the
cooling summer breezes.

Prior to World War I the Dreamland Casino and the Paradise Ballroom
catered primarily to West Side dancers while the South Side's White City
Ballroom and Midway Gardens and the North Side's Riverview and Arcadia
Ballrooms served dancers in their areas. Closer to downtown was the Colum-
bia Ballroom on North Clark Street and the Princess on Madison Street near
Ogden.

White City Ballroom was part of the large White City Amusement Park on the South Side at Sixty-third Street and South Parkway, now Dr. Martin Luther King Jr. Drive.[10] The Beifield family, owner of the downtown Sherman Hotel, operated White City beginning in 1904. White City had two dance venues: the larger was known as the Ballroom and had the largest dance floor in the city, at 33,800 square feet; the smaller dance venue was called the Casino. In the early days of its existence and true to its name, the park was duly painted white. A tall, lighted tower, said to cast a soft white glow in the sky, was the amusement park's landmark.

The first cabaret show in Chicago was staged at the White City Casino in 1912, according to a *Chicago Tribune* article, and featured a young Sophie Tucker.[11] The park claimed to produce the first outdoor grand opera programs in the city, and the concert brass bands of Kryl and Creatore entertained early visitors to the park.[12] Eli Courlander's orchestra played indoors for ballroom dancers in 1906 and 1907. In 1914 Cope Harvey's orchestra was hired to play for White City Casino dancers, and he and his musicians remained there almost continuously until the early 1920s. Bert Kelly's band was another early dancing favorite as were the bands of Sig Meyer and Charles L. Cooke (known popularly as Charlie Cook, or as Doc Cook, for his doctorate in music), which played lengthy engagements at White City over the years.

The opening of the glamorous new Trianon Ballroom just four blocks to the east, however, sounded the death knell for the White City dance emporia. Dancers were attracted by the Trianon's size and its amenities, and the new air-cooling system provided comfort for indoor dancing in the summer. There was a fire at White City in 1927. The park's ballroom and roller-skating rink survived, but the landmark tower, along with a Ferris wheel and some other buildings, did not.

Doc Cook's orchestra was one of the last regular attractions to play for dancing at White City. The group left the ballroom in 1930. Throughout the early and mid-1930s Depression years, dancing in the large ballroom limped along, limited to Sundays only. On New Year's Eve 1932 the ballroom featured Verne Buck's orchestra and the White City Symphonic Band.[13] By 1933, however, the park was delinquent on its taxes and the same year went into bankruptcy.[14] Although condemned as a fire hazard in 1939, the ballroom continued to operate spasmodically, but in 1959 it was consumed by flames. The site now is occupied by a housing development.

The Midway Gardens, although not technically a dance hall, was a major early dance venue on the South Side. Located at 6000 South Cottage Grove Avenue, on the southwest corner of Sixtieth Street and Cottage Grove, it occupied the northern half of the block along the west side of Cottage Grove. Midway Gardens was a large complex consisting of a terraced outdoor garden and a smaller indoor winter garden and restaurant that was later converted into a ballroom. The complex was conceived by a group of culturally oriented Chicago investors led by Edward C. Waller Jr. and Oscar J. Friedman and built on part of the site of the former Sans Souci amusement park.[15]

Midway Gardens opened in June 1914 and was best known as one of the Chicago architect Frank Lloyd Wright's earliest triumphs, but it was financially troubled from the beginning. Ballets, symphony concerts, and other cultural events were presented in the sprawling, terraced outdoor garden that seated four thousand people. The new venue operated for only two seasons as the Midway Gardens. Late in 1915 the Schoenhofen Brewery Company bought the distressed property, renamed it Edelweiss Gardens, and more or less continued with the same type of musical programs until 1918, when it was closed for a year during World War I. It reopened the following year and began presenting vaudeville acts, such as Ted Lewis and company, and outdoor public dancing with Benson orchestras led by Walter Ford and George Mallen. By 1921 the brewery company–owner of Edelweiss Gardens, facing heavy losses because of Prohibition, could no longer afford to keep it operating.

After a two-year hiatus and a major renovation by two businessmen, Edward Diedrich and G. R. Hebert, owners of the nearby Midway Automobile and Supply Company, the winter garden opened for public dancing in late 1923 with Art Kassel and his orchestra.[16] It now was called Midway Dancing Gardens and was managed for a time by George O'Hare, Husk O'Hare's younger brother. The space that previously seated 850 diners was expanded to accommodate 2,500 dancers on a spacious 21,600-square-foot indoor ballroom floor, the third largest in the city at that time.[17]

Midway Dancing Gardens often has been confused with the entire Midway Gardens complex, the largest part of which was the massive outdoor garden. Outdoor dancing on two and later three separate cement dance floors for patrons of the Gardens occurred only after the Schoenhofen Brewing Company took over Midway Gardens. The indoor or winter garden, a restaurant and cabaret show room, wasn't converted into a public ballroom until Diedrich and Hebert assumed management of the property.

It is the Midway Dancing Gardens—the indoor ballroom—which is of most interest to this study. The prominent South Side booker and leader Cope Harvey is said to have hired the bands at the Dancing Gardens. Elmer Schoebel's Memphis Melody Boys and bands led by Floyd Town, Ralph Williams, and the pianist Mel Stitzel were booked for dancing at the venue following Kassel. The dance bands at Midway Dancing Gardens could best be described as "hot" bands, meaning they featured musicians that played contemporary music reflecting the rising interest in jazz music in the early 1920s. The ballroom drew much of its crowd from the nearby University of Chicago campus and from the greater South Side.

Midway Dancing Gardens, however, simply could not compete with the new and glamorous Trianon just two blocks down the street, and it closed its doors in 1926. This begs the question about Messrs. Diedrich and Hebert's business judgment in light of the Trianon's opening a full year before they opened the doors to their Midway Dancing Gardens. The latter building later was used briefly as a roller-skating rink but in 1929 it was torn down and replaced with a gas station and car wash.[18]

Midway Dancing Gardens had a short but dazzling life. The entire Midway Gardens complex, probably doomed from its beginning, lasted only sixteen years. It certainly fell far short of its developers' grandiose vision for a cultural oasis, and its demise was a bitter disappointment for its architect.

There were two Merry Garden Ballrooms, three if you count a ballroom of the same name within Riverview Amusement Park.[19] The two better-known Merry Garden Ballrooms, however, were operated by the former dance team of Ethel Kendall and Jack Lund. The South Side Merry Garden was at 6040 South Cottage Grove Avenue, just south of but in the same block as Midway Gardens. The dance hall, a building on the old Sans Souci Amusement Park grounds, opened for business in the late 1910s. Other Sans Souci buildings, neither related nor connected to the Midway Gardens, continued to be used after Midway Gardens was completed to the north.[20] Cope Harvey also provided bands for this venue and played there with his own orchestra.

Kendall and Lund's ballroom was profitable; in the early 1920s the duo built the Pershing Hotel, just four blocks south on Cottage Grove Avenue at Sixty-fourth Street, presumably with their ballroom earnings.[21] The South Side Merry Garden closed about 1921 or early 1922 when Kendall and Lund built a new ballroom of the same name at Sheffield and Belmont on the North Side. They were prescient in their planning; within the year the new Trianon Ballroom rose two blocks to the south of the Merry Garden on Cottage Grove Avenue. It was a year later that the Midway Gardens winter garden, just to the north, was made over into the Midway Dancing Gardens. By 1925 the building housing the Merry Garden was an auto showroom operated by Diedrich and Hebert, who were running Midway Gardens next door.[22]

❖ ❖ ❖

One of the most unusual conversions of an existing building for use as a dance hall was the transformation that resulted in the Dreamland Casino at 1701 West Van Buren Street. The building was built in 1910 as an ice rink called the Ice Palace and was first leased to investors hoping to establish a professional ice hockey league. A large rectangular building (it could hold up to two thousand skaters), it was built on an unlikely piece of property belonging to the Rapid Transit Lines under the elevated train tracks at Van Buren and Paulina Streets, a point where routes from the north and south joined a major east-west line to the Loop. Large windows were installed in the roof to allow El passengers to view the skaters. The large curving, canopied entrance on the southwest corner of Van Buren and Paulina Streets was brightly illuminated with light bulbs and had large stained-glass windows above.[23] Two squat, brick towers framed the entrance.

Professor Frank Bement reopened the building as a combination ballroom and roller skating rink in 1911 with J. Louis Guyon as dance master.[24] Guyon took over the lease from Bement in 1914 and the place became known as Guyon's Dreamland. Both Bement and Guyon were sticklers for "chaste dancing" and proper etiquette, and they demanded appropriate behavior on the dance floor. Guyon's strict Victorian ideas on proper dancing led him to reject the tango and one-step as "immoral dances," but he looked approvingly on the more conventional two-step and the waltz. Guyon prospered running the Dreamland and left in 1917 to build his own ballroom.[25]

Patrick "Paddy" Harmon, a West Side promoter and sportsman, assumed the lease for the Dreamland operation.[26] The politically well connected Harmon, a bit more liberal in his thinking than Bement and Guyon had been, eased up a bit on dancers, allowing them to do some of the popular dances of the day. Harmon, however, never allowed things to get out of hand. Soon after taking over the Dreamland, Harmon hired Charles Elgar's small orchestra in 1916 to replace Frank Cavallo's orchestra, which was an unusual move because Elgar was a black bandleader from the city's South Side. Elgar became so popular with the young neighborhood dancers that his band remained on the stand of the giant ballroom until 1922. That year Doc Cook and his band from the Riverview Park ballroom followed Elgar. Harmon knew Cook, a black bandleader originally from Detroit, through the Riverview Ballroom, for which Harmon had the dancing concession.

The elevated tracks running above the Dreamland, as expected, caused a significant noise problem in the ballroom during Elgar's tenure there. Someone suggested that the $25,000 Barton organ, left over from the ice rink, be played along with the band at those times when a train crossed overhead. The organ would swell in volume to cover the noise, then resume its normal volume thereafter. The band, in the meantime, had been moved to the organ platform in the middle of the floor for easier coordination with the organ.

After the arrival of Cook's orchestra, Cook, himself an organist, is said to have continued the tradition of playing the Barton to mask the noise of the passing trains. He also added some of the loudest musicians he could find: the trumpeter Freddie Keppard and the clarinetist Jimmy Noone, both from New Orleans.[27] Being the promoter he was, Harmon staged big parties at holiday seasons, especially Christmas, at which time he often distributed gifts to thousands of West Side neighborhood children, for whom he was like a benevolent uncle.[28]

In 1930 Paddy Harmon was fatally injured in an auto accident on Northwest Highway near Palatine in the northwest suburbs. His widow, Mae (also injured in the auto accident), and his nephew Frankie continued to run the Dreamland. James Petrillo called the bandleader Joe Kayser and asked him to take his band into the Dreamland to help Mae and Frankie keep the ballroom going.[29] A year later Kayser and the popular ballroom manager Eddie Gilmartin bought interests in the operation, but the building still was owned by the Rapid Transit Lines, to which the Harmons, Kayser, and Gilmartin paid a monthly rent of six hundred dollars. Since the floor's banked curves for skaters were never removed, the new operators reopened the place as a combination roller rink and ballroom. Renamed the Playdium, it only lasted a few years and closed in 1934, a victim of the Depression.

Up on the North Side before World War I, the Marigold Gardens, an old-fashioned beer garden at Broadway and Grace Street, featured dancing in addition to cabaret shows both outside in the garden during summer and, during the rest of the year, in an indoor winter garden.[30] It was originally called DeBerg's Grove and was a vestige of the late 1800s European-style beer garden fad. Brass bands often were the featured entertainment. The site was thought to be the epitome of Chicago beer gardens on a grand scale.

Emil and Karl Eitel, who owned the downtown Bismarck Hotel, had bought the DeBerg property in 1896, changed the name to Bismarck Gardens, and later reinstated DeBerg's original entertainment policy of floor shows featuring cabaret acts. The property was billed as "nature's tree-roofed garden of music." Public dancing was added in 1910, and in 1914, on the eve of World War I, the Eitels changed the name to Marigold Gardens because of the growing hostility of Americans toward Germany and things German.[31]

The Marigold Room, from which the new name was taken, was the indoor or winter garden in which floor shows were presented. Over time, the Marigold became more of a cabaret than an outdoor beer garden.

The Chicago bandleader Paul Biese was the Marigold Gardens music director by 1916 and Carlos Sebastian staged the revues, called the Marigold Follies. The 1916–17 edition of the show featured a cast of sixteen young women and principals along with Biese's orchestra.[32] Floor shows continued to be the attraction during the early 1920s. They were produced by the Benson Organization until 1922, with the Benson Orchestra of Chicago directed by Roy Bargy.[33] The following year Ernie Young's agency took over the production of the shows and brought in Young's close associate Fred Hamm and his orchestra. From 1923 through 1926 the Marigold became a full-time two-part dance hall. The former garden was floored over and featured hotter bands, while the winter garden became a waltzes-only venue. Verne Buck and Herb Carlin's orchestras played for the dancers. More about the Marigold appears later in this book.

The Moulin Rouge, later the site of the Rainbo Garden, and the Green Mill Gardens were two early and significant dance venues located just a few miles to the north of the Marigold. Rainbo Garden was on Clark Street just north of Lawrence and the Green Mill Gardens was on Broadway at Lawrence. Both had outdoor summer gardens as well as indoor facilities for the winter months, and both became major Chicago cabarets in the 1920s. They will be treated in some detail in later chapters.

The Moulin Rouge property, at 4812–36 North Clark Street, began its life as an early roadhouse and restaurant that specialized in serving lunches in the 1890s to post-funeral parties from St. Boniface Cemetery across Clark Street. This was before the area, known as Uptown, became a part of Chicago. The Moulin Rouge became a dance hall, and the owner, Neals Buck, sold it to the long-time Chicago restaurant operator Fred Mann in 1918, who changed the name of the place to Rainbo Garden. This venue's important history as a popular dance location and major cabaret and restaurant began with Mann's proprietorship, which is discussed at length in a later chapter.

Several blocks to the east of the Rainbo was the Green Mill Gardens, one of the three largest summer garden entertainment spots in Chicago in the 1910s. Located at 4800–06 North Broadway Avenue, the Green Mill Gardens site, like that of the Moulin Rouge, had been a roadhouse and restaurant just after the turn of the twentieth century. From its location on the northwest corner of Lawrence and Broadway, it mainly served mourners from St. Boniface Cemetery a few blocks to the west. The Chamales brothers, Greek immigrants who were successful flower vendors on the South Side, bought the property in 1914. They remodeled and reopened the property that summer as the Green Mill Sunken Gardens.[34]

The Green Mill was unique in the United States because it was a sunken garden. Like the other outdoor gardens in Chicago at the time, however, there was an indoor or winter garden for indoor dining. The Chamales hired Miss Patricola and her twenty-five-piece orchestra as the main musical attraction for the opening, along with several vaudeville acts. After the opening, Patricola's orchestra, known as one of the best of the cabaret acts, remained as the primary drawing card and played return engagements annually until January 1917 when the troupe left to tour the Pantages vaudeville circuit.[35] Over time, the Green Mill, like the nearby Marigold and the far South Side Midway Gardens, added dancing to the bill of fare and by 1915 the Henry Theiss orchestra was playing on the bandstand.

Arnold Johnson's band played there for dancing in the years during World War I, according to Joe Kayser, who visited the Green Mill often with service buddies from the Great Lakes Naval Training Center, just north near Waukegan.[36] During the same period (1918–20) the drummer Tommy Rogers's ten-piece orchestra also played there with personnel that included at least five future Chicago bandleaders: Isham Jones (saxophone), Maurie Sherman, Sig Meyer (violin), Sol Wagner, and Arnold Johnson (piano). Ray Lopez, a New Orleans cornetist who had played with Tom Brown's band at the downtown Lamb's Café in 1915, also was one of the Rogers musicians.[37] The Green Mill is discussed further in a later chapter.

Just a few miles south along Broadway was the Arcadia, one of the earliest dance halls built after the turn of the twentieth century, before the concept of the modern ballroom was fully developed. A rather spartan building, about 225 feet long and 100 feet wide, with a curved, truss roof, the Arcadia was located at 4444 North Broadway. It made its official debut in October 1910 with an open house for the neighborhood.[38]

Built by Otto Price and John McCracken, the Arcadia, like the Dreamland Ballroom on the West Side,[39] was sited on property owned by the Rapid Transit Lines and was adjacent to the North Side elevated system workshops. The pianist Al Copeland and a seven-piece orchestra provided the music for the first dancers at the Arcadia in 1910.[40] Later, McCracken and Price hired other Benson Organization orchestras led by George Mallen and Sol Wagner.[41]

Paddy Harmon, Dreamland's operator, had leased the Arcadia building from McCracken and Price in 1923 for a reported $200,000.[42] Both the Arcadia and Dreamland prospered under his imaginative direction. The Arcadia, also used for roller-skating, was well appointed for the time but was neither as classy as the later Paradise Ballroom on the West Side nor as elegant as the Trianon, built more than a decade later.

The Rockford-based bandleader Joe Kayser, who was hired by Harmon to play at the Arcadia, said that the North Side hall was a more intimate room than the huge Dreamland and featured red, white, and blue lights and the requisite revolving mirrored ball hanging from the ceiling.[43] He said he never cared for the rather high bandstand, located on the north side of the hall, because it didn't allow any interaction between the band and the dancers.

Kayser was hired by Harmon to pep things up a bit musically. He heard about the Arcadia's opening through the bandleader Arnold Johnson, who ran a booking office in addition to his dance band.[44] Johnson and Kayser's friendship went back to the 1910s when Kayser played drums with a Benson orchestra, but despite their friendship Johnson could not book an out-of-town band.

Kayser contacted Paddy Harmon directly and came into Chicago to audition for the Arcadia job in 1924. The audition took place at the Dreamland Ballroom. Kayser said he and his musicians came in the back door of Dreamland so as not to attract any attention from the union. Doc Cook, the leader at Dreamland, also attended the audition to help Harmon evaluate Kayser's young band.

The Arcadia job was Kayser's introduction to Chicago. He and his men replaced Sol Wagner's band, but Kayser took his band back on the road after the first Arcadia engagement because he found that playing one-night engagements in the Illinois-Iowa-Wisconsin territory still was more lucrative than a steady ballroom job in Chicago.[45] Kayser later returned to Chicago to play at the Aragon, Trianon, and Merry Garden ballrooms and to lead stage bands at the large Diversey Theater on Clark Street and the State Theater in nearby Hammond, Indiana.

Paddy Harmon liked the job Cook had done to spice up the dance music at Dreamland and began using black as well as white bands at the Arcadia. Charlie Elgar and Clifford "Klarinet" King both worked at the ballroom. Dancing at the Arcadia ended briefly in 1926, but two years later Harmon hired Walter Barnes's Royal Creolean orchestra, a very popular black band from the South Side. The Barnes group remained at the Arcadia through the 1928–29 season and then spent part of the summer of 1929 at Harmon's West Side Dreamland.[46]

The Arcadia had shut down before 1930, the year Paddy Harmon died following a car accident. It remained vacant until 1931 when, under new management, it became a roller rink. It was leased in 1932 to Albert Hart and Michael Agazim for remodeling into an auditorium for dancing and other events.[47] That same year it reopened for dancing with Leon Bloom's orchestra. Dancing continued off and on through the 1930s but the Arcadia finally gave up its identity as a ballroom for that of a full-time roller rink.[48] A fire destroyed the building in 1959 and the site was cleared the following year.

Another converted building made into a dance hall was the Columbia Ballroom. Located just south of North Avenue on the east side of Clark Street, the second-floor dancing emporium was operated in the 1920s by Frank Mc-Guire, a dance master who kept a "special introducer" on hand to accommodate any shy man who found it difficult to approach a lady for a dance.[49] This neighborhood ballroom hired only local bands. Among those playing there was a colorful group of musicians led by the pianist Harry Plattenberg, called McGuire's Ice Cream Kings because they wore white suits. Sig Meyer's band and Jimmy Bell's orchestra from the South Side occasionally alternated on the bandstand.

Riverview was the North Side's equivalent to White City Amusement Park and opened the same year, 1904. George Schmidt, a wealthy Chicago businessman, conceived and built the park along the west side of Western Avenue between Belmont Avenue on the south and what later became Lane Technical High School on the north. The former shooting and hunting park on more than seventy acres featured most of the amusement rides and attractions of a state fairground. Riverview's main entrance was at Roscoe and Western Avenues.

Schmidt built one of the earliest dance pavilions on the North Side, a large wooden building at the south end of the park on the Belmont side. It was designed originally for summer use only. James A. Tinney, the manager, hired the pianist Ralph Foote to play dance music during the seasons of 1905 through 1909.[50] This predated by about five to nine years the dancing craze that hit Chicago and much of America. Later, an dance orchestra led by Tomasco replaced Foote.

In 1918 the Riverview management hired the black leader Doc Cook and his orchestra to play for both dancing and roller-skating year around.[51] Cook had been working in Detroit and was booked through the office of the Detroit bandleader/booking agent Ben Shook. Shook himself planned to fulfill the Riverview contract but at the last minute had a conflict and sent Cook instead.

Cook remained at Riverview through the end of the 1921–22 season. In addition to being a bandleader, he was a composer and arranger of some repute. While at Riverview he wrote a number of tunes including "I've Got the Blue Ridge Blues" (1918) and "Daisy Days" (1920).[52] It was a good job but it was a back-breaking schedule. Cook's Society Orchestra was featured at various venues within Riverview Park such as the Roller Rink, Palace Ball Room, Casino, and Merry Garden Ballroom (this ballroom was in the park and should not be confused with the nearby freestanding Merry Garden built in 1921) and on the bandstand in the park.[53] Ray Parker, originally with Tomasco's orchestra, led a dance band in the Merry Garden Ballroom at Riverview during the winter of 1920.

During the 1920s the park also hired other attractions such as the bandleaders Charlie Straight, Roy Bargy (then directing the Benson Orchestra of Chicago at Marigold Gardens), and Paul Biese (then working at the Pantheon Theater and the Edgewater Beach Hotel). The three leaders were known on Emerson records as The Imperial Three. Straight also appeared at the Roller Rink with his band in January 1921 to play for the "I Love You Sunday" party, an event named after a tune Straight had written.[54]

Elmer Kaiser's band and Frank Schmidt and his "Million Dollar Orchestra" replaced Doc Cook when he departed in 1922, but the Riverview summer ballroom could no longer attract the dancing crowd after the modern, air-cooled Merry Garden (1922) and Aragon (1926) Ballrooms opened nearby, providing year-round comfort.[55] While the ballroom later catered mostly to those attending the amusement park, the roller rink operated into the 1950s but was destroyed by fire.

The Princess, one of the earliest converted dance halls on the city's West Side, was a former Salvation Army training school located at 1519 West Madison Street. Al Turk's band was on the bandstand from the mid-teens to the early 1920s. Mike Parsons, a trombonist, succeeded Turk as leader of the band and, in 1923, Jules Goldberg's Princess Serenaders took the stand.[56]

The Princess was a medium-sized (8,500 square feet), upstairs ballroom in a rough neighborhood that a decade later became one of the city's skid rows.[57] The nine-piece Turk band, known at various times as the Princess Orchestra, Al Turk and His Oriental Serenaders, or Al Turk and His Turks, was a good but unremarkable ballroom dance band, as reflected in his limited recordings (Olympic and Okeh).[58] When Turk and his musicians occasionally played one-nighters out of town, most often booked by Turk himself or by Walter Ford, the Turk band was billed as the Oriental Serenaders, and for college dates it was called the Fraternity Aces. It was never booked for road engagements as the Princess Orchestra.

Danceland, another West Side dance hall, was built in 1921 at 3825 West Madison Street, near Homan Avenue, and had a fairly large dance floor—

13,500 square feet.[59] It was a ballroom of many names, first called Driscoll's Danceland. Pinky Aarseth's twelve-piece Benson band was the first band to play there but by the end of the first year Driscoll was losing money so he gave the band two-weeks' notice and closed the ballroom doors.

Danceland later reopened as the Brilliant Ballroom. In the mid-1920s it was named the Playdium (not to be confused with the old Dreamland Ballroom that was renamed Playdium in the early 1930s). The popular bandleader Arnold Johnson and his orchestra were hired to play for dancing at the Playdium. Johnson had been a fixture in the city in the 1910s and early 1920s at the Green Mill Gardens. From 1927 through the mid-1930s the huge ballroom became a cabaret and restaurant briefly called the Pla-mor Café in 1928, but a year or two later it became the Golden Pumpkin Chinese Restaurant, which will be discussed later.[60] Then, in the late 1930s and early 1940s, it was returned to a dance hall and called the Park Casino Ballroom. The building later was converted to a bowling alley but then lay dormant for many years. It was destroyed by fire in 1990.

J. Louis Guyon broke new ground in the dance business when he built his new Paradise dance hall on Crawford Avenue (now Pulaski Road) near Washington Boulevard, on the West Side. The Paradise, though called a dance hall at the time of its construction, was probably the first modern ballroom in Chicago to be designed and built from the ground up expressly for dancing, and it became a prototype of sorts. It was a nicely appointed dancing facility with air cooling for year-round operation. The emphasis was on moral dancing in decent surroundings. As noted earlier, Guyon had been dance master and then proprietor of the Dreamland, but he longed to have a more modern facility where he could implement fully his vision of an inviting and wholesome atmosphere where well-behaved dancers could enjoy themselves.[61]

The architect Francis M. Barton designed the facility to Guyon's specifications and it was built in 1918. Guyon also built an apartment hotel nearby, at the northwest corner of Washington Boulevard and Crawford Avenue, which was aptly named the Guyon Apartments.

Guyon had very definite ideas on how close dancers should be to each other. According to the bandleader Jules Herbuveaux, who both played in and led the Paradise orchestra in the early 1920s, the 25,500-square-foot dance floor easily held five thousand people. He said, "They could have put 10,000 people in there but they [Guyon] made them dance ten inches apart; anything less than that [and] you got thrown ... out. ... It was a very nice place."[62] Guyon was a stickler on maintaining that ten-inch separation, but he still managed to put enough dancers in his new ballroom that by 1922 he was said to be making a hundred thousand dollars a year.[63]

Jules Herbuveaux joined the Paradise orchestra in 1920 or early 1921. At the time, the group was led by the violinist Gordon Pouliet, a former symphony player from Minneapolis. The saxophone—Herbuveaux's instrument—was then coming into its own in dance bands, and Herbuveaux succeeded Pouliet as leader within the year.[64] Pouliet then joined Fred Hamm's orchestra at the Marigold Gardens as a violinist.[65] Herbuveaux's band recorded in New York for Okeh as the Guyon's Paradise Orchestra and continued to play at the Paradise until spring 1925. On Monday nights the group would travel to Villa Olivia, the Elgin-area estate of Charles Erbstein, an attorney and radio pioneer, and play over Erbtein's station, WTAS.

Herb Carlin's Benson Organization band followed Herbuveaux into the Paradise in 1925 and was in turn followed by a long list of bands over the years, including those led by Louis Panico, a former Isham Jones trumpeter, and by Charlie Agnew, formerly of the Dell Lampe Trianon Orchestra. Guyon died in 1944 and the ballroom was taken over and managed by a group headed by Herbert Beifield, formerly of White City.

In 1946, just after the close of World War II, Charlie Agnew returned to the ballroom to play for regular dancing and Henry Gendron played for the over-forty dancing. Later, the bands of Boyd Raeburn and Emil Flindt played engagements there. Flindt practically became the house band for several years in the late 1940s. Used for other purposes and then deserted in later years, the ballroom building was destroyed by fire in 1972.[66]

For its day, the Paradise was a high-class and well-appointed ballroom, and it also was the first major ballroom to be built in Chicago with the emphasis on moral dancing as well as decent surroundings. In these areas Guyon and the Juvenile Protective Association agreed. The Paradise was, in a sense, the harbinger of the new Trianon Ballroom and others to follow.

# 5 The Trianon, the Aragon, and the Modern Ballroom Era

IN December 1922 Andrew and William Karzas, two successful South Side businessmen, stunned the dancing and entertainment worlds when they opened their new, majestic Trianon Ballroom at Sixty-second Street and Cottage Grove Avenue. It was light years beyond J. Louis Guyon's vision of a setting for moral dancing in well-appointed surroundings. The Trianon was mammoth, its decor elegant—some would say posh—and its giant oval floor was the second largest in the city.

Dancing in Chicago would never be the same again; in fact the Trianon sent shock waves through the entertainment industry nationwide. It set higher standards for ballroom design, decor, and operation, not to mention size, and it seemed to eliminate any doubt as to whether or not ballroom dancing was just a fad. It was the modern quintessential ballroom, a metaphor for the times, and in the following years numerous ballrooms bearing the Trianon name began springing up in other cities and towns, but few of them rivaled the original in Chicago. In short, it was the first "ballroom" worthy of the name. To call it a dance hall, which many did at first, was to demean all that it represented. More important, Chicago dancers began deserting other early dance halls in favor of the Trianon. Within ten years, they would be lining up at Cottage Grove and Sixty-second Street before the doors opened.

The Trianon was constructed amid an early 1920s building boom in Chicago, especially in entertainment buildings. The boom was, in part, a release of a pent-up demand caused by the curtailment of construction during 1917 and 1918, when vital materials were diverted to the war effort. Paralleling the boom was a dramatic shift in architectural styles and significant improvements made in construction technology, which influenced the builders of the many new, so-called "atmospheric" theaters then being erected. More about these theaters will follow in chapter 11.

An important feature in these new structures was air cooling, a predecessor to modern air conditioning, which significantly improved customer comfort. More important, it gave managers a distinct marketing advantage: they could keep their new theaters open year-round, profiting from the additional months of operating revenue previously lost during summer shutdowns.

Andrew and William Karzas, the Trianon's builders, were Greek immigrants who had owned restaurants and nickelodeons and who were then operating several movie theaters.[1] They were keen observers of the current theater-building trends (their Woodlawn Theater was built in the new atmospheric style) and also were aware of the growth of ballroom dancing as a pastime. Their crowning achievement was addressing both trends in their new ballroom.

Designed by the theater architects Rapp and Rapp and modeled on the Grand Trianon Palace in Versailles, France, the Trianon Ballroom cost $1.2 million to build. It was financed through the sale of $1 million worth of building bonds. Beautiful did not begin to describe the interior of the new atmospheric ballroom. A grand staircase led to the ballroom on the upper level, which had a 29,580-square-foot dance floor and could accommodate up to three thousand dancers. Brocades, velvet, marble, and crystal were used lavishly throughout the building.[2]

To create a big splash for the Trianon's opening, Andrew Karzas, the ballroom's managing partner, hired Paul Whiteman and his orchestra, then probably the best-known dance orchestra in the country, to play for a charity ball on opening night and for the first week of dancing. Meanwhile, Roy Bargy led a fifteen-piece house relief band made up of musicians from the Benson Orchestra of Chicago, to which Bargy had added some musicians from the Paul Sternberg Orchestra then playing at the downtown Palace Theater.[3] The Bargy orchestra remained at the Trianon as the main attraction after Whiteman's departure, but for only about eight months of what originally was to have been a one-year engagement. Andrew Karzas in the meantime shopped around for an outstanding orchestra he could showcase at the new ballroom. Bargy's booking was handled through the Ernie Young agency, which had assumed management of the band at the end of 1922 when Bargy temporarily broke away from the Benson office.

Early in 1923, Andrew Karzas hired the well-known New York composer and arranger J. Bodewalt Lampe ("Creole Belles" and "Visions of Salome") as music director for the Karzas brothers' three theaters, the Trianon, and the new Karzas-owned radio station, WMBB. Bodewalt Lampe was charged by Andrew Karzas to organize a good dance band for the Trianon. Lampe thereupon called on his son Dell, an experienced conductor mostly of theater bands, who put together a nineteen-piece orchestra of high-caliber East Coast musicians.

The Lampe orchestra opened in September 1923, replacing Bargy's crew. The new orchestra was too large to fit on the ballroom's regular bandstand, located in an alcove on one side of the oval dance floor, and so a special platform had to be constructed for the orchestra at the ballroom's north end. The temporary bandstand soon was made permanent and became the main location of the orchestra.[4] The original bandstand was used when a second orchestra was needed. Lampe's orchestra, later reduced to twelve pieces, stayed until 1929. A second band, frequently led by Wayne King, Al Morey, or Charlie Agnew—all Lampe sidemen—almost always played on the side bandstand on weekends, thus providing continuous dancing.[5] Business had been good at the Trianon but Karzas quickly realized that Lampe's house band alone was not drawing the young dancers to the ballroom as expected, and he tried to break the band's contract. When that failed, he began hiring local and road bands to alternate with Lampe's group in hopes of livening things up for the young dancers.

In 1933 Jan Garber's orchestra hit the jackpot with dancers at the Trianon after he switched to a sweet band that was a Guy Lombardo sound-alike. With the airtime he received from the Trianon over WGN, his popularity grew and soon dancers were coming to the ballroom from all over the Midwest. Garber played long annual engagements through 1936, and Andrew and William Karzas and their investors, after struggling for eleven years to find a successful formula for the Trianon, finally were in box-office heaven.

Toward the end of 1935, however, they got a surprise. Garber, their cash-cow attraction, wanted to break his contract. He was getting so popular that on one seventy-one-stop one-nighter tour in 1935 (booked by MCA, of course) he took in an average of $1,100 a night, which was pretty big money for the Depression years.[6] With all this cash coming in, Garber was anxious to capitalize on his growing popularity and spend more time on the road than his Trianon contract allowed. To resolve the impasse, Garber agreed to buy out his long-term Trianon contract for $47,000, to be paid over time at $500 a week.[7]

Andrew Karzas, the managing partner, in the meantime, began searching for a "new Jan Garber" for his South Side wonder ballroom. He came close during 1935–39 when he attracted not just one but two bandleaders, Ted Weems and Kay Kyser. Weems was a veteran leader who was based in the Chicago area and had played at the Trianon and many other Chicago venues in the late 1920s and early 1930s. He now became a regular at the Trianon each season and featured a singer named Perry Como. Kay Kyser, a big hit for several years at the Blackhawk, had quickly risen to national prominence with his *Kollege of Musical Knowledge* radio show. Like Weems, Kyser played several long engagements at the Trianon before 1940. Practically every major dance band in the country played at the Trianon over the next ten years but the Karzas management preferred the sweet bands, those melody-oriented bands like Guy Lombardo, Jan Garber, Weems, and Kyser. During the years of World War II the bandleaders Lawrence Welk and Don Reid played at the Trianon so often they almost became "house" bands.

In 1946 and 1947 the city's growing black population, formerly living west of Cottage Grove Avenue and north of Sixty-third Street, began moving east and south. Until this time the Trianon, like many large entertainment enterprises in the then de facto segregated city, had an all-white policy. Now the black population was demanding entry to the Trianon, the Tivoli Theater located one-and-a-half blocks to the south, and many other formerly all-white venues. This resulted in a series of demonstrations and other disruptive incidents outside the Trianon in the early 1950s. These developments combined with limited parking for the dancers' cars severely affected attendance at the Trianon and it closed in 1954. The building was leased to various groups but finally fell to the wrecker's hammer in 1967 and was replaced by a moderate-income housing project.[8] The demolition of the building symbolically ended the era of grandiose ballrooms, just as the building of the Trianon had started the trend in 1922.

With the success of the Trianon assured by 1925, the Karzas brothers formed a syndicate and immediately began planning to build a similar glamorous ballroom on the North Side—the Aragon—on Lawrence Avenue just east of Broadway. The architects Ralph Huszagh and Boyd Hill (affiliated with John Eberson, an architect of atmospheric theaters) conceived the design for the Aragon to simulate a Moorish castle courtyard in Aragon, an ancient kingdom that preceded modern Spain.[9] The new facility was officially opened on July 14, 1926, with a giant ball for the Fraternal Order of Elks, then having its national meeting in Chicago.

With 21,036 square feet of space for dancing, the Aragon had the fifth-largest ballroom floor in the city, exceeded only by those of the Midway Dancing Gardens, Paradise, Trianon, and White City. The Aragon was every bit as sumptuous and classy as its sister ballroom to the south. Projected clouds moved across a light-blue ceiling that simulated the sky. The lighting could be adjusted to create the effects of different times of the day or evening. A grand staircase ascending to the second-floor ballroom was copied from the Trianon and, to accommodate two orchestras, the Aragon bandstand was two-tiered, the second stand slightly above and behind the first. There were curtains for the front and back bandstands, each of which had a separate lighting system.

Remembering his early difficulties in hiring the proper orchestra for the Trianon, Andrew Karzas now sought the advice of James C. Petrillo. The "right" band could make or break the new Aragon. Petrillo recommended the Oriole Terrace Orchestra, headed by Ted FioRito and Dan Russo as co-leaders.[10] The band had just completed its fourth year at the ritzy Edgewater Beach Hotel on the North Side and was playing at the downtown Palace Theater. FioRito and Russo, who also owned a partnership in radio station WIBO with Nelson Brothers Furniture Company, were very popular with the Edgewater Beach Hotel clientele and had developed a large listening audience through their nightly broadcasts and Brunswick records.

Karzas hired the Oriole Terrace Orchestra and sent it to play an introductory engagement for one week at the Trianon while the Dell Lampe Orchestra was on vacation.[11] Once ensconced at the Aragon, however, the band had a difficult first few months. An acoustical problem that was discovered in the giant ballroom shortly after opening caused an echo when the band played, confounding musicians and dancers alike.[12] The dancers seemed to be the most confused, trying to figure out which beat they should be dancing to, that of the band or that from the echo. The farther the dancers moved away from the bandstand, the more troublesome the problem became. The band was a flop, Ted FioRito recalled in a magazine interview.[13]

A mismatch of the orchestra with the young Aragon dancers also may have been part of the difficulty. The Oriole Terrace band was used to playing for an older, mature dancing audience at the Edgewater Beach. Karzas could see the frustration of the Oriole Terrace Orchestra and the dancers and it must have seemed like Dell Lampe and the Trianon all over again. Karzas hadn't anticipated that the young dancers, who had flocked to the Aragon when it first opened, would begin drifting off to other nearby ballrooms. The acoustical problem was partially corrected but would continue to haunt other bands. Meanwhile, J. B. Lampe was trying to solve the problem. In the fall of 1926 he sent the banjoist Al Morey from the Dell Lampe Trianon orchestra up to the Aragon to lead a second band of hand-picked musicians to try and help the struggling Oriole Terrace Orchestra.[14] The Morey band appeared opposite the Oriole Terrace Orchestra four nights a week. Morey and two other sidemen in Lampe's Trianon group, Charlie Agnew and Wayne King, had led occasional relief bands at the Trianon on weekends.

Getting yet another band was the least of Karzas's worries now as he tried to terminate what seemed to be an ironclad one-year contract with the Oriole Terrace Orchestra. In a surprising move, he solicited help from Jules Stein of MCA to resolve this predicament, although the Trianon had never hired an MCA band until that point.[15] The connection with Stein may have come via Ernie Young, who is credited with booking Roy Bargy's band for the Trianon.[16] Young was an early partner of Stein.

For whatever reason, Stein was brought in as the problem-solver. He turned out to be as good a negotiator as he was a salesman. He convinced FioRito and Russo to tear up the contract with Karzas and gracefully leave the Aragon as soon as possible, thus removing the immediate impasse. The final solution unexpectedly gave the Oriole Terrace Orchestra to Russo.[17] Meanwhile, MCA began booking the Russo orchestra and helped FioRito form a new one. A public announcement of the agreement was made in early January 1927 with the news that the FioRito-Russo group was leaving the Aragon and would play for the one-week grand opening of Schoenstadt's new Piccadilly Theater in Hyde Park, beginning January 24.[18]

MCA immediately was rewarded with some business for helping Karzas solve his problem with the Oriole Terrace Orchestra and brought in two bands—Henry Gendron and Don Bestor—to play continuously for Aragon dancers. Al Morey's house band returned after Gendron and Bestor left the ballroom, but in the spring of 1927 Morey left the Aragon to accept an engagement as stage band leader at the Publix Theater in Des Moines, Iowa. Enter Wayne King, Bodewalt Lampe's second reserve leader at the Trianon, who was sent to the Aragon to succeed Morey as leader of the house band. Along with King came copies of the Dell Lampe Trianon waltz library. Each Friday evening was waltz night, and every third dance (during which four to six tunes were played) consisted of waltzes. J. B. Lampe reportedly went to the Aragon to rehearse the band himself; he wanted King to become the "Waltz King."

King did fulfill Lampe's wish and, in the process, became a big draw at the Aragon box office. By the early 1930s, with Garber at the Trianon and King playing most of the year at the Aragon, things were looking good for the Karzas brothers. King returned for long annual engagements at the Aragon until 1935, when he left to capitalize on his enormous popularity resulting from the orchestra's Victor recordings, their nightly WGN remotes, and the popular three-times-a-week *Lady Esther* broadcasts via NBC. The Karzas organization now faced yet another big challenge: how to replace Wayne King.

King's replacement was a new MCA band that had attracted some attention at the Beverly-Wilshire Hotel in Los Angeles: Orville Knapp and his

Band of Tomorrow.[19] Knapp employed unusually exaggerated dynamics and used several unconventional dance orchestra instruments, including French horns and a Hammond organ. In addition the band carried both a tuba and a string bass. Obbligatos were not furnished by the usual trombone or violin but were sung by the female vocalist.[20]

The Band of Tomorrow opened on October 5 with a large advertising barrage, but it ran into trouble almost immediately with the Aragon dancers.[21] Knapp's subtle and soft music was quickly swallowed up by the cavernous Aragon ballroom, bewildering the dancers.[22] If the dancers had had trouble with the FioRito-Russo Orioles ten years earlier, trying to determine which beat to dance to, they could hardly hear the Orville Knapp band. The recalcitrant acoustical problem was only partly to blame. While Knapp's group was a very good dance band, it was just too innovative for the Chicago dancers. In short, it was the wrong band in the wrong place.

Karzas called in Jules Stein, who was now booking nearly all of the Aragon bands and who necessarily shared the problem. Stein, by then managing more than a hundred bands, brokered another creative deal. Distilled to its essence, the deal involved a band trade: Orville Knapp for Freddy Martin. By November 15, 1935, Knapp was out of the Aragon and in Denver at the Cosmopolitan Hotel for six weeks.[23] Freddy Martin's band, then playing at the Waldorf-Astoria in New York, opened at the Aragon in February 1936. Orville Knapp's band then moved into the Waldorf-Astoria. Happily, both Martin and Knapp prospered at their new venues, but unfortunately that summer Knapp was killed in a plane crash near Boston. He was only twenty-eight years old.[24]

Martin's melodic band featured only tenor saxophones in the sax section. He was a big hit at the Aragon and he stayed for four years. When he left to pursue other opportunities, Karzas brought in another young West Coast band led by Dick Jurgens. The youthful Aragon dancers immediately identified with the new group. Jurgens became as popular with the Aragon crowd over the next ten years as Wayne King had been. Four future bandleaders—Eddy Howard, Harry Cool, Ronnie Kemper, and Buddy Moreno—emerged from the Jurgens band. It was a very entertaining group of young musicians. They were talented and added just enough comedy, tomfoolery, clever songs, and audience participation stunts to the mix to maintain maximum dancer interest.

Andrew Karzas died suddenly in 1940 from a heart condition and his brother, William, assumed control of the Aragon and the Trianon.[25] Eddy Howard, the only one of the four Jurgens alumni to develop a national name as a leader, became a regular Aragon attraction in the 1940s and early 1950s, riding high on such big Mercury Record hits as "To Each His Own," "Rickety Rickshaw Man," and "I Wonder, I Wonder."

Aside from Howard's annual visits, no one band, with the exception of the Teddy Phillips orchestra, would ever dominate the Aragon after Jurgens. Instead, a parade of sweet bands played at the giant North Side ballroom from then on, including those led by Larry Fotine, Ray Pearl, Ernie Rudy, and a host of others. There were still occasional one-night or weekend appearances by national name bands like those of Harry James, Guy Lombardo, Clyde McCoy, and Vaughn Monroe.

In 1958 William Karzas retired and turned over the day-to-day management of the Aragon to his son, Andrew, who continued to operate the ballroom until September 1963 when William died. Andrew sold the Aragon to Oscar Brotman and Leonard Sherman, who, in 1964, brought back Wayne King for a nostalgic weekend to close the ballroom.[26] King's well-advertised return "for the last time" was as much a publicity stunt as anything, but it turned out to be as formal a closing as the old ballroom would have. The giant floor was converted into a roller rink and the building later went through several transitions, including becoming a discotheque called the Cheetah. After several owners, a few superficial facelifts, and some minor alterations, however, the Aragon remains basically the same as it was when it opened in 1926.

The size and location of the Trianon and Aragon—both marketing advantages when they opened—worked against them in later years when more and more dancers arrived in autos. There was very little parking space. Both were near or, in the case of the Aragon, adjacent to elevated stations. Major streetcar routes passed by or near their doors.

Despite the ballrooms' standard-setting elegance and modern management, some dancers were intimidated by the size of the dance floors and the sheer number of people. The lack of adequate parking facilities, especially after World War II when automobiles came into wide use, took its toll. These factors led to the construction of a host of smaller, more intimate ballrooms throughout the city in the 1920s and later. Some were built above or adjacent to neighborhood movie theaters, which were erected in large numbers during this period.

The trend toward new and smaller ballrooms was driven by the fact that there were few if any entrepreneurs willing to finance massive dancing structures. With the exception of the Aragon in 1926, the trend was clearly away from such large halls as the giant White City Ballroom, the Paradise, or the Trianon Ballroom, all of which had dance floors exceeding twenty-five thousand square feet in size. The smaller floors of the neighborhood venues seemed to satisfy the dancers' need for a more intimate feeling.

The new, smaller, 1920s vintage ballrooms—some of which probably were built in the late 1910s—were located, with a few exceptions, at or near major shopping areas at key street intersections across Chicago, which at first was a distinct advantage in attracting primarily neighborhood or area dancers. A number of these smaller ballrooms became significant showcases for Chicago dance bands and attracted big crowds, especially where the ballroom had remote broadcast lines.

Several other smaller ballrooms, such as the Oriental Ballroom, the Silver Slipper, and the Castle Gardens—the latter owned by Husk O'Hare and his brother George—were started in the Loop during the 1920s and served residents living closer to the city, business people working downtown, and visitors less dependent on autos in later years. The Oriental Ballroom was located on the top floor of the Oriental Theater building at 20 West Randolph Street and drew a downtown crowd that probably was different from the dancers at the outlying ballrooms. The Oriental Ballroom opened in 1926, about the same time as the theater on the first floor, and thrived in the late 1920s.

A variety of bands played at the Oriental Ballroom. The Herbie Mintz orchestra, which played there through the late 1920s and into the 1930s, was perhaps most closely associated with the venue. The black leader and booker Dave Peyton had a second band at the Oriental in 1927 playing opposite Mintz. Peyton was no stranger to downtown locations by this time, although the white Local 10 allowed few other black bands to play in the lucrative Loop area. Al Hausburg picked up the lease for the ballroom and operated it in the late 1930s and the 1940s.

George O'Hare's Castle Gardens on Quincy, just west of State Street, was an upstairs place that featured mainly his brother Husk O'Hare and one or the other of Husk's many orchestras, or occasionally a black jazz band from the South Side. Sol Wagner's band provided the music for years at A. C. Eichner's Silver Slipper, 184 West Randolph Street. There was another, unrelated Silver Slipper Ballroom at Sixty-third Street and Cottage Grove Avenue.

One of the more successful North Side neighborhood ballrooms was the Merry Garden Ballroom. Located at 3136 North Sheffield Avenue, near Belmont, it was built by Ethel Kendall and Jack Lund. As described in the last chapter, it was the second of two ballrooms of that name. It opened on Labor Day, September 5, 1921. Thirty-one years later, with ballroom dancing losing out to television as a nighttime entertainment option, it closed. The first orchestra on the bandstand had been that of Verne Buck. A parade of bands followed Buck's orchestra through the 1920s, led by Rex Maupin, Jess Hawkins, Hal Hiatt, Jack Russell, and Joe Kayser.[27]

The 1926 opening of the Aragon a few miles north and east hurt the Merry Garden somewhat, but the Merry Garden catered to a large North Side and West Side crowd and, with its more intimate midsized dance floor (14,355 square feet), was a cozier facility. It prospered for two decades. Joe Kayser, back from his venture as a stage bandleader in Kansas City, organized a new Chicago band for the Merry Garden in 1928. According to his band payroll for November 22 of that year, he had the jazzmen Jess Stacy on piano, the drummer Danny Alvin, the trumpet player Muggsy Spanier, and the hot saxophonist and clarinetist Maurie Bercov, capitalizing on the growing popularity of jazz music with the young dancers.[28] A year later Kayser was still drawing big crowds with his band, both at Merry Garden and during summers at Municipal Pier.[29]

The Merry Garden's dance floor was about half the size of the Trianon's, but it still was big enough to host special events. In 1929 and 1930, the promotion-minded Kendall and Lund staged world's championship marathon dances, one of which continued for 2,780 hours.[30] Charlie Agnew took over the Merry Garden house band in the late 1930s and became a favorite of the dancers. He later played other key Chicago locations and began touring the country as an MCA band with a good deal of success. Traveling bands also played engagements at the North Side ballroom, including Ray Pearl, Lawrence Welk, and Ace Brigode. Following the ballroom's closure in 1952, the building was used as a warehouse until 1961 when it was razed for a parking lot. It was an ignoble end to a popular dance spot and certainly signaled the growing impact of television and other diversions on the public's entertainment habits.

Practically every neighborhood in the city had one of these small, boutique ballrooms by the end of the 1920s but at many the dancing was on weekends only. On the West Side there were the Byrd Ballroom on Madison Street near Cicero, the Keyman's Club almost across the street, the Lions Club at Grand and North Avenues, the Crystal Ballroom on North Avenue near California, and the Cinderella on Madison west of Central. In Cicero there was the Olympic. On the South Side were the Casino Moderne at Sixty-third Street and Drexel Boulevard; the Silver Slipper (earlier the Cinderella) at Sixty-third and Cottage Grove; and the Granada at Sixty-fourth and Cottage Grove. Things were much the same on the North Side. The Cascades Ballroom was located at Sheridan and Wilson; a little farther to the east was the Wilshore Ballroom, on Wilson at Lake Michigan. The Wilshore was a summer-only dance spot nicely situated to catch the lake breezes. At Broadway Avenue and Grace Street, just north of the Marigold Gardens, was Andy Anderson's Chateau.

Anderson operated the small, intimate Chateau Ballroom on the second floor of the Chateau Theater building, at 3810 North Broadway Avenue. It was typical of most of the smaller neighborhood ballrooms. Built in 1920 or before, the Chateau's 6,600-square-foot dance floor served the neighborhood dancers and featured mostly local bands—Lynne Hazzard, Gordon Birch, Gay Claridge, Carl Sands, and others.[31] By the 1960s both the theater and the ballroom had been renamed the Vogue. The Crystal Ballroom at 2701 West North Avenue, just east of California, was similar to the Chateau in size and character. It featured dancing mainly on the weekends and used mostly local bands.

The Byrd Ballroom, 4728 West Madison Street near Cicero, like the Chateau and Crystal ballrooms was located over a theater of the same name. The Byrd's most active period was in the 1940s and 1950s when the bandleader Carl Schreiber leased the facility on weekends. Schreiber was head of Personalized Orchestra and Entertainment Services and booked other bands as well as his own. During this post–World War II period, the Byrd drew a large crowd from the West Side and west suburbs.

Just across the street from the Byrd was the Keyman's Club, at 4711 West Madison. The facility, which included a very large ballroom, was designed to house the club's many social activities and also was available for rent or lease. The club sponsored regular public dances using local bands and operated through the 1930s and 1940s. In the late forties, the Keyman's Club brought in some name bands and top talent for its events.

Several entrepreneurs built ballrooms to serve dancers in the outlying precincts of Chicago and in the suburbs; two of the venues, Madura's Danceland and the Melody Mill, had surprisingly large dance floors and accommodated large numbers of people. Madura's Danceland, at 114th Street and Indianapolis Boulevard in Hammond, had started out as a dance hall built in 1917, shortly before World War I. The Madura family began operating it in 1929 and it became one of the earliest ballrooms on the city's far Southeast Side.[32]

Michael Madura managed the ballroom and was succeeded later by his son Mickey. Like most of the other outlying Chicago ballrooms, Madura's Danceland featured local or territory bands as the main dancing attraction, with occasional one-night appearances by name bands. It operated three or four nights a week. The ballroom was destroyed by fire in 1967.

The Willowbrook Ballroom is located at 8700 South Archer Road in suburban Willow Springs. It was built as the Oh Henry by John Verderbar and
his two sons, Rudy and Eddie, in 1930 and continues to operate under the
Willowbrook name, the last of the Chicago area's major dance venues from
the thirties and forties.[33] It replaced a previous 1920s-era pavilion destroyed
by fire. The Oh Henry was billed as the "ballroom with the country club
atmosphere" because of its English Tudor style of architecture and garden-
like setting. It had a 5,000-square-foot dance floor—small compared to other
ballrooms—which gave it a certain amount of intimacy.

The Oh Henry had a house band, Kenny's Red Peppers, in the early years
but in 1934 Verderbar decided to hire Emil Flindt's Varsity Band to meet the
changing times. Flindt, a veteran dance-band leader originally from Clinton,
Iowa, remained at the ballroom until 1938. Ray Herbeck, leader of a fresh
young California sweet band, replaced Flindt, stayed for the 1938–39 season,
and was the first of many non-Chicago traveling bands the Verderbars hired.
Name bands like those of Ben Bernie, Art Kassel, and Clyde McCoy occasionally played one-night engagements.

Because the Aragon and Trianon demanded and received "mileage protection" from the major booking organizations, the Verderbars had to seek
out new territory bands to play at their ballroom. Mileage protection meant
that a band that played in either of the Karzas ballrooms could not play in another ballroom within a certain distance—usually fifty miles—for a specified
amount of time thereafter. With help from booking agencies, however, Verderbar did identify bands that were on the way up and hired them before
they got into the Aragon-Trianon web. Ray Pearl's band from Pennsylvania,
Chuck Foster and Don Reid's bands from California, and Tommy Carlyn
from Pittsburgh were all Verderbar discoveries. Several gained a measure
of fame from their frequent local and network remote broadcasts via WGN,
WBBM, and WENR.

Headliners like Guy Lombardo, Jan Garber, Sammy Kaye, Dick Jurgens,
Eddie Howard, Freddy Martin, Lawrence Welk, and Wayne King made occasional guest appearances, especially in the fifties and early sixties after the
demise of the Aragon and Trianon. The Verderbars, sensitive to the drop-off
in attendance at the ballroom, added a large restaurant in 1955 and renamed
the Oh Henry the Willowbrook. The local bands of Teddy Lee, Norm Ladd,
Freddy Mills, Andy Powell, and Will Carroll and a few bands from adjoining
states played for dancing. In the late 1980s the restaurant was closed to the
general public and was used only as a catering facility.

The Willowbrook continued to operate until 1997 under the management of a third-generation Verderbar, Pat Verderbar Williams (Eddie's daughter), and her husband, Richard. They sold it to new owners who operate the ball-room and its large catering facilities. The Willowbrook outlasted the Aragon and the Trianon.

Another suburban ballroom, the Melody Mill Ballroom at 2401 South Des Plaines Avenue in west suburban North Riverside, was a relative latecomer to the dancing business. Opened on New Year's Eve 1931 with a popular local band led by Jack Russell, the ballroom got off to a rousing start in spite of the Depression economy and remained open until 1984. Ben Lejcar and his fam-ily had gotten into the ballroom business almost by accident. A contractor, he took over the building when the owner defaulted to builders in 1931 during the early part of the Depression.[34] The Melody Mill was easily visible from Twenty-second Street, two blocks to the north, because of the small windmill on the roof.

Following a format similar to that of the older Oh Henry, the Mill engaged a series of local and territory bands through the years with occasional name bands hired for one-night engagements. In the 1940s and 1950s many of the bands played engagements that lasted several weeks or months. The three-hundred-pound Tiny Hill and his shuffle-rhythm orchestra, an unknown band from Decatur, Illinois, came into the Mill in 1938 for a short stay. Soon, he was broadcasting from the Mill on the CBS and Mutual networks, recording for Okeh and later for Mercury records ("Angry," "Sioux City Sue," and others), and appearing on the *Your Hit Parade* network radio show. Dancers waited in block-long lines for the ballroom to open. Another big attraction at the Melody Mill was the Ralph Marterie orchestra, a Chicago-based post–World-War II success. He is credited with drawing the largest crowd ever at the Mill, 5,500 people on a New Year's Eve in the 1950s. Through the years, though, mostly sweet territory bands played at the Melody Mill. Larry Fotine, Larry Faith, and Leo Piepper were just a few of them.

The Mill even had its own song, "When It's Moonlight on Melody Mill," which became a familiar tune through the many radio remotes from the ball-room. The words and melody were credited to the owner, Ben Lejcar. Needless to say, it was a "must play" for the bands that appeared there. Three bands made recordings of the tune: Tiny Hill, Larry Faith, and Al Pierson.[35] The Melody Mill was officially closed on April 29, 1984. More than three thousand loyal patrons crowded into the ballroom to dance for the last time to the music of Freddy Mills.[36]

The Chevy Chase Ballroom in suburban Wheeling, just north of the Cook County line on Milwaukee Avenue, dates back to the early 1920s when the original complex, called Columbian Gardens, was built by the Knights of Columbus.[37] In 1928 it was renamed the Bon Aire Country Club by the new owners, William Skidmore and William Johnson, who later were proprietors of the Lincoln Tavern in Morton Grove. Skidmore and Johnson remodeled the property and expanded it to accommodate more diners and provide space for a show room.

Freddy Martin's orchestra, which had been at the Aragon, and popular local bands like Henri Lishon's played for dancing at the handsomely appointed club and accompanied name acts and chorus lines performing on the elevated dance floor. The Bon Aire's dance floor was about half the size of the Willowbrook's but was able to accommodate four hundred to five hundred people. WGN and other Chicago radio stations did remote broadcasts of the bands from the Bon Aire during the 1930s and 1940s.

Both Skidmore and William Johnson had died by the early 1950s and Johnson's brother Joseph changed the name of the property to the Chevy Chase Country Club, where he began sponsoring public dancing. The country club was purchased in 1977 by the Wheeling Park District and renovated in 1997–98.[38] Public dancing continued one or two nights a week in the remodeled ballroom until 2001. Teddy Lee, Steve Cooper, and Vito Buffalo were the main bands to furnish music there. Occasionally, traveling territory bands, such as the Jack Morgan band or the Don Glasser–Lois Costello orchestra, played one-night engagements.

## Swinging and Swaying through Middle Age and Beyond

By the mid-1940s there was a growing number of older dancers—dubbed the over-thirty crowd—who were no longer comfortable in the larger ballrooms, most of which catered to younger dancers. The Chicago entrepreneurs Al Hausberg, James Glyman, and John Burke were among the first to open several small, specialized ballrooms that accommodated this demographic group. The dancers were over thirty years of age (often over forty) and most were single, but they still loved to dance. Above all, they wanted a dancing environment where they could meet others the same age. Coincidentally, this occurred just as ballroom dancing in Chicago generally was losing favor in the post–World War II forties. As time passed, the crowd got older and, though "over thirty" no longer sufficiently described their age bracket, the term was still used to classify the ballrooms. The dancers became acquainted over the years and the small ballrooms were like clubs.

Glyman and Burke leased several small vacant theaters, eventually buying them and converting them to boutique ballrooms. On the South Side, they took over the Sun Theater at 7219 South Wentworth Avenue and the Boulevard Theater on Kedzie Avenue at Fifty-fifth Street. In converting the buildings to ballrooms, they leveled the theater floors and installed hardwood dance floors and bars. The two men did the same thing to the Embassy Theater on the West Side, at Fullerton Avenue just east of Pulaski Road. The local dance bands of Teddy Lee, Freddy Mills, Dan Belloc, Gay Claridge, Tony Barren, and Don McClain filled these jewel-box ballrooms with dancers. Occasionally a name band would play a one-nighter, drawing even bigger crowds of dancers now in their fifties or older, but forever "over thirty."

The veteran ballroom operator Al Hausburg identified this market in the 1940s and prospered through the sixties with his Lions Club on the West Side and the downtown Oriental Ballroom. In the forties he had leased a small ballroom over the Milford Theater on the North Side. Located at 3311 North Pulaski Road, at the intersection of North Pulaski (formerly Crawford Avenue) and Milwaukee Avenue, it became his most profitable and enduring property. Hal Munro's orchestra was a long-time favorite at the Milford along with many of the bands that played at the Embassy Ballroom, for the number of organized dance bands in the area had dwindled significantly by the 1960s and musical choices were difficult. But the older dancers were loyal and returned each week, sometimes several nights a week, to the few remaining ballrooms. Alas, over-thirty dancing as such, the last vestige of ballroom dancing in Chicago, came to an end with the closing of the Embassy and the Milford. The over-thirty dancers—and there are still many of them at this writing—now patronize the two surviving ballrooms, the Willowbrook and the Glendora. Both establishments are in the southwest suburbs and now make their money mostly on banquets.

Social dancing, so popular from the 1920s through the 1940s, gave rise to a very large and profitable ballroom business in Chicago. The ballrooms were significant dance venues through the years, but they became less and less important after 1950. By the 1960s only a few of the newer ballrooms still were operating.

Being in the ballroom business in the 1930s and 1940s was like being on a roller coaster ride. Business slowed dramatically in the early thirties during the economic depression and many operators were forced to cut back their dancing schedules or shut their doors. The 1940s and World War II, on the other hand, were boom years for most of the city's dance venues but it was the last hurrah for both dancers and dance bands.

Chicago's ballrooms hired many dance bands, but they weren't the only employers of the bands. During the 1920s, hotels and cabarets, later called nightclubs, competed vigorously for dance bands to supply music for dancing and for floor shows, which were now gaining popularity. By the thirties hardly a major metropolitan hotel in the nation was without a dine-and-dance room prominently featuring a dance band. In fact, dance bands became so important to hotels that many hostelries advertised their dance bands widely to attract out-of-town guests.

# 6 Early Downtown Chicago Hotels Join the Dance Party

THE early hotel orchestras, which began entertaining diners in Chicago's major downtown hostelries by 1910, were different from the dance bands of the day in both composition and repertoire. For the most part they were string ensembles, discretely hidden from view behind screens or on balconies as they played light classical music and polite popular tunes. Over time, however, these ensembles emerged from their hiding places and developed into versatile orchestras that could not only furnish background music but also play for dancing. They eventually provided accompaniment for floor shows that became a popular part of the entertainment in some hotel dining rooms by the mid-teens.

MCA's idea of rotating bands and the enormous boost the bands received from radio helped move this process along and fifteen years later made the bands into major draws. By the late 1930s, dance bands became the main entertainment attractions in hotel dining rooms throughout the nation, for which the hotels willingly paid top dollar. A 1938 advertisement in *Billboard,* the show business weekly, estimated that hotels in the United States spent more than ten million dollars each year for dance bands and talent for the floor shows.[1] It was big business indeed.

The College Inn of the Sherman Hotel was the first of the major early downtown hotel club rooms to add a dance floor to accommodate diners inclined to dance. As the dancing idea spread, competition developed among the large hotels and they began seeking the best or most popular dance orchestras in town. Occasionally they employed out-of-town groups to compete with the growing number of ballrooms and cabarets, which were drawing large crowds.

By the early 1920s, most major downtown hotels were important employers of dance bands and began advertising their bands to attract new customers. Remote broadcasts from the hotel dining rooms were the most potent means of delivering this message to the public. These broadcasts helped the Sherman Hotel's College Inn, the Terrace Garden of the Morrison, and the Balloon Room of the Congress Hotel dramatically increase business. In the late twenties the LaSalle Hotel joined the parade of hotels broadcasting their dance bands.

The earliest of the modern downtown hotels were the Congress, which opened in 1893, and the Blackstone, which began in 1910, both on Michigan Avenue; the LaSalle, erected in 1909; and the Sherman, built about 1910. The LaSalle was in the heart of the city's financial district, at Madison and LaSalle Street, and the Sherman, a few blocks north on Randolph between Clark and LaSalle Streets, was in what became the entertainment district. The Morrison Hotel, later famous as headquarters for the Cook County Democratic Party as well as the host of a string of top performers and dance bands, was another early arrival. Located on Madison at Clark, it was built in stages; the first section opened in 1911. From the late 1910s forward, many of the big downtown hotels had floor shows and dancing. The Loop hotels and those along Michigan Avenue catered to upscale travelers and businessmen with expense accounts. Some of the more affluent local citizens, however, did frequent the dining rooms and later the show rooms of the hotels.

The famous Sherman Hotel, or Sherman House, as it was often called, was the third of three hotels by that name erected on the Randolph Street site between LaSalle and Clark Streets. Joseph Beifield (sometimes spelled Byfield), a successful Chicago garment manufacturer, acquired the property in 1901 and built the new building between 1909 and 1911.[2]

The College Inn, one of the best known cabarets in the country, predated the opening of the new hotel, having begun in the basement of an earlier Sherman Hotel on New Years Eve 1910.[3] Rigo and his Gypsy Orchestra, a well-known musical group of the day, played dinner music for the guests. Some time later the dance team of Maurice and Walton, stars of Broadway and of the Continent and peers of the famous Castles, appeared in the College Inn. The duo was the first of several dance teams to grace the floor of what the Beifields claimed was the first nightclub in America. In 1914 the College Inn introduced ice shows, which were a novelty at that time.[4] Walter Blaufus's orchestra had been at the hotel since 1912 or before and accompanied the skaters and entertainers.

A series of small groups of from four to six musicians worked as a relief band and played for dancing in the College Inn as early as 1912. Between 1914 and 1917 the Chicago saxophonist Paul Biese and the San Francisco banjo player Bert Kelly, among others, led combos there. "Bert Kelly's Jass [*sic,* also sometimes spelled Jaz] Band" got high marks in the trade publication *Variety*, which called the group "an established favorite." The publication also credited Kelly—correctly or incorrectly—with introducing "Jaz [*sic*] Orchestras" in and around Chicago.[5]

Another room, the Bal Tabarin, called Chicago's original dance supper club, was opened in 1911 atop the Sherman Hotel and had its own entrance on Lake Street. Featured at the Bal Tabarin shortly after its opening was the famous dance team of Maurice and Walton.

By the late 1910s, the Edgar Benson organization was presenting the floor shows at the College Inn, complete with a dance band, in exchange for the cover charges. This was the compensation policy Benson and other show producers used with most hotel and cabaret clients. Paul Biese and his popular orchestra, a Benson organization, were back in the College Inn for one year beginning in 1920.[6] The soon-to-be-famous Isham Jones and his band, another Benson attraction, followed Biese and played each season through 1925, the year when Benson lost the contract for the College Inn but not, apparently, for the Bal Tabarin.[7]

Jones had one of the best dance bands in the city at that time. Jones's 1921 Brunswick recording of the "Wabash Blues" featuring the trumpeter Louis Panico became a big hit for the band and helped draw visitors to the College Inn. Jones's recordings and the ensemble's nightly broadcasts via radio station WLS, then also located in the Sherman Hotel, reinforced the band's popularity.[8]

According to reports, the records made money for both Brunswick and Isham Jones. One account said Jones had received more than a half million dollars in royalties from Brunswick Records by 1923.[9] The twenty-eight-year-old Jones and his famous recording and broadcasting orchestra also were being paid $3,500 a week in 1922 to play for just two hours a night, according to a *Chicago Defender* article.[10] In those days of show-business hype, however, there is no assurance that any of these figures were accurate.

Isham Jones's success at the College Inn, enhanced by the nightly broadcasts from the room, gave the Beifields (by now Joseph's sons Eugene and Ernest were involved in the hotel's management) the idea to remake the College Inn into a celebrity room. Such a room, they reasoned, would draw even bigger crowds, especially out-of-town visitors. They proceeded to hire well-known stage entertainers of the day such as Joe Howard, Mae Murray, Bee Palmer, and Ted Healy to star in the College Inn floor shows.[11]

When Benson lost the College Inn business in 1925, Isham Jones left for New York.[12] Jones's replacement for the summer was Vincent Rose and his orchestra, who had been recording for the Victor label. To replace Jones in the fall the Beifields hired Abe Lyman and his California band, a non-MCA group. Lyman had developed a reputation playing at the toney Coconut Grove of the Ambassador Hotel in Los Angeles. It was only a short engagement, however, since the Lyman band had already played an earlier engagement at the Congress Hotel's Balloon Room, succeeding the Coon-Sanders band, and was heading to New York on its first trip to the East.

The long-term house band led by Maurie Sherman took over for the rest of the season. Sherman originally was a violinist with Isham Jones and began leading another Benson orchestra in 1924, playing at both the hotel's Bal Tabarin in the evenings and for afternoon tea dancing and occasional evening sessions at the College Inn. His orchestra remained at the hotel until the mid-1930s, probably one of the longest continuous local hotel engagements for a Chicago orchestra at that time. A 1928 review of the Maurie Sherman orchestra, then being booked by MCA, reported that among the group's personnel were several former Isham Jones sidemen: Carroll Martin, trombone; Herb Quigley, drums; John Kuhn, tuba; and Maurie, himself.[13] Jack Chapman's Benson organization continued to play in the hotel's Bal Tabarin until the mid-1920s because Benson still retained that room as a client.

Joseph Beifield died in 1926, followed by his son Eugene a few years later. The day-to-day management of the hotel and of the College Inn now fell to the other son, Ernest (Ernie), and to Frank Bering. In 1927 the Sherman Hotel signed up with MCA to provide dance bands. In addition to Maurie Sherman, MCA began showcasing its growing inventory of bands. Ray Miller, Lloyd Huntley, Sleepy Hall, Red Nichols, Ted Lewis, and Dan Russo all were late-1920s attractions at the College Inn. Ernie Beifield continued to use the one-dollar cover charge to pay the bands and entertainers.[14] What money the College Inn management saved on the cheaper MCA bands, it put into advertising.

In 1930 the room was expanded and the Beifields hired Ben Bernie's New York–based band. It was the beginning of a long relationship for Bernie and the College Inn. The following year Bernie introduced his soon-to-be-famous celebrity nights at which show business personalities then in Chicago stopped by and performed. The Merriel Abbot dancers, a chorus line, also was added to the show. By now NBC too was carrying nightly coast-to-coast remotes from the room. Later, the Pabst Brewing Company sponsored the Ben Bernie show each week in an effort to keep alive its brand name during Prohibition and to advertise its malt mix to home brewers.

The Coon-Sanders band, after a season-long run at the Hotel New Yorker, returned to Chicago in April 1932 to begin a much-heralded engagement at the College Inn, succeeding Ben Bernie. The band's co-leader, Carlton Coon, had developed an infected jaw, however, and his condition worsened.[15] He died of blood poisoning in Chicago on May 4, after the band had opened at the Sherman. It turned out to be a gloomy period for the Nighthawks, who were popular in Chicago after long runs at the Blackhawk.

If Coon's death had occurred four or five years earlier, it probably would have rocked the young MCA organization, especially coupled with Paul Biese's death in 1925. Coon's death may not have caused a significant problem for MCA in 1932 other than the loss of some good commissions, but it signaled the end of the Coon-Sanders band. Ben Bernie returned in the fall and for the next three years was one of the most popular attractions not only in Chicago, but nationally through his nightly NBC hookup. Whether or not the Coon-Sanders orchestra, had it survived, would have enjoyed similar success can be only a matter of speculation.

George Olsen's band featuring his wife, Ethel Shutta, as the vocalist, followed Bernie and was another popular attraction at the College Inn. This entertaining combination played several successful seasons at the College Inn during the mid-1930s. Frankie Masters, Don Pedro, Al Trace, and Buddy Rogers, who was married to the popular silent screen actress Mary Pickford, also were bandleaders who were popular with College Inn patrons during the 1930s. Al Trace played in the Celtic Café, another room in the hotel, and for the College Inn afternoon shift. His group also played occasionally as relief band at night for nearly four years.[16] By this time an engagement at the College Inn was considered one of the best jobs for musicians and bands in the city and, because of the nightly NBC broadcasts, could make a band famous.

Ernie Beifield and his partner, Frank Bering, signaled a big change in policy in February 1939 when they remodeled the College Inn. The room was renamed the Panther Room of the College Inn and began featuring the "Cavalcade of Swing," a parade of swing bands. This continued for the next six years, making the room with the new tropical rain-forest decor the Midwest's swing mecca.[17]

Ernie Beifield's new swing-band policy in the Panther Room was an immediate success. Over the next few years, he acquired a reputation in the business as one of the most astute entertainment proprietors in the country.[18] A younger, more "hep" crowd patronized the room now so closely identified with swing music. Even the floor-show acts took a back seat to the bands.[19]

World War II ended in 1945 and the Panther Room and its swing policy ended three years later. Sensing a change in public tastes, Beifield again re-

modeled the room and dropped the Panther Room tag. He and Bering called it
the College Inn once again, and over the next two years they staged a series of
revues singling out the music of such popular composers as George Gershwin
and Cole Porter. The pianist Bill Snyder's band played for the show's singers
and dancers and, at intermissions, for dancing. The curtain fell on the revues
in 1950, impresario Beifield's last production. He died later that year at age
sixty.[20]

In yet another incarnation, the fabled old College Inn became the College
Inn–Porterhouse. Frank York, a New York violinist and bandleader, formed
a crew of strolling violinists who dressed in cowboy-styled shirts and trousers
and paraded around the redesigned room, which now had a western motif. By
the late 1960s the room, again renamed the College Inn, returned to its more
traditional entertainment policy. The last floor show was in 1971 and featured
a cast of twenty-four with Peter Palmer's local fifteen-piece orchestra. The
intermission pianist, Hots Michaels, survived at the College Inn until 1973,
but his departure that year signaled the end to music at the Sherman Hotel.
By the end of the seventies the hotel was demolished to make way for the
new James R. Thompson State of Illinois Center.[21] A hotel that enjoyed one
of the highest profiles in the nation for dance bands ended as a pile of rubble
seventy years after it began.

Another early modern hotel in the Loop was the twenty-two-story LaSalle,
located at Madison and LaSalle Streets. When built in 1909 by E. J. Stevens,
it was said to be the world's biggest hostelry.[22] Prior to World War II it was
considered not only one of the city's most famous hotels but also one of the
classiest. The LaSalle had regular cabaret entertainment in the 1910s. Edgar
Benson had the contract to provide the acts and the orchestra and, without
any hard evidence, it is assumed there was also dancing. The two most active
public rooms in the hotel were the Blue Fountain Room, a favorite lunching
spot for socially prominent Chicago matrons and a posh dining room at night,
and, in the forties, the Pan American Room.[23]

Jean Goldkette's orchestra played for dancing by 1922 and then Carl Rupp
led his Benson music-makers there in 1923. Two years later George Nachstadter's orchestra entertained the patrons and played for dancing.[24] Gus C.
Edwards's dance orchestra was broadcasting from the LaSalle via WMAQ,
the "Daily News station," in 1927. Other Benson bands led by E. E. Sheetz,
Jack Chapman, Doc Davis, and Lew Diamond, according to contemporary
advertisements for the hotel, played for dancing in various dining rooms.[25]

Gus C. Edwards, now a partner in the Kennaway booking office, succeeded
Benson as the agent for both the LaSalle and the new Stevens Hotel, the latter

on Michigan Avenue, in the late twenties. Things got a little more exciting in the dance band department by the very early 1930s when Husk O'Hare had a three-year run in the LaSalle's Blue Fountain Room. The early 1930s orchestras of George Devron and Del Coon also played there. Both O'Hare and Devron also played long engagements at the Stevens (later named the Conrad Hilton) Hotel.

Hit hard by the Depression in the early 1930s, the LaSalle Hotel closed the Blue Fountain Room until 1936 when it reopened with Bob McGrew's band. In the next several years Buddy Fisher and the English-born pianist Little Jack Little and their bands entertained listeners and dancers. By the end of the 1930s, the Blue Fountain Room management discovered it could do as well financially with small combos. The groups playing in the room included the hot violinist Stuff Smith's sextet (with Jonah Jones on trumpet) and the Bob McGrew combo. Stuff Smith did especially well in the Blue Fountain Room, bringing in $2,300 profit in March 1939.[26]

In the 1940s, true to its name, the Pan American Room featured a string of Latin bands with Jose Cortez and Ralph Morrison leading the parade in 1944. It became the main show room at the hotel in the 1950s and was renamed the Lotus Room. Avery Brundage, the financier, had bought a 96 percent interest in the hotel in 1941 and sold out in 1970, but not before a fire destroyed part of the hotel in 1946 killing sixty-one and injuring two hundred, ending the hostelry's reputation as one of the world's safest.[27]

The Morrison Hotel, the LaSalle's neighbor one block to the east at Madison and Clark Streets, was built in sections between 1911 and 1931. It was oriented more toward flashy entertainment than was the staid LaSalle and it tried to attract show business people as guests. To this end, the owner and general manager, Harry C. Moir, frequently placed full-page ads in entertainment trade publications in the 1920s announcing that the hotel had reserved the fortieth and forty-first floors especially for its "theatrical guests."[28]

The Morrison began featuring small bands for dancing in its short-lived Booster's Club as early as 1914; Bert Kelly's small combo was one of them. Behavior in the club must have been raucous because it was closed by court order on January 8, 1916. A few days after the Booster's Club was shuttered, another Morrison Hotel room called the Fox Trot Club was criticized along with several other spots in town by a morals court judge for allowing all-night dancing and drinking involving young girls and men.[29]

In 1919 John Wickliffe's Ginger Band was booked into the Morrison's posh

Terrace Garden room. The band was said to be the first black band to play a white downtown Chicago hotel and very likely the first black band to play a regular engagement in the Loop.[30] With dancing firmly established as an integral part of hotel entertainment by the early 1920s, the Morrison designated its basement Terrace Garden room as its cabaret or dine-and-dance room. It was referred to later also as the Terrace Room and the Terrace Casino.

Moir signed on with the Benson Organization to furnish music for the room. Benson sent Austin Mack and his Century Serenaders to play there before 1923. Mack was followed by Roy Bargy's fine band in March 1924. Bargy, however, left shortly after the engagement began and joined the Isham Jones band as pianist/arranger, as noted earlier. Just about a year later Benson reportedly lost his contract for the Morrison's Terrace Garden although the agreement probably continued until the end of that season because a Benson band under Don Bestor's leadership was still playing there in May.[31]

One of Benson's former bandleaders, Art S. With, who now had his own booking agency, signed a contract to provide the Morrison with orchestras. Between the fall of 1925 and 1927, With assigned several of his dance bands to the Terrace Garden. Ironically, the leaders of many of them, such as Ralph Williams, Fred Travers, and Gus C. Edwards, were former Benson leaders. In 1928, the Art Kassel band began a season-long engagement at the Terrace Garden, which was said to be Kassel's first location engagement in the Loop.

By 1929 Gus Edwards, now an executive with the Kennaway agency, held the Morrison contracts and was hiring both dance bands and club acts.[32] George Devron, a Kennaway band, was brought into the Terrace Garden, where it remained until spring 1930. The Florida-born bandleader Pedro Avalor, later to become well known as Don Pedro, in 1932 played the first of many Chicago engagements at the Morrison.

Chicago's hotels, restaurants, and nightclubs pulled out all the stops as the city hosted the world's fair of 1933, called the Century of Progress. The Morrison opened the Terrace Garden for late afternoon tea dancing in 1933 with Jack Russell's orchestra. Smaller hotels and other venues also added music to their offerings and, after the enormous success of the fair in the first year, geared up for the 1934 season. The Morrison, now working with MCA, brought in Clyde Lucas and his California Dons from the West Coast.[33] The band was heard on WENR, KYW, WMAQ, and the NBC-Red network. Stan Myers and then Enrique Madriguerra followed in 1935. The following year, Sophie Tucker, "Last of the Red Hot Mamas," was the star at the Terrace Garden for what amounted to her comeback.[34] The trombonist and composer Jack Fulton led the orchestra.

The success of the French Casino, the former Rainbo Garden on the North Side, during the world's fair apparently did not go unnoticed by the Morrison's managers. In the summer of 1936 following Sophie Tucker's departure, they remodeled the Terrace Garden and rechristened it the New French Casino. Working with MCA, which operated the original French Casino, the hotel hired Ted FioRito's band, a chorus line, and a New York producer and launched the new room, which also later was known as the French Parisian.[35] Lou Breese's band later came in to play for the show with Charlie Agnew's group for dancing. In 1937 Maurie Sherman's band moved from the Sherman over to the Morrison to take over Agnew's spot.[36]

In later years the Terrace Garden again became a restaurant, and entertainment was discontinued. The Boston Oyster House and a new hotel-top restaurant in the tower section of the Morrison became major centers of attention as the big-band era died after World War II. The hotel was sold in 1963 to its neighbor, the First National Bank, and was torn down the following year to make way for the bank's new high-rise headquarters.[37]

The Congress Hotel, 520 South Michigan Avenue, is one of the oldest hotels in the city but it didn't begin its name-band dancing policy until well into the 1920s. It was erected originally as an annex of the Auditorium Hotel, just across Congress Street to the north, to accommodate the increased number of guests expected at the 1893 World's Columbian Exposition. Later, as an independent hotel, the Congress acquired a cachet of its own and became a favorite stop for many celebrities, including at least nine U.S. presidents, from Grover Cleveland to Franklin D. Roosevelt.[38] Ironically, the Auditorium Hotel fell out of favor and by the 1930s was bankrupt.

Concert and dance music provided by local orchestras was featured in the Congress's main dining room beginning in the 1920s. Then, in April 1924, hotel management hired the Paul Whiteman Collegians, an orchestra made up of young college men, to play in the hotel's new dine-and-dance room called the Balloon Room. That summer the Kansas City Nighthawks, led by Carlton Coon and Joe Sanders, had been doing big business at a north suburban roadhouse called the Lincoln Tavern. During the Nighthawks' stay, Jack Huff, the Lincoln Tavern manager, introduced Coon and Sanders to the Congress Hotel's general manager, H. L. Kaufman.[39] As a result of this meeting, Kaufman hired the Nighthawks for the Balloon Room during the 1924–25 season, beginning that October.

These two engagements—the Lincoln Tavern and the Congress—gave the

Kansas City band almost a full year of work in Chicago during which it was seldom absent from the nighttime airwaves. At the end of its first season on the Congress Hotel bandstand in April 1925, the Chicago-born Abe Lyman and his California Ambassadors followed the Nighthawks.[40] Lyman's band was a popular attraction in Los Angeles.

The Coon-Sanders band played a second season (1925–26) at the hotel based on the polite yet somewhat enthusiastic reception of the Congress's society clientele, which was sophisticated but restrained. Local bands led by Husk O'Hare and George Mallen also played in other rooms at the Congress. Now alert to the growing interest in dance bands, Kaufman began booking MCA bands such as Ace Brigode and his Virginians, Charles Dornberger, and Ben Bernie and his Roosevelt Hotel Orchestra from New York.

The parade of out-of-town bands continued into the early 1930s but they were mostly sweet and conservative groups that played for equally conservative patrons. The Congress's dining room, variously known as the Grill or, later, the Popeiian Grill, was host to the bands of Fletcher Henderson and Vincent Lopez, the latter doubling during his engagement between the hotel's Joseph Urban Room and the 1933 Century of Progress. Later the Congress became known as a "graveyard for bands" because of the large number that played there and literally died from lack of attention.[41]

That reputation changed, however, when the hotel's biggest musical attraction to date (and perhaps for all time) opened on November 7, 1935. The swing band of Benny Goodman, a Chicago native, began a one-month booking in the Joseph Urban Room that eventually was extended until the following May. The band was organized in New York for the NBC network radio program *Let's Dance*, but it had struggled during a road tour with poor turnouts all the way to the West Coast earlier in the year. Finally, at the Palomar Ballroom in Los Angeles, its last stop, the band received an enormous welcome from dancers.[42]

Chicago's swing fans were waiting breathlessly for the Goodman band's arrival and neither they nor the band were disappointed. The band's driving four-four tempos and exceptionally well played arrangements, many of them by the black arranger and leader Fletcher Henderson, set the room afire, musically speaking. The first-ever swing concerts, sponsored by the Chicago Rhythm Club, were held at the Congress during Goodman's stay. Sunday afternoon was the usual time for these concerts, which were packed with musicians and swing fans alike.[43]

The band did remote broadcasts frequently via WGN and over an NBC network wire installed at the hotel. The former Chicago bandleader Jules

Herbuveaux, now an NBC producer, went over to the Congress to do the mike setups for the Goodman band's first network broadcast. According to Herbuveaux, Goodman had worked for him on occasion in the 1920s and they remained friends. Herbuveaux said Goodman "was scared to death, this was his first band, practically, with a wire and on the road. We had a heart-to-heart talk. I said I don't think you can miss. He took off from that point."[44]

In was an odd coupling—the Goodman band and the staid old Congress Hotel. But the venue now became the early swing hangout for Chicago. The dance bands playing at the hotel immediately prior to Goodman were decidedly not swing bands. Before Goodman, only the Coon-Sanders Nighthawks and perhaps Abe Lyman's California band playing at the Congress in the mid-twenties had been as musically challenging relative to the times.

Congress Hotel management was exultant over the success of the Goodman aggregation that season (the band drew record attendance). An irony lay in the fact that management had been reluctant at first to book the Goodman band at all. What is more significant, Goodman helped put swing music on the map as an accepted style of dance music among white audiences.

Ben Pollack and Duke Ellington followed Goodman in the spring of 1936. The Joseph Urban Room closed for remodeling and enlargement that summer, during which the Congress installed multilevel seating. A rotating stage and bandstand were on the lowest level. The Casa Loma Orchestra, then rising in popularity, was the first to play in the bigger room, now called the Rococo Room.[45] In the summer of 1942, shortly after the beginning of World War II, the Congress and the Stevens, its neighbor down the block, suddenly were taken over by the U.S. Army to quarter army students being trained to be radio operators.[46]

Following the war, Albert Pick, head of a large Chicago-based hotel supply company, took control of the Congress, adding it to his portfolio of other hostelries. About the same time, a newly named room, the Glass Hat, emerged in the hotel. Located at first on the east or Michigan Avenue side of the building, it was later moved to a larger area on the south or Harrison Street side. Dance music was supplied by the bands of Will Back, Don Ragon, Wayne Muir, and Joe Vera. Dick Sarlo and his quartet were hired in 1952 to play on Muir's off nights—Sunday and Monday—and for tea dancing on Saturday afternoons.

Sarlo continued as the relief band at the Glass Hat, playing the rest of the week at other locations.[47] Three years later he became entertainment director, booking bands and entertainment for the Pick chain's other twenty-three properties. Sarlo in 1962 began playing full time in the enlarged Glass Hat. He took an interest in hotel management and began working days at the Congress to learn the business. When the Congress was sold to the Americana chain in 1976, Sarlo was appointed general manager of the hotel, and he remained in the position until 1980. He maintained his Congress Hotel office well into the late 1980s, continuing to book bands and talent and produce shows. Today at the old Congress, now under new management and called the Congress Plaza, no dance music is heard except at private parties.

The Blackstone Hotel, at 636 South Michigan Avenue, just to the south of the Congress, was a venerable edifice that played host to many American presidents. However, it was probably the least adventurous musically of the older Chicago hotels. The Blackstone had been a gathering place for the city's rich and famous from its opening in 1910. Tracy and John B. Drake, who later erected the Drake Hotel several miles to the north, built the Blackstone.[48] Prior to the 1930s Irving Margraff, a local Benson maestro, and his string ensemble played dinner music and a bit of dance music in the main dining room, but it was very formal and guests wore evening clothes. In 1933 Al Kavelin's group became the first name band to appear there and featured the pianist Carmen Cavallaro, later to be a leader of his own dance band. Kavelin returned for several seasons to appear in the hotel's intimate and posh Mayfair Room, on the Michigan Avenue side of the hotel.[49]

In 1944, caught up in the spirit of patriotism, hotel management agreed to lend its prestigious Mayfair Room for a war-bond jazz concert featuring the hot jazz violinist Stuff Smith, the trombonist J. C. Higginbotham, and the trumpeter Hot Lips Page, all popular jazz musicians.[50] This break in tradition was a one-time occurrence.

"Piano-bands," or bands dominated by or prominently featuring a pianist (often the leader), seemed to be well received at the Blackstone ever since the Kavelin orchestra's appearance. A series of such groups followed Kavelin, including those led by Neil Bondshu and Dick LaSalle, in the Mayfair Room.[51] The smaller Balinese Room to the west of the lobby featured smaller groups. Leading such groups in the Balinese Room, which claimed to have the country's only copper dance floor, were the pianist and arranger Jimmy Blade, the saxophonist and singer Dick Sarlo, and later Hal Otis, a flamboyant violinist and pianist.

Time did not treat the Blackstone kindly. As it passed through the hands of a series of owners, it lost much of its luster. In the 1970s and early 1980s the former Balinese Room became Flaming Sally's, with a red decor and a policy of offering Dixieland jazz. The bands of Jim Beebe and Bill Reinhardt filled the room with two-beat rhythms. Later, the well-known Chicago jazz promoter Joe Segal moved his Jazz Showcase operation into the room. In the

Mayfair Room, a "solve-it-yourself" detective play replaced the dance bands and floor shows in later years and ran for several seasons. The hotel, now closed, is for sale for possible conversion into upscale condominiums.[52]

There were a number of other early hotels in the Loop and surrounding downtown Chicago area that were considered to be commercial or business-men's hostelries; many of them presented music for dancing at one time or another. In the late 1910s, the bandleader and booker Bert Kelly had small dance combinations working in the Fort Dearborn Hotel (on the southeast corner of LaSalle and Van Buren) and at the Grand Pacific Hotel (on the northwest corner of Clark and Jackson), where floor shows also were presented at that time.[53]

The Beifield family and Harry C. Moir, early twentieth-century Chicago hoteliers, were pioneers in opening their dining rooms to dancing. They recognized the growing interest in ballroom-style dancing and provided their dining-room guests with dance bands and floor space to show off their latest dance steps. Both were also among the first to present floor shows; the Sherman Hotel claimed to be the very first. The Beifields not only presented ice shows at the College Inn but had gone out of their way to emphasize dancing by hiring Maurice and Walton and other dance teams, who, during their performances, displayed for patrons the grace and beauty of the dance.

Dancing was not always viewed as socially acceptable by certain segments of the public in the early 1900s so it took courage on the part of these astute hoteliers to experiment with these new policies. Their judgment, however, was vindicated because floor shows and dancing in hotel dining rooms became a nationwide trend by the end of the 1920s.

Guy Lombardo's Royal Canadians, one of the most famous dance bands in America, had its first major success in Chicago in 1927–28 at the Granada Café. The band always drew large crowds when it returned to town in later years, as demonstrated in this photo of an appearance at the Willowbrook Ballroom in 1967. (Photo by author, © 1998 Charles A. Sengstock Jr.)

Wayne King remained enormously popular with dancers nationally for more than fifty years after his initial success at Chicago's Aragon Ballroom. He continued to make twice-annual tours. (Photo by author, © 2000 Charles A. Sengstock Jr.)

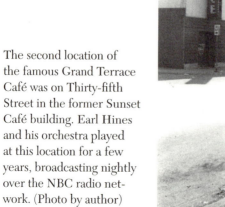

The second location of the famous Grand Terrace Café was on Thirty-fifth Street in the former Sunset Café building. Earl Hines and his orchestra played at this location for a few years, broadcasting nightly over the NBC radio network. (Photo by author)

Bandleader Jan Garber survived the demise of the dance bands and the rise of rock and roll. He continued to make records and tour widely until the 1970s and was especially well liked by Chicago audiences. (Photo by author)

The veteran bandleader and booking agent Joe Kayser (left) began booking the bands for Al Hausberg's "Over-Thirty" Milford Ballroom after he retired from MCA. Hausberg (right) kept the Milford open through the 1970s. (Photo by author, © 2004 Charles A. Sengstock Jr.)

In 1921 the Green Mill Gardens added the two-story building in the center of this photo, which housed the new indoor cabaret upstairs. The giant Balaban and Katz Uptown Theater, built in 1923–24, occupies what was once the outdoor Green Mill Sunken Gardens. (Photo by author, © 2004 Charles A. Sengstock Jr.)

Bandleader Freddy Martin and his orchestra followed Wayne King into the Aragon in 1936 and stayed for four years. This photo was taken in the 1960s when Martin and his band returned for an engagement. (Photo by author, © 2004 Charles A. Sengstock Jr.)

The stage-band policy featuring Paul Ash was introduced in Chicago at the McVickers Theater on Madison Street in 1925. (Photo by author, © 2004 Charles A. Sengstock Jr.)

Between 1928 and the early 1950s there was no dance band venue in the
United States better known than the Blackhawk Restaurant on Wabash Avenue
in Chicago's Loop. (Photo by author, © 2004 Charles A. Sengstock Jr.)

The Aragon Ballroom on Lawrence Avenue still stands, eighty years after it opened, and is used occasionally for dancing and special occasions. (Photo by author, © 2004 Charles A. Sengstock Jr.)

The Faith Tabernacle now occupies the former Marigold Gardens winter garden building at 817 West Grace, just west of Broadway. The outdoor gardens
were to the left, behind the building. (Photo by author, © 2004 Charles A.
Sengstock Jr.)

Opposite page: It was big news in 1928 when the Coon-Sanders Nighthawks
returned to the Blackhawk Restaurant for their annual engagement. (Courtesy
of Don Roth)

*Coming*
SATURDAY Night, Sept. 29

COON-SANDERS
ORIGINAL
NIGHTHAWK
ORCHESTRA

Plus A CORPS OF
*Famous* ENTERTAINERS

Reserve Your Table NOW!
*Telephones - Randolph 5419 - Dearborn 6262*

BLACKHAWK
RESTAURANT
Wabash Ave. — Just South of Randolph

Fred Mann built the new Rainbo Garden building on Clark Street just north of Lawrence Avenue in 1922 to house a large indoor cabaret called the Rainbo Room. The sign hanging from the marquee advertises the Isham Jones orchestra. (Photo by Kaufmann and Fabry, courtesy of David R. Phillips)

Opposite page, top: Ben Bernie, "the old maestro," was a major attraction during the early 1930s at the College Inn of the Sherman Hotel. (Photo by Maurice Seymour courtesy of Ronald Seymour)

Opposite page, bottom: The performers, band, and patrons posed for this summer evening photo of the Rainbo Garden outdoor garden sometime before 1920. (A79918, Lake County [Illinois] Discovery Museum, Curt Teich Postcard Archives)

The Trianon Ballroom, Sixty-second Street and Cottage Grove Avenue, is shown here as it appeared in 1922 just after it was completed. The towers on the roof were for radio station WMBB, owned by the Karzas family and located at the ballroom. (Photo by Chicago Architectural Photographing Company, courtesy of David R. Phillips)

Opposite page: Jules Herbuveaux and his orchestra played at the Paradise Ballroom on the West Side and at the Palmer House before moving to WMAQ and NBC in 1928 to become the house band. (Photo by Kaufmann and Fabry, courtesy of David R. Phillips)

The first floor-show revues presented in Chicago were at the venerable North American Restaurant on State Street in 1915. Larger than most cabarets, the restaurant had an elevated stage that afforded customers good views of the acts and the band. (R74135, Lake County [Illinois] Discovery Museum, Curt Teich Postcard Archives)

Director Roy Shield and the studio orchestra for NBC–Chicago, shown here sometime in the early 1930s, were featured on *The Carnation Hour.* (Photo courtesy of Mrs. Thomas Barber)

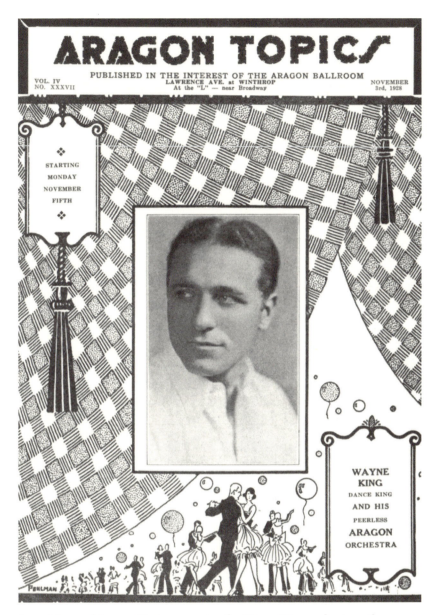

# ARAGON TOPICS

**PUBLISHED IN THE INTEREST OF THE ARAGON BALLROOM**
LAWRENCE AVE. at WINTHROP
At the "L" — near Broadway

VOL. IV
NO. XXXVII

NOVEMBER
3rd, 1928

❖
STARTING
MONDAY
NOVEMBER
FIFTH
❖

WAYNE
KING
DANCE KING
AND HIS
PEERLESS
ARAGON
ORCHESTRA

PEHLMAN

A 1928 issue of *Aragon Topics* promotes the Wayne King orchestra—then unknown—as its attraction. King's group later became one of the most famous dance bands to originate in Chicago. (*Aragon Topics* courtesy of Andrew Karzas)

**ARAGON ☾ TOPICS**

Lawrence Near Broadway      Uptown Square — At the "L"

Vol. I.      THURSDAY, JUNE 9, 1927    ⬤ 287      No. 39

**PAUL ASH — "RAJAH OF JAZZ"**
Saturday, June 11
**And His Entire Merry-Mad Musical Gang Here**
Alternating With Al Morey and His Original Royal Syncopators

*Milton Watson and Others Here Saturday, June 11th*

Paul Ash was the most famous bandleader in Chicago and occasionally left his post as director of the Oriental Theater stage band to make guest appearances around the city. Here Ash and his band are being promoted for a 1927 appearance at the Aragon Ballroom. (*Aragon Topics* courtesy of Andrew Karzas)

Charles "Charlie" Straight's band was an early and much-admired Chicago dance organization. The group played for many years at the Rendezvous Café on the North Side and was quickly signed by MCA in the mid-1920s. Straight's band preceded the Coon-Sanders Nighthawks into the Blackhawk Restaurant in 1926 and traveled the MCA circuit of Midwest venues. (Photo courtesy of the Chicago Federation of Musicians)

A lighted billboard announced the Coon-Sanders Victor Recording Orchestra as the current attraction at the famous Dells roadhouse on Dempster Road in Morton Grove. The sign helped guide patrons to the entrance along the dark suburban road. (Special Collections, Kansas City Public Library, Kansas City, Missouri)

Sol Wagner's band, a popular Chicago ballroom and cabaret group of the 1920s and 1930s, played a summer-long engagement in 1935 at a resort in South Haven, Michigan. (Photo courtesy of Bud [Buddy Shaw] Shiffman)

Henry Weber, a veteran opera and radio conductor, spent twenty years at WGN, where he was music director, but he was best known for directing the orchestra on the *Chicago Theater of the Air* radio show heard on the Mutual network. His vast knowledge of operas allowed him to condense the WGN presentations into one hour. (Photo courtesy of WGN Radio)

Opposite page: The popular comedian Joe E. Lewis (center) visits Kay Kyser's band at the Blackhawk Restaurant during a 1934 WGN remote radio broadcast. Pierre Andre, a WGN announcer, is at the right. (Photo courtesy of WGN Radio)

The title "Idol of the Airlanes" was conferred upon Jan Garber (left, holding violin) while he was playing at Chicago's Trianon Ballroom. Don Shoup is at the right with the guitar and the drummer Lew Palmer is in the background in this early 1930s photo. (Photo courtesy of WGN Radio)

The former Chicago bandleader Ted FioRito, who was as well known for writing music as he was for playing it, views a sheet-music collection of his hit songs in a special display in 1969 in Scottsdale, Arizona, where he had retired. (Photo courtesy of Jonathon Marshall)

## MERRY GARDEN BALL ROOM

at Belmont on Sheffield Avenue

*Telephone Buckingham 3500*

CHICAGO

MANAGEMENT
ETHEL KENDALL
AND
JACK LUND

BILL FOR JOE KAYSER AND BAND WEEK ENDING AND ENCLUDING NOVEMBER 22nd, 1928.

| | | | |
|---|---|---|---|
| DAN ALVIN; DRUMS, SEVEN SESSIONS @ $15.00 per session---------- | | | $105.00 |
| JESS STACY, PIANO, " " " " " " | | | 105.00 |
| J. CORSELLA, TROM. SIX SESSIONS " " " " | | | 90.00 |
| H. MALANO; " ONE SESSION STRAIGHT SCALE | | | 10.00 |
| H.L. ELSNER, BASS, SEVEN SESSIONS " " | | | 80.00 |
| D. SHERWOOD, VIOLIN, " " GUARANTEE FOR SEVEN SESSIONS | | | 85.00 |
| J. FINLEY, SAX, " " SCALE AND DOUBLING------------ | | | 109.00 |
| D. ALTIER, " " " " " " | | | 109.00 |
| M. BERCOV, ; " " " " " | | | 109.00 |
| M. SNYDER, BANJO, FOUR SESSIONS " " " | | | 64.00 |
| H. WILLIAMS " THREE SESSIONS @ $16.43 per session | | | 49.29 |
| JOE BILLO, COR. SEVEN SESSIONS, GUARANTEE FOR SEVEN SESSIONS | | | 85.00 |
| M. SPANIER, " " " " " " " | | | 105.00 |
| JOE KAYSER, " " GUARANTEE | | | 135.00 |
| LEADER, " " 13 men | | | 84.00 |

FINLEY, ALTIER and BERCOV, REHEARSAL TUESDAY NOVEMBER 19th @ $3.00 per man

9.00

1373.79

The payroll for Joe Kayser's Merry Garden Ballroom band in 1928 indicates that several 1920s Chicago jazz musicians were among the eleven members: Danny Alvin (drums), Jess Stacy (piano), Maurie Bercov (saxophone), and Muggsy Spanier (trumpet). (Courtesy of Joseph R. Kayser)

Opposite page: Joe Kayser was a well-known dance-band leader in northern Illinois before he brought his band to Chicago's Arcadia Ballroom in 1924. (Photo courtesy of Joseph R. Kayser)

J. Bodewalt Lampe (center), music director of the Aragon and Trianon Ballrooms, is flanked by the bandleaders (from left) Al Morey, Wayne King, Joe Kayser, and Dell Lampe. Both Morey and King played with Dell Lampe's orchestra and led second bands on weekends. (Photo courtesy of Joseph R. Kayser)

The Art Kassel "Kassels in the Air" band was a homegrown Chicago unit that was booked by MCA in the 1920s and became a big attraction from coast to coast. (Photo courtesy of Nick Sisk)

Frank Westphal's orchestra played at the inauguration of the new Rainbo Room of the Rainbo Garden in 1922. (Photo courtesy of the Chicago Federation of Musicians)

Louis Panico, who played the famous trumpet solo on the Isham Jones Brunswick recording of "Wabash Blues," later was a well-known bandleader and spent many years at the Canton Tea Garden in downtown Chicago. (Printed by permission of Conn-Selmer, Inc., a Steinway Musical Instruments Company)

One of the largest restaurants in Chicago, the Golden Pumpkin specialized in Chinese food, dancing, and floor shows. (119804, Lake County [Illinois] Discovery Museum, Curt Teich Postcard Archives

The sumptuous appointments of the Aragon Ballroom's palatial dance floor and surrounding area, like those of its sister ballroom the Trianon, were light years ahead of the facilities in other ballrooms of the day. (Photo by Chicago Architectural Photographing Co., courtesy of David R. Phillips)

# 7 The Beat Goes On

DANCE bands had become a big factor in drawing patrons to hotel dining rooms by the mid-1920s. Isham Jones validated that fact by demonstrating his band's importance to the Sherman Hotel's bottom line during his four successful years in the College Inn, entertaining patrons and broadcasting his music through nightly remotes.

Many new hotels erected after 1920, both in downtown Chicago and in the growing number of outlying commercial areas of the city, quickly embraced the dine-and-dance policy and designated at least one or more of their public rooms to include dancing. Based on the success of the College Inn and the Morrison's Terrace Room, many hotels began presenting floor shows of various types. By 1930 there were few major hotels in cities big and small in the United States that had not literally and figuratively jumped on the "band wagon."

Chicago's newer hotels were certainly more modern and often bigger than those built at or before the beginning of the twentieth century. Of the newer hotels, the Palmer House on State Street and the Bismarck on Randolph Street replaced older hotels of the same names. The Stevens Hotel was opened in 1927 on Michigan Avenue just south of Congress Parkway. Farther north on Michigan, Tracy and John B. Drake erected their namesake hotel at Oak Street.

The original Palmer House, at State and Monroe Streets, probably the best known of Chicago's hotels, was completed just two weeks before the Great Fire of 1871. The hotel and the rest of Chicago's downtown area were totally destroyed. The hotel's replacement across the street was larger and more elaborate and became *the* hotel in town.[1]

Potter Palmer's sons, Honoré and Potter Jr., built the present Palmer House on the same site in two sections. The first opened in 1924, the second in 1927. Music had been a part of the hotel's hospitality all along but, characteristic of the times, little note was made of what musical groups appeared there until just after World War I. Louis Alberti and his orchestra, a Benson organization, was one of the first groups to be identified as playing at the Palmer House prior to 1920 and included a young West Side trumpet player named Louis Panico.

The first section of the 1920s Palmer House to be built was the eastern section, located between Wabash Avenue and the midpoint between Wabash and State Street to the west. The main dining room in this new section was called the Victorian Room and, in the mid-1920s, featured Jules Herbuveaux and his orchestra for dinner music and dancing. Herbuveaux had previously been at the Paradise Ballroom on Chicago's West Side.

The nearby Empire Room opened in the Palmer House for luncheons and early dinners for theatergoers in 1927, and the violinist Ralph Ginsburg's five-piece string ensemble was hired away from the Blackhawk Restaurant to provide the evening dinner music.[2] By then the Blackhawk was well on its way to becoming a dance band mecca. (More about this in chapter 8.) The beautiful mirrored, green, gold, and ebony Empire Room didn't make its debut as a nightclub, however, until May 1933. The Palmer sons decided to go into show business on the advice of a consultant who foresaw the demand for this kind of show room after the repeal of Prohibition, which came later that year.

Veloz and Yolanda, a sensational ballroom dancing act, opened the Empire Room to much publicity and ballyhoo generated by the hotel's press agent, Al Fuller.[3] The dance team, which remained at the Empire Room for thirteen months, made many return appearances and by 1935 carried its own orchestra led by Shep Fields. George "Spike" Hamilton, a West Coast leader, formed a new orchestra to play for the dance act in 1936.[4] (Hamilton was to become the father of the movie star and television personality George Hamilton.) Jerry Shelton, a flashy accordionist who had been with the Fields band, later took over leadership of the V&Y orchestra.

Ted Weems's Chicago-based band succeeded the Veloz and Yolanda troupe in November 1934, beginning a new Palmer House name-band policy, which continued through World War II.[5] Tommy Dorsey, Guy Lombardo, Ray Noble, Hal Kemp, and Tommy Tucker played in the room over the next few years. In 1941 the Griff Williams orchestra was engaged to follow Tommy Tucker and played for what turned out to be a record engagement—forty weeks.[6] Williams had a lot of experience playing in San Francisco hotels and, most recently, the Stevens Hotel in Chicago. He and his piano-led staccato tenor band were a big hit with the society-crowd clientele of the Empire Room.[7]

By November of that year, Williams had broken two attendance records: the biggest Saturday night since Veloz and Yolanda in 1935, and Ray Noble's attendance record of seventy days, which Noble had established the previous year. The WGN wire clearly was helping draw crowds to the posh room.

Griff Williams's drawing power literally was music to the ears of the hotel's vice president, Edward T. Lawless, who signed Williams to a contract calling for sixteen weeks a year at the Palmer House.[8] In December 1942, Lawless amended the agreement with Williams to a contract "for the duration [of World War II]." Williams didn't quite fulfill his contract. The band pulled out in January 1944 for a road tour to make way for the entertainer Hildegarde.

Williams was not on the road very long. He enlisted in the Navy in February 1944 and was assigned to the Great Lakes Naval Training Center in nearby Waukegan where, as a lieutenant j.g., he was the assistant to the banjo ace and vaudeville entertainer Eddy Peabody, who was in charge of the music and entertainment program there. In 1945, as World War II ended, the hotel magnate Conrad Hilton purchased the Palmer House for twenty million dollars.[9] The Williams orchestra returned to the Empire Room the following year amid much hoopla and celebration. But times had changed and the group soon began spending much of its time at major locations outside Chicago. In the next decade there followed a parade of other hotel bands, most of them led by pianists such as Henry King and Carmen Cavallaro.

In 1957, the local leader Ben Arden formed what became a house band, which remained at the Palmer House for a record-breaking seventeen years, backing a string of glitzy shows booked by the hotel's entertainment director, Merriel Abbot, and featuring top show-business names such as Maurice Chevalier, Nelson Eddy, Sophie Tucker, and George Gobel. It also made Arden's band the longest-running hotel band in Chicago, a title formerly held by Maurie Sherman at the Sherman Hotel in the 1920s and 1930s. Arden and his band were replaced at the Empire Room by the veteran Chicago dance- and show-band leader Frankie Masters and his eleven-piece orchestra.

It soon became apparent that the Empire Room could no longer operate profitably and continue to bring in the top-name acts now accustomed to performing in the large, big-budget Las Vegas show rooms. The singer Peggy Lee was engaged to play the Empire Room in September 1975.[10] She reportedly was paid twenty thousand dollars a week. Other entertainers were said to be asking for even more than that plus a cut of the cover charges. For her engagement, Lee required a thirty-five-piece orchestra, about twenty-four musicians more than in the house orchestra. On the other side of the economic equation, the Empire Room held only five hundred people, not enough, even at top prices, to support week after week such a large overhead (there was a ten-dollar cover charge during Peggy Lee's engagement). As a result, the Palmer House management on January 19, 1979, closed the posh show room. The last show featured the comedienne Phyllis Diller. A Chicago leader, Norm Krone, and his orchestra played for the show and for dancing.[11]

The Empire Room reopened for dinner in October 1979 with Victor Lombardo's orchestra and a singer. Polly Podewell, a local vocalist, brought her voice and a five-piece unit into the Empire Room early in 1980.[12] In May of that year Norm Ladd, a Chicagoan, and his eleven-piece band succeeded Podewell to play for dancing in the room and remained until the following year when the hotel discontinued its music policy altogether.

A few blocks west and north of the Palmer House was the Bismarck Hotel. Located at 171 West Randolph Street, at the corner of Randolph and Wells Street, the Bismarck was in the heart of Chicago's entertainment district. A businessman's hotel, it was just one block west of the LaSalle Street financial district, across and down the street from the Sherman Hotel, and a short walk from State Street.

The first Bismarck, dating back to 1894, was in the building occupied by the former Germania Hotel. The owners, Emil and Karl Eitel, razed the old Bismarck, and a new complex designed by the theater architects Rapp and Rapp was built in 1926. It occupied the north half of the block along Randolph Street between LaSalle and Wells. The Bismarck Hotel was on the west; the Palace Theater was to the east; and the Metropolitan Office Building was around the corner to the south along LaSalle Street.[13]

Two of the earliest dance bands to play in the hotel's main dining room were the Flamingo Orchestra and the orchestra of Cope Harvey, the South Side leader and booking agent. Things picked up musically when the Eitels decided to upgrade their main dining room, turning it into a dine-and-dance venue. They redecorated the main dining room and renamed it the Walnut Room in August 1931 and hired the local bandleader Art Kassel and his band for the 1931–32 season.[14] The Kassel band continued to play there most seasons until the late 1940s.

Other bands also played long engagements at the hotel but Kassel put the hotel on the map via his nightly broadcasts and his imaginative radio call, "Kassels in the Air." Over the years, the Mutual, NBC-Red and NBC-Blue networks, and several local stations, including the powerhouse WGN, carried his band up to three times a night from the Walnut Room. Art's composition (with Mel Stitzel) and theme song "Doodle-Doo-Doo" became familiar in the hotel dining room and was heard on the airwaves for nearly twenty years.

The Walnut Room had small floor shows, usually a dance act, a singer, and an occasional animal or magic act. There were three shows a night to accommodate the before- and after-theater traffic in the thirties when many of the nearby North Loop legitimate theaters were still active.

Control of the hotel and adjacent properties passed from the Eitel family to Arthur Wirtz, a real-estate magnate, in 1956. By then the bloom was off the rose for big bands, most nearby theaters had closed, and all but a few of the upscale retail stores on State Street had closed or moved to North Michigan Avenue. The hotel still stands, and after changing hands again and undergoing an extensive renovation it was reopened as the Hotel Allegro in 1998.[15] The North Loop theater district also is being revived and three of the major old-line theaters have been extensively remodeled and reopened.

The Stevens Hotel, the largest hotel in the world at the time of its completion in 1927, was located at 720 South Michigan Avenue, in the block south of the Blackstone Hotel. It was the brainchild of Ernest Stevens, son of the family that built the LaSalle Hotel in 1909, which at its completion had been deemed the world's largest.[16] Three dance orchestras—those led by Jack Chapman, Armand Hand, and Paul Ash—played for several thousand guests at the May 1927 grand opening in the hotel's giant grand ballroom. Ash had achieved local stardom as the leader of the Oriental Theater stage band and probably attracted the most attention that evening. Roy Bargy was the featured pianist with the Armand Hand orchestra and, in the weeks following, led a band that played for diners and dancers in the smaller dining room called the Boulevard Room.[17] The grand musical style in which the hotel was opened perhaps was a signal of the importance dance music would have in the years ahead.

The hotel went into receivership in 1932, however, and into bankruptcy in 1935. Business was slow during the Depression but music for dinner dancing and accompaniment of floor shows continued to be provided by Frankie Masters and others. As noted earlier, the U.S. Army took over the Stevens in 1942 for housing military radio operator trainees.[18] Back in regular civilian control by 1943 and 1944, management hired the name bands of Harry James (with Frank Sinatra), Duke Ellington, Bernie Cummins, and George Olsen to attract customers.[19] All played in the Boulevard Room. Conrad Hilton bought the property in 1945 for $7.2 million, made it his chain's flagship, and renamed it, predictably, the Conrad Hilton.[20] Hilton management continued the music and floor shows in the Boulevard Room with Don McGrane and other dance bands until 1947 when it changed to featuring ice shows.

Merriel Abbot produced the first ice show, a spectacular called "Iceland Fantasy"; Chuck Foster's band played for the show and for dancing. An ever-changing parade of new dance bands came into the Boulevard Room with each ice show,[21] but when Frankie Masters, a big Chicago favorite, brought in his dance band to accompany an ice show, he stayed for five shows. Later, he returned and stayed five years (1952–57), during which he accompanied eleven ice shows. That was the end of the formal entertainment at the hotel. Totally remodeled in the mid-1980s, the hotel is still one of Chicago's finest and largest, but music is heard only for special occasions.

Several miles to the north of the Stevens was the Drake Hotel, built by Tracy and John B. Drake at Walton Street and Michigan Avenue. It was located on what became by 1980 the fourth most valuable parcel of land in the city, valued at $12.9 million.[22] The hotel was opened in December 1920 at the north end of that section of North Michigan Avenue now known as the "Magnificent Mile," a stretch of exclusive stores, shops, and hotels that runs north from the Chicago River to Oak Street. Through the years, the Drake attracted a wealthy and prestigious clientele to its dining rooms, but like its sister hotel, the Blackstone to the south, it maintained a staid, very formal atmosphere until the 1930s. During the 1920s, Edgar Benson had the music concession and put Jack Chapman and his orchestra in as the first regular purveyors of music. Radio station WDAP, soon to be WGN, then broadcasting from the Drake in 1922, put Chapman's orchestra and, later, Henry Selinger's Drake Concert Ensemble on the air each night.[23]

The music at the Drake was always muted and designed to fit nicely into the background. Reeds and strings were emphasized, and there was a period in the later 1920s when Drake management discouraged the use of any brass at all in its orchestras. Bobbie Meeker, a violinist who came out of the Benson Orchestra of Chicago and succeeded Chapman at the Drake in 1934, had a brass-less group during an earlier engagement in 1928. About this time the Drake management was beginning to take note of what was happening at other downtown hotels and decided it better get on the name-band wagon.

Clyde McCoy was the hotel's first name-band. McCoy and his band, then becoming popular from their hit Columbia recording of "Sugar Blues," remained in the Drake's Gold Coast/Silver Forest Room for eighteen months. The room with two names was the Silver Forest Room in the summer, with open skylights, bare floors, light-colored decor, and silver leaves shimmering on the ceiling; in the winter, it was the Gold Coast Room, which was carpeted and was painted in different seasonal colors.[24]

Earl Burtnett and his very popular band from California, Vincent Lopez,

Paul Whiteman, Wayne King, and the English bandleader Jack Hylton all played for the floor shows and dancing in the Drake's glamorous dining and show room.[25] In 1941 the larger Gold Coast/Silver Forest room was vacated in favor of the adjacent but smaller Camellia House. Here more intimate shows, usually featuring a chanteuse, were presented each night among the fresh white camellias and black banquettes, and smaller orchestras were used for the floor shows and dancing.

The orchestra of the pianist-leader-arranger Jimmy Blade holds the record for playing the longest engagement at the Camellia House: sixteen years, from 1951 to 1967.[26] Bill Snyder, another Chicago pianist-leader, famous for his 1950 hit record of "Bewitched, Bothered, and Bewildered," succeeded Blade and remained until 1970, when the Camellia House ended its show policy. The room went through several revivals with the local bandleader Dick Judson playing for seven seasons. Paul Meeker and his group also played in the room. Then, in 1975, Victor Lombardo, Guy's youngest brother, brought his small group into the room for the season to play for dancing and a small floor show.[27] The Drakes sold the hotel in 1979 to new owners who not only kept the exclusive flavor of the hostelry but also enhanced it with an extensive renovation of the property in the mid-1980s.[28]

Farther north were the Ambassador Hotels East and West, two small hostelries located at the intersection of State and Goethe Streets. They acquired cachet with Hollywood film stars and other entertainers because they were small, intimate, and famous for their service. The better known of the two, the Ambassador East, became a watering hole for the rich and famous mostly because of its elegant dining and show room, the Pump Room.

From the late 1930s into the 1970s, the hotels were under the management of the Sherman Hotel's Frank Bering and, until his death in 1950, Ernie Beifield, who used all their show business know-how in crafting the Pump Room into a venue that dripped with glamour. Turbaned waiters served food from flaming swords, a showy gimmick borrowed from the College Inn, where it was used a few years earlier. Hollywood and New York show business personalities making coast-to-coast trips on the splendid trains of the day were met at the depots by Ambassador Hotel limousines, which then ferried them to the Pump Room for their between-train stops.

A long line of dance bands, big and small, played in the Pump Room through the years, but the longest-running band engagement of all was that of the Chicagoan David LeWinter's musical crew.[29] LeWinter's talented musicians, all of whom doubled and tripled on instruments, were booked into the room in 1945 and didn't leave until 1963. Twenty-four-year-old Stanley Paul, a New York pianist, formed a band for the Pump Room to succeed LeWinter and, like his predecessor, caught the patrons' fancy. Paul stayed until 1972 and, since leaving, has become one of the city's top society bandleaders.

At that point LeWinter and Paul played alternating engagements until 1974. Then Romeo Meltz, who for years had been leading the combo at the Ambassador West's Buttery, moved across the street to play in the Pump Room, where he remained until it closed in 1976. The Pump Room was redecorated that year and reopened under the Lettuce Entertain You restaurant chain management, which has tried to maintain in the jet age the glamorous image the room had in the railroad age, but without music.[30]

The Sheraton Hotel on North Michigan Avenue, the Westin (formerly the Continental) Hotel just south of the Drake, the St. Clair, the Brevoort, the Hamilton, the Eastgate, the Midland, and the Atlantic hotels, all in or near the Loop, had entertainment and dance bands through the years. In the late 1930s and early 1940s the Sheraton, at 505 North Michigan Avenue, earlier known as the Medinah Athletic Club, was host to the Catholic Youth Organization (CYO) dances held on weekends. Gay Claridge's and Mickey Prindl's bands were two of the many musical groups to play at this venue for the CYO dances.

The Tally-Ho was the hotel's main dining and entertainment room and featured local Chicago bands such as that of Hal Munro. Later, small combos were hired for the smaller New Horizons Room in the late 1940s and early 1950s. The pianist Joe Vera and his group, featured earlier at the Congress Hotel, played in the New Horizons Room for several years. The remodeled and expanded hotel today is called the Intercontinental and has no regular music.

The Beifields, Harry Moir, the Palmer brothers, and H. L. Kaufman were the pioneers in putting dancing and floor shows into hotel dining rooms in downtown Chicago. Their willingness to take risks with new forms of entertainment not only became a factor in how people chose their hotels but, in the process, helped build the dance bands into popular attractions.

There were other entrepreneurs in the city who worked their business magic in the outlying neighborhoods and precincts of Chicago. The city by 1920 had a population of 2.7 million people and was growing rapidly, pushing its boundaries to the south, west, and north. These entrepreneurs noted the trend and built the many hotels that dotted the city's outlying areas, creating little oases for dancing and entertainment most often located in or near the growing number of commercial and retail centers. Among them were the Southmoor and Pershing hotels on the South Side, the Graemere to the west, and on the North Side the very large and impressive lakeside resort called the Edgewater Beach Hotel.

The elegant Edgewater Beach, in the 5300 block of North Sheridan Road, was a gleaming jewel along Chicago's lakefront to the north of the downtown. William M. Dewey, a strict disciplinarian and a man of high principles, managed the Edgewater Beach. He took seriously his duties of providing impeccable service and first-class entertainment to his affluent clientele. Today such a hotel would be called a "destination resort" because it had all the amenities of a resort—shops, meeting rooms, tennis courts, swimming pools, several restaurants, a fine beach along the lake, dancing, and classical concerts at the dinner hour and on Sunday afternoons.

Before 1920 Dewey hired Paul Biese and his nine-piece crew, probably the best-known orchestra in the city before Isham Jones, to play for dancing in the main dining room. Here guests could gaze at the lake through large windows overlooking the water. Biese played the Edgewater Beach for several years.[31] He also played long engagements during the 1920s at the nearby Pantheon Theater, at 4650 North Sheridan Road, about a mile south of the hotel. Biese died suddenly at age thirty-eight following an engagement near Cincinnati in October 1925, as noted earlier.

In the 1920s there were dinner concerts in the huge main dining room (it was said to seat one thousand people) by a string ensemble directed by Joseph Gallicchio, which gave way later in the evening to dance bands. Elaborately produced floor shows were introduced later in the hotel's life, often with a chorus line. William Dewey made a risky but ultimately favorable decision in early 1922 when he hired a brand-new orchestra from Detroit to replace Paul Biese for the summer. Co-led by Dan Russo and Ted FioRito, the orchestra had been organized especially to open a new restaurant that fall in Detroit called the Oriole Terrace, owned by J. L. Woods.[32] In anticipation of that opening, the orchestra had recorded several sides for the Brunswick label that unexpectedly became quite popular.

The band became a big attraction that summer at the Edgewater Beach, helped along by its records. The group returned to Detroit at the end of the engagement, as planned, but Woods's restaurant closed a short time later. Paul Biese's band, meanwhile, did not return to the Edgewater Beach that fall for some reason, so William Dewey went to Cleveland, where the FioRito-Russo orchestra had landed following the Oriole Terrace's closing, and rehired that group. It didn't take long for the Oriole Terrace Orchestra to regain its popularity with Edgewater Beach dancers and diners alike and it became one of the most popular in the city.

FioRito had written his first big hit, "Toot Toot Tootsie, Goodbye," and the band recorded it on Brunswick just before going back to the Edgewater Beach in the fall of 1922. As noted in chapter 3, the band's guitarist-singer, Nick Lucas, popularized the tune through nightly broadcasts from the hotel via WEBH, a station located in the Edgewater Beach. Lucas's vocalizing on "Toot Toot Tootsie" and two other FioRito tunes, "Charlie My Boy" and "No, No, Nora," helped him establish a career as a successful vaudeville performer.

When the Oriole Terrace Orchestra left for the Aragon in the fall of 1926, Gus Edwards, a booker, brought in a couple of dance bands from his list of clients over the next three years. Joe Gallicchio, who had been affiliated with the hotel since earlier in that decade, continued to direct the concert sessions until Ferdinand Steindel succeeded him. Both FioRito and Russo appeared at the hotel again with their respective new orchestras, and in 1930 Charlie Agnew's Chicago band, now booked by MCA, was hired for the spring season. Harry Sosnick and Phil Spitalny followed Agnew with their orchestras. Spitalny had not yet organized his all-girl orchestra, which in the 1940s was a big hit on network radio.

Paul Whiteman, a bit down on his luck because of the music slowdown during the early years of the Depression, lived in Chicago from 1930 to 1932.[33] Working part-time in the downtown NBC studios, the Whiteman band needed a steady Chicago job at night beginning in early 1931, at the conclusion of its engagement at the South Side Granada Café. NBC was then also booking dance bands, including Whiteman's, through its Artists Bureau and ended up easing Phil Spitalny's orchestra out of the Edgewater Beach Hotel to clear the way for Whiteman.[34] Following Whiteman at the Edgewater Beach was a parade of local and name bands.

Gus Edwards, now representing the Consolidated Radio Artists Bureau, introduced to the Edgewater Beach patrons one of his young discoveries, Orrin Tucker, in 1938. Tucker, from suburban Wheaton, and his made-to-order hotel band were well received by the staid Edgewater Beach clientele. As the 1940s dawned and competition from the downtown hotels increased, the floor shows, now being produced by Dorothy Hild, an ex-dancer and the Edgewater's entertainment director, became bigger and flashier with a full-fledged chorus line. The main dining room, renamed the Marine Dining Room with a nod to its magnificent view of Lake Michigan, presented a new floor show each month. The shows went on seven nights a week but the bands later only played for five, so relief bands were required for the off nights.[35]

During the summers, the bands played for dancing outside on the Beach Walk, an area along the hotel's Lake Michigan beachfront. The changeable

Chicago weather frequently forced musicians and dancers alike to flee in-doors to the Marine Dining Room. The June bugs, which often got caught in the saxophonist's keys, caused some unusual musical effects. The hotel lost its lakefront beach and the Beach Walk in the early fifties when Lake Shore Drive was extended north to Hollywood Avenue.

Wayne King, who had played at the Edgewater Beach Hotel on several oc-casions in the thirties, assumed leadership of his post–World War II orchestra at the hotel in 1945 when he returned to civilian life. He had been in the army at nearby Fort Sheridan, running the music and entertainment programs there and at other local military bases. In 1944, Emil Vandas, a violinist with King's prewar orchestra, had taken over part of the Eddie Oliver band with which he was then playing at the Edgewater Beach and built an orchestra around the Oliver men. In reality Vandas was organizing the new Wayne King postwar orchestra for his old boss.[36]

The hotel was sold in 1947, and in 1954 the Marine Dining Room was shuttered, ending a run of more than thirty years featuring outstanding floor shows and top dance bands. The hotel went into bankruptcy in 1967 and was torn down in 1970.[37]

Several hotels had been built in the late 1910s and early 1920s on the South Side in the Hyde Park area near the lake and the University of Chi-cago campus. Most prominent were the Del Prado, the Windermere, and the Southmoor. All three catered to an affluent white clientele and by the 1920s had a high percentage of residential guests. Over to the west along Cottage Grove Avenue was the Pershing Hotel, located just south of the Sixty-third Street intersection, at Sixty-fourth Street.

The Southmoor Hotel, 6646 South Stony Island Avenue, was the most mu-sically prominent of the Jackson Park hotels featuring dance bands in the late 1920s. Located across the street from the southwest corner of Jackson Park, the hotel hired Ben Pollack, a native Chicagoan then living on the West Coast. Pollack brought his band, called the Californians, into the Venetian Room for the 1926–27 season. Playing with the group were several Chicagoans earlier hired by Pollack: Gil Rodin, a tenor saxist, and Harry and Benny Goodman. The engagement lasted a little over a year and Pollack and his bandsmen ap-parently drew such big crowds that the management did away with the floor show.[38]

Art Kassel's band followed Pollack in 1927 and the black bandleader Hughie Swift succeeded Kassel to complete the 1927–28 season.[39] Two local bands led by Ralph Williams and Dick McPartland, respectively, played at the hotel most of the time until the Depression forced the hotel to shut down its dancing and entertainment offerings. The bandleader George Foster reopened the Venetian Room for dancing in 1939 but by the end of World War II there were no more regular musical attractions at the hotel.[40]

The major retail center of Sixty-third and Cottage Grove, a mile directly west of Jackson Park, became an entertainment district in the 1920s. The Trianon, one block north, and the Pershing Hotel, at the corner of Sixty-fourth and Cottage Grove, were the anchors. The hotel was built around 1924 by the former dance team of Ethel Kendall and Jack Lund, who also owned the first Merry Garden ballroom at 6040 Cottage Grove Avenue. Within walking distance of either the Trianon or the Pershing were the giant Tivoli Theater and two ballrooms, the Cinderella and Midway Gardens.

The Pershing catered to a white clientele in the 1920s and 1930s and had several cocktail lounges and a fairly large ballroom (7,175 square feet). The hotel hired both black and white bands. The ballroom was leased out to promoters during much of the 1920s. Dave Peyton, a booker and bandleader, installed one of his dance bands in the second-floor ballroom of the newly opened hotel in 1925 to accompany Ernie Young's elaborate floor show. Ralph Jones directed the Peyton orchestra. For a time the ballroom was operated by a longtime entertainment entrepreneur, Al Tierney (sometimes spelled Tearney), and was called the Pershing Palace Café, later Club Bagdad. A white band fronted by the Benson agency's Walter Ford alternated during this period with Peyton's ten-piece band, which later was led by the saxophonist Ralph Brown.[41] About 1927 MCA put Bernie Cummins and his Ohio-based road band into the Pershing. But it was mostly local leaders such as Charlie Pierce who furnished the music for dancing on weekends only.

In the early and later 1930s the hotel ballroom was leased by David and Maurice Solovy and operated as a public ballroom.[42] Johnny Maitland and other local bands usually played at the Pershing in this period. The Solovys later took over the old Cinderella across Cottage Grove Avenue and renamed it the Granada. In addition to these South Side venues, they also operated at times during the 1930s the Marigold Gardens, Green Mill Gardens, and Wilshore Ballroom, all on the North Side.

An investment group that owned the older Du Sable Hotel at Oakwood Boulevard and Cottage Grove Avenue purchased the Pershing in the early 1940s. The black community by this time was moving south of Sixty-third Street and the hotel became a center of musical activity that leaned heavily toward jazz.[43] Clarence Black's combo provided dinner-and-dance music in the smaller Pershing Show Lounge (later called the Persian Lounge) on the first floor in the early forties.

Jimmy Dale, a white bandleader (his real name was Harold Fox and he was a member of the Fox family tailors on Twelfth Street), had what amounted to the house band in the Pershing's ballroom during the late 1940s. The Dale band always attracted outstanding young Chicago jazzmen, including the trumpeter Gail Brockman; saxists Gene Ammons, Lee Konitz, and Johnny Griffin; and a valve trombone player named Cy Touff. McKie Fitzhugh, a black disc jockey and entrepreneur, hosted many special kinds of dances in the ballroom that attracted crowds of up to two thousand dancers. In the basement of the hotel there was a nightclub, later called El Grotto, that featured black bands, combos, and fairly elaborate floor shows. Ethel Waters and the bands of Earl Hines (who had a business interest in the El Grotto), Eddie South, Walter Dyett, and Charlie Parker all appeared in the lower-level nightclub in the forties.[44]

On the West Side, across the street from Garfield Park at Washington Boulevard and Homan Avenue, was the Graemere Hotel. Like the hotels near Jackson Park, the Graemere had primarily residential guests. Through the late 1930s, Don Pedro's orchestra was regularly featured in the hotel's Glass House show room. Early in 1939, the pianist Joe Vera took over Pedro's band, but during the 1940s and 1950s the hotel booked only small combos and comedians for its show room, which was just off the lobby.

The depressed economy during the early 1930s had a powerful impact on Chicago hotels, and many owners went bankrupt or defaulted on their mortgages and/or property taxes. But by 1935, the U.S. government's Reconstruction Finance Corporation (RFC) or companies with leases from the RFC had taken over management of many of the larger downtown properties. In the process, many of the show rooms were shuttered for months at a time to reduce the flow of red ink. However, thousands of visitors came to Chicago to attend the Century of Progress, which significantly helped the hotels weather 1933 and 1934.

Of the older major downtown hotels, the Morrison went bankrupt in the early 1930s. Ernie Beifield's Sherman Hotel was bankrupt by 1934 but Beifield regained control in 1938.[45] The Congress Hotel was taken over by the RFC in the 1930s and, as noted earlier, was later bought by Albert Pick.[46] The Stevens Hotel went into receivership for back taxes and default on bonds in 1930. It was taken over by the RFC and later leased to an operating company. The Blackstone the same year passed into the hands of an insurance company on a defaulted mortgage loan.[47]

Other hotels weathered the Depression years quite well. The Drake stayed afloat in spite of the family's loss of the Blackstone. The Palmer House, said to be the longest continuously operated hotel in America, went through the economic downturn relatively unscathed.[48] According to Jules Herbuveaux, the most recent Palmer House (completed between 1924 and 1927) never had a mortgage in all the years of its operation.[49] As noted above, the Palmer family sold it to the Hilton Hotel chain in 1945.

Of the Chicago hotels to have modern dance bands regularly in their dining rooms, the Sherman was probably the earliest, followed by the Morrison, the LaSalle, and the Palmer House. The Fort Dearborn and Grand Pacific hotels both had Bert Kelly dance bands playing for hotel patrons. While other downtown hotels probably had dance bands, the leaders' names are hard to find in contemporary publications before 1920. It was an era when neither dance bands nor their leaders had yet gained any celebrity.

Over the next fifty years, most downtown Chicago hotels and many in the outlying areas moved the dance bands from obscurity to prominence in their main show rooms, where they became the main attractions. Hotels and dance bands during this time became inseparable business associates. In 1938 it was estimated that hotels in the United States spent more than ten million dollars each year for dance bands and talent for the floor shows, according to an advertisement in *Billboard*.[50]

This prosperous partnership between dance bands and hotels—in Chicago at least—finally ended in 1981 when the Palmer House brought down the curtain on regular dancing in its main dining room. The dance band era actually had ended years earlier but the Palmer House seemed unwilling or unable to give up so quickly on the fine old tradition that had begun so many years before.

# 8 Dance Bands Thrive in Chicago's Cabarets and Restaurants

CHICAGO'S dance bands and orchestras broadened their charter significantly in the city's early twentieth-century cabarets and restaurants, quickly becoming first-rate show bands. In addition the cabaret orchestras became not only an integral part of floor shows but often a central part of the production. In the process, the bandleader became a popular personality.

"Cabaret" was a generic term used to refer to those establishments between 1910 and 1930 that served food and liquor, provided dancing, and presented some form of musical entertainment on a dance floor, usually one that was surrounded by customers seated at tables (thus, a floor show). The intimacy that was established between performer and audience in this arrangement seemed to have great appeal.[1] In some of the bigger drink-dine-and-dance venues, however, the shows were presented on an elevated stage for improved sight lines.

The cabaret idea originated in Paris about 1880, spread through Europe, and found its way to the United States by the early 1910s. Many small tavern and saloon owners, anxious to clean up their often sleazy image, made room for a dance floor, added a singer or a dancer, perhaps a musician or two, and became a cabaret overnight, at least in name. "Café" was another name for a cabaret and became the preferred term by the late 1910s. Many cabarets, in fact, used the term in their names, thus giving rise to places like Café Royale, the Arsonia Café, and the Bagdad Café.

Cabarets were not universally well accepted new institutions. Like some dance halls, many cabarets were located in disreputable parts of the city or catered to a rough crowd. In a 1916 series of exposés, the *Chicago Herald* called cafés and dance halls "thorns in the side of virtue."[2] The paper pointed out in another of its articles that even the movies of the day portrayed the cabaret as a symbol of vice, but it allowed that some of these venues were quite properly run.[3]

Restaurants, on the other hand, were public dining rooms where food was the main attraction. Alcoholic beverages often were available and small string ensembles often played soft background music for the diners in larger establishments. By the mid-1910s, however, the lines dividing cabarets and restaurants became blurred as more and more restaurants began installing entertainment in the form of floor shows. The North American Restaurant on State Street was credited with inaugurating the first floor-show revue in 1915, while some of the other upscale downtown restaurants such as Rector's had only orchestras and occasionally presented dance teams or singers.[4]

Things changed quickly after the North American Restaurant began its floor-show revues, which were fairly large spectacles. The concept of presenting a number of vaudeville-type acts integrated according to a theme and performed on the dance floor or a low stage was as novel as it was popular, and it spread quickly to smaller clubs.[5] Lewis Erenberg, in his *Chicago History* article "Ain't We Got Fun," suggests that it was the patrons' ability to be close to celebrities and gangsters and their perception of a certain amount of "risk" and "danger" that added immensely to the cabarets' popularity.[6]

Playing music in Chicago's early 1900s cabarets and restaurants offered a somewhat insecure existence to the musicians, whose profession was already uncertain. The cabarets were not known for their longevity; like their owners, they came and went. Apart from the hotel dining rooms there were a number of prominent Chicago restaurants in the central downtown area in the pre-1920 period: the North American, Rector's, and deJonghe's French Restaurant were just a few of them.[7] Other venerable restaurants were Henrici's, Silver's, Chapin and Gore's, the Richelieu, Kinsley's, and King's. Schlogl's and the Red Star Inn were the best-known German restaurants and were both located just north of the Loop.

The North American Restaurant, operated by Louis Eckstein and Abe Franks, was a fine-dining establishment located in the North American Building, 36 South State Street.[8] At their first floor-show revue, in 1915, Eckstein and Franks featured Miss Patricola's orchestra, a well-known touring vaudeville group of the day, which had played at the opening of the Green Mill Sunken Gardens a year earlier.[9] Four additional performers and eight chorus girls were also in the show. No first name is ever given for Patricola in the publicity or music trade publications. The Patricola band worked as an act rather than as a dance band since James Henschel's orchestra provided the music for the show and for dancing. By 1920 Henschel, a violinist, was a well-known conductor around town and later led the pit orchestra at the Great States (later State and Lake) Theater for Orpheum circuit vaudeville shows.

The acts and bands for the North American were booked through Morris Silver of the Western Vaudeville Managers Association (WVMA, an arm of the Orpheum circuit) rather than through Edgar Benson, who had cornered much of that type of downtown business by then.[10] Over the years, Silver, a prominent agent, also booked acts for the Moulin Rouge, the Terrace Garden of the Morrison Hotel, and the Congress and Grand Pacific hotels.[11] In later years, Silver went to work for the Balaban and Katz Theater chain.

Just south of the North American and around the corner on Monroe Street was Rector's Restaurant, a very high class establishment. In 1915 its name was changed to Café Royale, but it maintained its upscale clientele and featured public dancing and small shows.[12] In something of a booking coup that year, Café Royale's management was able to hire the famous dancers Vernon and Irene Castle, who were starring at the nearby Illinois Theater in their own show called *Watch Your Step,* with music by Irving Berlin.

The Castles ambled over to the Café Royale after the theater to perform their specialty numbers twice a night. A Benson orchestra accompanied their fancy stepping and that of the patrons. Shortly after the Castles took to the road with their show, they were replaced by Maurice and Walton, who had performed at the Sherman Hotel five years earlier.[13] The Café Royale continued operating into the 1920s but was taken over in 1925 by Joe Spagot, who ran it under his name.[14]

Two of Chicago's finest restaurants of the 1910s and 1920s, deJonghe's and Henrici's, didn't have any music but they were so well known they deserve mention. DeJonghe's was just across the street from the Palmer House on Monroe Street and considered the city's finest French restaurant.[15] It closed in the early years of Prohibition when Mr. deJonghe apparently felt that dinner without wine was not dinner at all. Henrici's, located just west of State Street on Randolph, openly advertised that it had no music on its premises, but that didn't faze its famous clientele.

## Cabarets and Cafés

Some of the earliest major cabarets in and near the central city were Lamb's Café on the northeast corner of Clark and Randolph and George Silver's across the street. Lamb's Café, an upscale watering hole for Loop business people and politicians, in 1915 received some unexpected and at first unwanted publicity when the manager, Smiley Corbett, hired an early New Orleans jazz band. About the same time, several smaller but popular clubs and cabarets, such as Casino Gardens on North Clark Street and De l'Abbee Café in the Normandie Hotel at Van Buren and Wabash, also brought in small New Orleans bands to capitalize on the sudden interest in this strange-sounding but appealing new music.

While these venues are beyond the scope of this study, the music is notable for its influence on many of the dance band musicians and leaders. The spirit and excitement of the new jazz music gradually was absorbed into the dance music played by many of the city's dance bands, and a number of the early jazz musicians later found steady work in commercial Chicago musical groups. Ironically, more information seems to be available in the latter-day literature about early jazz bands and the Chicago clubs where they played before 1920 than about the dance bands and cabaret orchestras.

South of the Loop were Colosimo's, on South Wabash just north of Twenty-second Street near the old Levee red-light district; Freiberg's Hall, on Twenty-second Street just east of State Street; and Schiller's, on Thirty-first Street east of State. Colosimo's was owned by James "Big Jim" Colosimo, a larger-than-life operator of brothels and other enterprises associated with vice, who was just entering the bootleg liquor business at the time of his murder in 1920 at the age of forty-nine. City judges, aldermen, and a variety of politicians acted as pallbearers at Colosimo's funeral, giving some indication of Colosimo's political influence.

Colosimo's was a colorful place. There had been a number of restaurants at the site for over eighty years but they attracted little attention until Big Jim bought the building in 1914 and remodeled it into a cabaret with his ill-gotten gains.[16] It became a showplace and celebrity hangout in the 1910s, known for its entertainment and excellent Italian spaghetti sauce, and it continued operating until 1945.[17]

The infamous prostitution area south of the Loop called the Levee—an area roughly bounded by Nineteenth Street on the north, Twenty-second Street on the south, State Street on the east, and Clark Street on the west—was closed down in 1912. But the neighborhood remained ridden with illicit activity. Big Jim Colosimo's glitzy café just to the east of the old Levee was a little island of class, at least on the surface, in an otherwise rough neighborhood of the First Ward. Celebrities, opera stars, and politicians along with a variety of gangsters and wealthy socialites were said to have patronized the restaurant-cabaret for the food but also for the small, good floor shows and bands.[18] Colosimo's was shut down briefly in 1926 during a federal government crackdown but otherwise seemed immune to Prohibition enforcement activities.[19]

The Arsonia Café on West Madison Street near Paulina was one of those small taverns that became a cabaret, but in the transformation it soon was a colorful and successful drinking oasis that, like Colosimo's, attracted show business performers and the sporting crowd. It was just sleazy enough to appeal to the occasional wealthy Chicagoan out slumming.[20] Although the owner, Mike Fritzel, was early to spot the New Orleans jazz craze and capitalize on it by hiring a black Crescent City jazz band, his café wasn't a major Chicago dance venue by any stretch of the imagination.

Fritzel and his brother "Dutch" were from western Nebraska.[21] They opened Arsonia Café in 1903. Calling the place a café perhaps was stretching things a bit. Along with booze and chop suey, small shows of five or six entertainers were presented on a canvas awning thrown over the carpeting. At first a piano player accompanied by a xylophonist and drummer provided the musical support for the acts.[22] Later Fritzel brought in Pinky Aarseth, who led a six-piece band there for many years thereafter.[23] Federal agents padlocked the Arsonia in 1928 for a Prohibition violation, but Fritzel was only beginning his fifty-year career as one of Chicago's premier nightclub entrepreneurs. The best was yet to come.

East of Fritzel's and north of the Chicago River was the Erie Café, located at the corner of Clark and Erie Streets. It opened in the teens and continued to operate until the 1940s. Known for its good food, the café in its early days featured entertainment and small musical groups that often had a distinct jazz edge. The talented pianist Elmer Schoebel was one of the leaders there around 1920 with a group that later formed the core of the New Orleans Rhythm Kings at the Friar's Inn across town.[24] In later years, however, the Erie Café became known more as a restaurant than a dine-and-dance venue.

Another early cabaret was the Winter Garden Café, opened in 1916 on premises formerly occupied by the old Vienna Café in the Consumers Building, 214 South State Street. S. Roth, the new owner, remodeled the interior, added a custom-built dance floor, and installed a floor show with eight principals and a chorus line of four. Sig Salleme led the orchestra that backed the show and accompanied dancing from 7 P.M. until 1 A.M.[25] "Winter Garden" wasn't a unique name and it was claimed by at least two other clubs in the 1920s.

One of the rowdiest of the early Chicago cabarets was Freiberg's Hall, at 18 East Twenty-second Street on the southern fringes of the infamous Levee, between State and Wabash. It was a wide-open cabaret that later, as the Midnight Frolics, roared into the 1920s. Ike Bloom, whose real name was Isaac Gittelson, opened the place as Freiberg's Hall in the late 1880s and it quickly earned a seamy reputation. B-girls and female "dance instructors" lined the bar of the club, ready to solicit drinks and snuggle up on the dance floor with the predominantly single male patrons.

Bloom had considerable political clout in the early years of the century as a confidant to First Ward co-aldermen Michael Kenna and John Coughlin. The hall was closed down by Mayor Carter Harrison in August 1914, but it reopened again in December of the following year, courtesy of the new mayor, William "Big Bill" Thompson.[26] More about Freiberg's Hall and the Midnight Frolics follows in the next chapter.

Farther south, Al Tierney, a longtime Chicago entertainment entrepreneur and a politically well connected man, operated the Grand Auto Inn at 338 East Thirty-fifth Street, just west of what was then called Grand Boulevard. Over the years it was only one of Tierney's many establishments. Grand Boulevard was renamed South Parkway and, later, Dr. Martin Luther King Jr. Drive. Tierney's name for the inn reflected the growing use of automobiles during the 1910s, which allowed people more mobility.

The clientele was white although the inn was located in a neighborhood in transition from a predominantly white population to a black one. The Auto Inn operated sporadically during the 1910s and early 1920s, becoming the Plantation Café in 1924. Music was an integral part of the proceedings at Tierney's establishment, and in about 1915 or 1916 the Chicago bandleader and booker Bert Kelly installed Clint Brush's small band at the inn.[27] The Plantation Café, under new management, became a "black and tan"; that is, it catered to a mixed audience of blacks and whites.

When Prohibition began on January 1, 1920, it further complicated the already dicey business of running cabarets and restaurants that formerly served alcoholic beverages. Enforcement of the new laws evolved into a series of ever-changing and confusing government and police strategies resulting in raids, arrests, legal actions, and outright closures of some establishments. Prohibition, however, did not decrease the number of cabarets and restaurants operating in the city. On the contrary, the number of new establishments actually increased, and many of the places were larger and more elaborate than the older venues.[28]

To keep business coming through their doors even though they could no longer sell liquor, the cabaret and restaurant entrepreneurs simply presented more elaborate floor shows.[29] Some of the shows featured top-name acts from the vaudeville stage. Most of Chicago's large cabarets and restaurants by then had first-class dance bands that also accompanied the performers in the floor shows, which by now had become a standard offering in these establishments. As the role of the dance bands expanded, these ensembles were acknowledged for the first time in the trade-press cabaret reviews. The bandleaders Paul Biese, Charlie Straight, Ralph Williams, and Isham Jones were among the earliest to gain some recognition in this period.[30]

As more large cabarets and restaurants came on line during this period, more dance bands were required. But there was one location in Chicago where all the bands wanted to appear: the Blackhawk Restaurant. By 1930 it had become the most prestigious dance band address in the United States. The Blackhawk Restaurant was located at 139 North Wabash Avenue on the eastern perimeter of the Loop. It became a shrine of sorts—a Mount Olympus—to bandleaders all over the United States because playing there could catapult a band to fame with the help of the WGN broadcast line. Several thousand remote broadcasts emanating from the bandstand of this fine-dining establishment during those years also made it one of the best known restaurants in the nation.

As exciting a venue as it became in later years, it all began very quietly when Otto Roth opened the new eatery in December 1920, almost a year after Prohibition began.[31] The restaurant was named for the famous Illinois Eighty-sixth Blackhawk division of the U.S. Army, which had established an enviable record during World War I. Paul Biese's orchestra played for afternoon tea and Frank Westphal's band for evening dancing at the Blackhawk, but only during the first few weeks. Both were Benson bands and quite popular in Chicago at the time. Other Benson orchestras—Charlie Straight's and Ralph Williams's to name two—also played there between 1921 and 1926 for special occasions, but dance music definitely was not a regular feature. Ralph Ginsburg's string ensemble, in fact, more appropriately set the tone for the dining establishment by providing semiclassical music for luncheon and dinner guests.

When Otto Roth agreed to hire the Coon-Sanders Kansas City Nighthawks through MCA for the 1926–27 season, it was a serious change in strategy for the restaurant, resulting in a significantly bigger overhead. Roth redecorated and built a bandstand on the long north wall of the restaurant, which was a narrow room running east and west. Radio broadcast engineers hung drapes over the mirrors on the wall behind the band to deaden the room noise for the nightly broadcasts over WBBM, later WGN.

As previously mentioned, MCA assigned Charlie Straight to play for two weeks in September until the Nighthawks returned to Chicago from their summer road tour.[32] Once the Coon-Sanders crew arrived, the Blackhawk would never be quite the same again. The band played hot arrangements that could be called jazz-inspired but not jazz, and the co-leaders' vocal duets were among the highlights of the band's performance. The Nighthawks hit the road again in the spring of 1927 and local bands appeared at the Blackhawk during the slow months. George Konchar's orchestra was one such summer substitute, and for years a small combo called the Four Horsemen provided the music during Chicago's hot months.

The Nighthawks didn't return the following fall but stayed on the road until December. Roth hired Ben Pollack's California band to open the season in late September. Pollack had an outstanding group of young musicians, including two future leaders, Benny Goodman and Glenn Miller, and had been working in the Chicago area. The Pollack band drew a lot of local and visiting musicians to the Blackhawk but Roth noticed a big drop in revenues. The Californian's Blackhawk engagement, while musically successful, was not very rewarding at the cash register.

Coon-Sanders and company did return to the Blackhawk in January 1928 and it must have seemed to Otto Roth like every night was New Year's Eve. The restaurant did land-office business, which was interrupted only briefly in February 1928 when federal agents raided the Blackhawk and eleven other establishments around Chicago. No liquor was found and the restaurant re-opened a few days later, but the place was momentarily caught in the web of prohibition enforcement.[33]

The band left the Blackhawk in the spring of 1931, eventually heading for New York once they had fulfilled their now-routine road tours in October. Awaiting them in New York was a season-long engagement at the Hotel New Yorker and a regular network radio show. In their absence that summer Roth redecorated the restaurant, adding a new silver-foil ceiling in the main dining room in an attempt to spark things up and help people forget about Coon and Sanders. Roth couldn't have known it at the time but the Coon-Sanders Nighthawks never would play at the Blackhawk again.

The following year—1932—a young but seasoned band led by Hal Kemp was booked into the Blackhawk. MCA had signed the band earlier in the year and the group had already played an engagement at the Trianon Ballroom on the South Side.[34] Kemp and his band, originally from the University of North Carolina, had appeared at New York's Hotel Manger, made several long road tours, and had been to Europe and back by the time they arrived at the Blackhawk. Although Kemp's ensemble was a good solid band, it hadn't created much excitement anywhere. But that soon changed when it arrived at the Blackhawk.

In the next two years the Kemp band played three separate engagements at the Wabash Avenue restaurant. Its final engagement was during the summer of 1934, which was the second and most successful season for the Century of Progress world's fair and an exciting time to be in Chicago. Prior to the band's introduction to the Blackhawk, it had just settled on a unique and subtle new style orchestrated by the pianist-arranger John Scott Trotter. With an emphasis on muted trumpets and low-register clarinets, the pleasing new sound fit well into the art-deco world of the early 1930s and was ideal for radio broadcasts.

The nattily dressed Kemp band was as exciting to watch as it was to hear. Late in the evening the musicians would line up at the front of the bandstand and, with the lights low, play from memory tunes like "Stardust" as they swayed from side to side. This might not sound particularly creative today, in an era of sophisticated, visually oriented audiences conditioned by years of television viewing, but in 1933 it was an impressive sight and helped create a romantic mood in the room.

During the first year of the Century of Progress, WGN and the Blackhawk had broadcast a one-hour show at midnight every Monday called *Midnight Flyers*. WGN's Pierre Andre, the program's host, was called the pilot, and between the band's numbers he presented news of the fair and various attractions around town. Celebrities often stopped by to visit with Kemp, Andre, and whatever band was playing.[35] The show was a big attraction on the early-morning airwaves for Midwest listeners and for many fair-goers who crowded the restaurant.

The second year of the fair, the Kemp band's Monday night show was called *Celebrity Night*, and performers, actors, musicians—even whole bands—would stop by the Blackhawk to say hello and entertain. The idea of *Celebrity Night* was copied from Ben Bernie's popular show broadcast from the Sherman Hotel. Due to Kemp's big radio buildup (there were up to three regular fifteen-minute broadcasts a night) from the Blackhawk, the band's haunting theme song, "When the Summer Is Gone," became an airwaves favorite. The group went on to great success at the Pennsylvania Hotel in New York and elsewhere.

Ever mindful of the restaurant's image, Roth remodeled again in the mid-1930s, removing several pillars in front of the bandstand to improve sight lines. He also installed a new soundproofed canopy over the bandstand, supported from above and trimmed with shiny brass tubing, behind which was indirect lighting. These changes improved the visual presentation of both the bands and the acts that participated in the small floor shows staged each night.

Kay Kyser and his dance band, another young and struggling road band, followed Kemp. Like Kemp, Kyser was originally from the University of North Carolina. The band was seeking a unique voice to distinguish it from the large numbers of other bands. Some 1928 Victor recordings made by the Kyser group demonstrate their "vanilla" style, which was devoid of any special sound or identity. But with the help of MCA, Kyser and his arranger settled on a new sweet style prior to opening at the Blackhawk in the fall of 1934.

The band immediately attracted the attention of customers and listeners. Its new style was reminiscent of Guy Lombardo's approach but in addition featured bubbling muted trumpets and a pair of trombones playing fills that slid around between the saxophones. The ever-present trombone obbligato also was a key part of the Kyser style, especially on his theme song, Walter Donaldson's "Thinking of You." Funny-hat novelties and song titles sung by a male vocalist completed the formula, keeping audiences musically and visually entertained.

The band's biggest boost, however, came from the Monday midnight radio broadcast that Kay inherited from the Kemp band. Celebrity nights continued on Monday nights for a while until the unions ended gratis appearances by musicians and performers. Without musical guests, the Monday night broadcast needed a tuneup, a new approach to attract listeners.

The band began staging a primitive version of a musical quiz show, calling audience members to the microphone and asking them to identify short phrases of a song played by the band. MCA quickly took control when it saw the possibilities for a new radio show. By 1935 the agency was providing complete shows not only to individual stations in large markets but, more important, to the networks: bands, singers, comedians, writers, producer, everything.[36]

Don Roth thinks it was MCA's Lew Wasserman who came up with the name for the show, an opinion confirmed by Dennis McDougal in his book *The Last Mogul.*[37] A more polished version of the Kyser idea was developed further with the help of Wasserman, the WGN writer-producer Fran Coughlin, and others.[38] The result was *Kay Kyser's Kollege of Musical Knowledge,* which debuted on WGN. The show hit the jackpot, and both listenership and attendance at the Blackhawk skyrocketed. A delighted Otto Roth raised the minimum charge per person from $1.00 to $2.50, a pretty steep price for that time.[39]

Due to the fan mail it drew, the weekly broadcast quickly moved from its Monday-night time slot on WGN to the full Mutual Network in 1937, to Tuesday evenings on CBS, and ultimately to NBC, sponsored all along by the American Tobacco Company. All of this quite obviously was engineered by

MCA.[40] The *Kollege of Musical Knowledge* was the first popular musical quiz show but MCA quickly developed the *Beat the Band* show, featuring the Ted Weems orchestra originating in Chicago's NBC studios in the Merchandise Mart. The Kyser band's success was assured from that point forward and the group appeared on stages throughout the country and in movies. The show continued on radio into the 1940s and eventually went on television, but it never was as successful as it had been on radio.

The last of the dance bands to receive the "Blackhawk treatment" and be lofted into the rarefied heights of musical fame in the late 1930s was the Bob Crosby orchestra. Bing Crosby's younger brother and a singer with Anson Weeks and others, Bob Crosby was the leader and frontman of a group of bandsmen who had played for Ben Pollack.[41] After some success in New York, where it had a network radio show, the band came into the Blackhawk for the first time in March 1938. Playing a unique brand of big-band Dixieland, the Crosby band was one of the first hot or swing bands ever to come into the Wabash Avenue eatery. The Crosby band's nightly broadcasts via WGN and the Mutual Network worked that old "Blackhawk magic" and, aided by its growing number of Decca recordings, the band's reputation was made.

Jan Garber, the trombonist Jack Teagarden, and the xylophonist Red Norvo and his wife, the vocalist Mildred Bailey—the latter two then known as "Mr. and Mrs. Swing"—all led bands at the Blackhawk in the thirties, but none caught the public's attention like Coon-Sanders, Kemp, Kyser, and Crosby before them. Don Roth said that Teagarden, who won a coin toss with Glenn Miller for the Blackhawk slot, didn't draw well at all.[42] The band was too loud. Due to the configuration of the long, narrow room, with the bandstand on one of the long walls, the sound from the band bounced off the opposite wall and overpowered the restaurant patrons.

By contrast, Johnny "Scat" Davis followed Teagarden and, according to Roth, drew far bigger crowds. Many other bands appeared at the Blackhawk over the years, but none ever elicited that warm, fuzzy feeling from Roth and the Blackhawk patrons like Coon-Sanders, Kemp, Kyser, and Crosby had.

Ironically, Joe Sanders, "the Old Lefthander," and his band played many return engagements at the Blackhawk during the late 1930s and early 1940s.[43] Since Carlton Coon's untimely death in 1932, Sanders had continued to tour with a band. Although he still drew large crowds of fans of the old Nighthawk band, the enchantment of the days with his partner Coonie were gone. Don Roth said that Sanders tried to hire Johnny Coon, Carlton Coon's son and also a drummer, to work with the band to give it the old Coon-Sanders name, but things never worked out. Johnny, however, later took a band out on the road under MCA's management and eventually became a television personality and producer in Chicago.

The bands played long hours at the Blackhawk, from 6 P.M. until 1 A.M., later on weekends, seven days a week. Between the dinner show and the supper show the band had about an hour off. In addition, there was Sunday tea dancing from 4 P.M. to 6 P.M. in the 1930s, which later became a family matinee from 3 P.M. to 6 P.M. These Sunday afternoon sessions attracted a lot of families, so the younger generation also was exposed to the music and excitement of the floor show.

After World War II, the restaurant went back to its successful policy of booking sweet bands. The Blackhawk also staged small revues featuring young, up-and-coming names like Barbara Cook, Joey Bishop, Pat Carroll, and others, but by 1952 customer enthusiasm for dancing and dance bands was flagging as entertainment habits changed. A 20 percent entertainment tax imposed during the war was still in force, adding to the already growing cost for a night out on the town. Following the final night of the Henry Brandon band's engagement in October of that year, the bandstand was disassembled over one weekend. Food became the whole show beginning the following Monday and until the Blackhawk closed.[44]

In 1989, Don Roth reviewed some the bands that had played the Black-hawk.[45] He recalled that the Coon-Sanders band was very popular and probably the most exciting, spending five years at the Wabash Avenue restaurant and establishing both the band and the restaurant as national attractions. The next most popular band was Hal Kemp's. Roth said Kemp was the most popular band with the 1930s dancers. Roth's appraisal of the Bob Crosby band was that it was loud and played an exciting style of orchestral Dixieland jazz, but it didn't draw that well at the door—certainly not like Hal Kemp. The Crosby band, however, got a lot of publicity out of the engagement, and its broadcasts attracted a lot of customers. Teagarden, according to Roth, did poorly at the door, where it counted. MCA had put a lot of money into the Teagarden opening at the restaurant, according to Roth, but it didn't show up in the gate receipts.

The venerable old Blackhawk Restaurant closed its doors in August 1984 after sixty-three years in business, and Don Roth sold the building to a large Chicago financial institution.[46] The building was demolished in 2003 to make way for another structure. The Loop had lost its cachet as the center of entertainment, and many of Chicago's fine hotels and stores relocated to North Michigan Avenue. Times clearly changed and Roth changed with them, concentrating on his restaurant in northwest suburban Wheeling, where it remains in operation.

The Friar's Inn, 343 South Wabash Avenue, at the corner of Van Buren, was an archetypal roaring-twenties cabaret. It opened its doors in 1921, just after Prohibition began. Mike Fritzel, proprietor of the Friar's Inn, had a lot of experience in running establishments offering booze, entertainment, and shows. His famous—some say infamous—Arsonia Café at 1654 West Madison Street had been a place where socialites from the Gold Coast often went to rub elbows with an assortment of characters, including gamblers, show folk, and neighborhood people.[47]

By 1921 when he opened the bigger, flashier Friar's Inn in a basement space at the northeast corner of Van Buren and Wabash, Fritzel knew exactly what he wanted in a cabaret, but it would have to be without booze. The place had been operated first as the Boulevard Café in the early teens. In 1916 George Silver had made it into a fine-dining restaurant called Silver's and later changed the name to Friar's Inn. Fritzel bought the café from Silver, who was in financial trouble, and remodeled it to his specifications.[48]

For his opening entertainment lineup, Fritzel brought along from the Arsonia the Pinky Aarseth band to play for the floor show and to provide intermission dance music. High-quality food for his patrons was also top on his agenda, continuing a policy started by George Silver. Interestingly, good food was a tradition Fritzel would maintain with his successor venues, the Chez Paree and Fritzel's.

The Friar's Inn was open almost twenty-four hours a day with one band playing the evening shift till midnight and another taking the stand until the early hours of the morning. A number of dance bands followed the Aarseth combo in the following several years, three of them with connections to New Orleans. In keeping with Fritzel's inclination to hire hot bands, as he had at Arsonia, he brought in a band that had been playing locally; about half of the musicians were from New Orleans and half were from Chicago or the Midwest.[49] Eventually called the New Orleans Rhythm Kings, it was a group of rather independent-minded youngsters who enjoyed playing hot New Orleans–style music over the more mundane tunes that Fritzel now preferred for his dancers. They became rather famous locally because of a number of recordings they made for the Gennett label in Richmond, Indiana, and drew good crowds, including a number of Chicago dance-band leaders and musicians who were fascinated with the new sounds.

Merritt Brunies's more conventional dance band followed the New Orleans Rhythm Kings and played at the Friar's for a number of seasons.[50] Brunies was the older brother of the Rhythm Kings trombonist George Brunies. Wingy Manone, another New Orleans native but then living in Chicago, put together a band for a brief engagement at the Friar's Inn following Merritt Brunies.

The Chicago drummer Bill Paley succeeded Manone with a band made up of musicians from the Charlie Straight and Art Kassel bands.[51]

The federal authorities shut down Fritzel's club in 1927 for violating the Volstead Act and it never reopened. But in short order Fritzel opened or took over operations of a series of other establishments, including the Ansonia [*sic*] on East Chicago Avenue and the Tent at State and Bellevue, both on the Near North Side. He also was said to be a manager or partner in the nearby Club Royale and in the Midnight Frolics on Twenty-second Street, on the Near South Side, seemingly keeping one step ahead of the federal agents. The Midnight Frolics was closed down the following year.[52] However, Fritzel's biggest and best-known club was to follow just before the repeal of prohibition in 1932.[53]

# 9 The Bands Earn Respect

THE bandleader and booker Bert Kelly established one of the most interesting Chicago cabarets to debut during Prohibition. In many ways Kelly's Stables was an archetype of a 1920s dine-and-dance club, complete with a small jazz band, a floor show, and plenty of room for dancing. It was north of the Chicago River, on the northeast corner of Rush and Hubbard, just across the street from what today is the giant Wrigley Building. During the 1920s that part of town was known as Tower Town, an area with a lot of artists and named after the Chicago Water Tower, a prominent landmark to the north. Kelly's Stables lasted just about as long as Prohibition. Federal agents shut it down in 1930, three years shy of Repeal.

Kelly's Stables attracted not only neighborhood artists but an affluent crowd from the nearby Gold Coast along Lake Michigan.[1] It literally was located in a three-story former stable and could accommodate more than seven hundred people. The first floor contained the main dining room and a dance floor where the small floor shows were presented. There were other dance floors and dining facilities on the two floors above.[2] Kelly had a preference for jazz music and was often credited with leading one of the first jazz bands in Chicago (at the College Inn). As a result of his partiality, a parade of former New Orleans jazzmen led the small groups that played there, including Alcide "Yellow" Nunez, the powerful cornet player Freddie Keppard, and the Dodds Brothers. Johnny Dodds on clarinet and Baby Dodds on drums continued playing at Kelly's until the place closed in 1930.[3] Ric Riccardo, an artist, moved into the building in the 1930s and established a restaurant that became a popular gathering place for artists and journalists. Phil Stefani's Restaurant now occupies the building.

Over in the south Loop area, nestled under the El tracks at 416 South Wabash, the Moulin Rouge Café was a pre-1920 cabaret that continued to roar through the twenties. Dining, dancing, and large, elaborately staged cabaret shows were the attractions at the Moulin Rouge. It opened in the late 1910s and hired only black dance bands until the late 1920s. The Moulin Rouge was one of six dance venues in the white areas of Chicago to employ black bands. This speaks to the influence the Moulin Rouge management and a few other entrepreneurs had with the white Chicago musicians union. Other venues that hired black bands in the white Local 10 jurisdiction were the Dreamland Ballroom on the West Side and the Arcadia Ballroom, the Riverview, and Municipal Pier ballroom on the North Side, all managed by Patrick "Paddy" Harmon; the west suburban Cotton Club, run by Ralph Capone; and the Green Mill Gardens on the North Side.[4]

Clarence M. Jones's orchestra was one of the earliest musical groups to play at the Moulin Rouge, broadcasting via KYW.[5] Following the Jones group in 1923 and remaining for the next three years were the trumpeter Jimmy Wade and his orchestra.[6] The violinist Eddie South, later to be called the "Dark Angel of the Violin" by Paul Whiteman, was the standup leader of Wade's orchestra, which by 1926 had expanded to eleven pieces. The band alternated between the Moulin Rouge in the winter and Albert "Papa" Bouché's "House That Jack Built" in the summer.[7] Bouché's club was later known as the Villa Venice and located on Milwaukee Avenue in unincorporated Cook County. Bouché also managed the Moulin Rouge in the early 1920s and produced the shows there.

By 1925, Ernie Young, the prominent Chicago showman and vaudeville booker, began producing the shows at the Wabash Avenue café.[8] The large shows were presented in three segments each evening with one-hour intermissions for dancing. When Wade left for New York in 1926, Eddie Richmond's white band moved into the Moulin Rouge. Richmond, a trumpet player, had been with the Five Kings of Syncopation, the little jazz band that backed Sophie Tucker on stage from 1919 to 1921. Frankie Masterman, a banjo player later to be known as the bandleader Frankie Masters, was a member of Richmond's nine-piece combination at the Moulin Rouge. The show room, by then owned by William R. (Izzy) Rothstein, was closed in 1927 for Prohibition violations during the federal government's crackdown on illegal booze.

The Moulin Rouge reopened a year later under the management of Mike Fritzel, who had recently lost his nearby Friar's Inn to a Prohibition violation closure. Although the Moulin Rouge name was changed to Club Royale, it was shut down again in 1929 for the same reason. In 1930 the club was reopened under a third name, Royal Frolics, by Dennis "The Duke" Cooney.

Cooney was said to have been Al Capone's lieutenant in charge of prostitution and, earlier in the century, closely associated with the First Ward coalderman and committeeman Michael Kenna.[9] Cooney was a good manager who at one time had owned and operated the Rex Hotel and Café at 2138 South State, in the heart of the Levee, an establishment that allegedly also served as a bordello.[10] He also was a political powerbroker in the First Ward and knew his way around town.

Cooney hired only white bands for his floor shows, and the Chicago leader Henri Lishon's nine-piece orchestra, a fine show band, got the nod. Lishon previously had been at the Midnight Frolics until a fire destroyed the club. He remained at the Royale Frolics off and on until 1938, backing the elaborate shows.[11] The bands of Mark Fisher and Al Turk followed Lishon's orchestra at the Royal Frolics in the late 1930s. Cooney closed down the place in the summer of 1939, reopened it briefly, and then closed it again for good in November.[12] It later became Jimmy Wong's popular Chinese restaurant. Ironically, the place had begun in the mid-1910s as a Chinese restaurant, the Mandarin Inn. Wong's closed in 1997.[13]

North of the Chicago River was the Chez Pierre, reportedly one of the four most profitable clubs in Chicago during the 1920s.[14] It ranks as one of the shortest-lived 1920s cabarets in Chicago, surviving about four years. It opened in 1924 on the third floor of a warehouse building at the southwest corner of Fairbanks Court and Ontario Street, not a booming area of nightlife. The building actually fronted on Fairbanks Court but the entrance was around the corner at 247 East Ontario. John Raklios and his partner, the impresario Pierre Nuyttens, operated the restaurant. The cuisine was French, the entertainment high class, and the patrons upscale, and in spite of its location the place drew big crowds.

The violinist Earl Hoffman, originally from Peoria, led a fine eight-piece string orchestra at the Chez Pierre during its four years of its existence, playing for dancing and accompanying the colorful revues staged by Nuyttens.[15] The club was one of the twelve cafés and restaurants raided by federal agents in February 1928 and, after a hearing, was shut down for one year and a day.[16] It never reopened under that management.

Al Tierney, the veteran Chicago cabaret owner and operator, had had good luck with his several venues over the years until he opened the Town Club south of the Loop. Tierney had a reputation for serving good food and producing lively and colorful floor shows. In 1925, he leased the second-floor ballroom of the new Pershing Hotel, at Sixty-fourth Street and Cottage Grove Avenue, to create the Pershing Palace. It probably was the largest cabaret on the South Side and had expansive floor shows produced by Ernie Young featuring ten principal performers and a chorus line of up to twenty dancers.

Tierney ran the Town Club on South Wabash about the same time but it was on a somewhat smaller scale than the Pershing Palace, having a chorus line of only six dancers. The show, created by the South Side producer Percy Venable, was composed of six acts, the chorus, and the band led by Emerson Brown.[17] Like so many other Prohibition-era clubs in Chicago, the Town Club was raided from time to time for various liquor violations and never survived the decade.

Over the years, Tierney had some good bands in his clubs, beginning with a Bert Kelly group at the old Auto Inn on Thirty-fifth Street, mentioned earlier. Tierney hired black South Side bands at the Pershing Palace (later called Club Bagdad) where Dave Peyton's contract orchestra led by the saxophonist Ralph Brown provided music for Ernie Young's shows.[18]

In the previous chapter, the discussion about Freiberg's Hall ended at 1915 when Ike Bloom remodeled the place and changed its name to the Midnight Frolics cabaret. It was a throbbing, all-night venue with a floor show, a chorus line of sixteen young women, a band, a dance floor, and a Chinese menu. Ralph Gillette and Jack Adler managed the cabaret, which was located at 18 East Twenty-second Street, just around the corner from Colosimo's.[19] With its new, dressed-up facade it now catered to an exclusively white clientele of out-of-town businessmen, show business people, socialites, the sporting crowd, and hoodlums. Al Capone, headquartered at the nearby Metropole Hotel in the late 1920s, was a frequent visitor and owned a 25 percent interest in the club, said to be among his favorites.[20]

Dance bands played an increasingly important role in the proceedings at the Midnight Frolics and over the years the cabaret employed some of the city's top name bands. In 1921 and early 1922, Jules Buffano directed the band at the club. Buffano, a pianist originally from St. Louis, came into the Midnight Frolics after the breakup in 1921 of the Five Kings of Syncopation, of which he, like Eddie Richmond, was a member. Austin Mack's orchestra followed Buffano to play for dancing and to accompany the floor shows produced by his brother, Roy.

Shows at the Frolics typically had five to eight acts consisting of a dance team or singles doing interpretive or acrobatic dances, singers, a comedian, and a master of ceremonies who also did comedy and songs.[21] Topping that off was a line of elaborately costumed chorines. One or two singers in the show would move among the tables during intermissions reprising some of the numbers from the floor show for tips. With such a big lineup, the show was usually done in four segments spread out over the evening with an intermission during which patrons could dance.[22]

Joe E. Lewis made his debut as master of ceremonies at the club in 1925, starting a career that would eventually make him one of the highest paid nightclub acts by the 1950s. In 1926 Charlie Straight's MCA band, just recently at the Blackhawk for a few weeks following a long stay at Kansas City's Muehlbach Hotel, moved into the Frolics to replace that of Austin Mack. The gala opening attracted a parade of big-name performers led by Sophie Tucker. Paul Ash, the Oriental Theater stage-band leader and probably the most popular bandleader in Chicago, came out for the opening at the Frolics between his theater performances especially to introduce Straight and his nine musicians to the audience. His presence at the Frolics in that capacity was an endorsement of Straight's growing celebrity.

The Midnight Frolics was shut down in February 1928, one of twelve Chicago night spots raided by federal agents looking for Volstead Act violations.[23] No liquor was found and it reopened in the spring of 1928 with Charlie Straight again providing the show and dance music. The colorful Ralph Williams and his eleven-piece Rainbo Garden show band, Charlie Kaley, and Charlie Agnew—all MCA attractions—appeared at the club over the next few years. In 1931 club management booked Henri Lishon's popular show band.[24] Lishon's engagement ended suddenly in 1934 when a fire swept through the club, taking with it the band's music library and all the instruments.

Ike Bloom did not limit his gift for managing successful nightclubs to the Frolics. By 1925 he also had opened the Deauville, a posh, north Loop cabaret at the corner of Dearborn and Randolph.[25] Ernie Young presented the floor shows, and Irving Rothchild's orchestra provided accompaniment and played for dancing.

There were a number of very nice cabarets on the city's South Side in the late 1920s; one of the most luxurious was the Grand Terrace on South Parkway near Oakwood Boulevard. When Edward Fox decided to open his new, state-of-the-art club on the city's segregated South Side, he intended it to appeal to a more affluent white audience. A former manager of two black-and-tan cabarets, the Sunset and the Plantation, Fox knew exactly what he wanted in the new Grand Terrace. He selected as the site the then-vacant Peerless Theater, remodeled it, and elegantly appointed the venue with carpeted floors, mirrored walls, colored lighting, and a combination dance floor and stage that could be elevated for the show.[26] The Grand Terrace opened in December 1928 with Earl "Fatha" Hines and his orchestra on the bandstand, a chorus line of ten, and four to five acts in the show.

Percy Venable, Fox's producer at the nearby Plantation and Sunset cafés, presented the first shows at the Grand Terrace. Business at the Grand Terrace was slow at first but the crowds really flocked to the club beginning in 1932, the year Hines began broadcasting, first on local station WEDC, and later on WENR, KYW, and via the NBC-Red network.[27] The World's Fair of 1933–34 also brought a lot of people into the club anxious to hear and see in person Earl "Fatha" Hines, the man and the band they had heard on the nightly NBC broadcasts.

Noting how popular Hines was becoming through his broadcasts and annual summer one-nighter tours, Fox signed him to what amounted to a "lifetime" contract. The trouble was, Hines wasn't being paid very much for his work at the club and Fox was pocketing most of the profits from the road tours. Fox hired other bands to replace the Hines band when it was traveling but those groups either lacked Hines's showmanship or had difficulty playing for the tough floor show. Erskine Tate, a theater-band leader, Carroll Dickerson, Fletcher Henderson, and Bill "Count" Basie headed just a few of them.[28] The one exception was Louis Armstrong's band, which played for a month at the Grand Terrace in the spring of 1938, about six months after the Grand Terrace moved from its South Parkway location to the old Sunset building at Thirty-fifth Street and Calumet.[29] The Fletcher Henderson and Andy Kirk bands followed.

Hines enlisted James Petrillo's help in breaking the contract with Fox, which essentially made Hines an indentured servant. Hines was a free man by 1939.[30] Walter Fuller, a former Hines sideman, and Lionel Hampton followed Earl's band when Hines left the club in 1940, but the club closed a few years later.

Some cabarets sputtered along for years doing moderate business; others came on the scene suddenly, gleamed brilliantly for a few years, and just as quickly faded away. Al Quodbach's Granada Café, formerly the Gingham Inn, was one of the latter establishments. It was said to be one of the four top moneymakers in Chicago in 1928 (along with Chez Pierre, Rainbo Garden, and the Club Alabam on the Near North Side), which was ironic because the Granada was located five blocks south of the Sixty-third and Cottage Grove entertainment district, at Sixty-eighth Street and across from the famous Oakwood Cemetery.[31] Quodbach was credited with running a very clean (and profitable) operation (no liquor) by providing good entertainment and charging only fifty cents per person to come in the door.[32]

Aiming strictly at a white audience, Quodbach, who was said to have begun as a cab driver, was well enough connected with the powers that be that he never seemed to have operating problems.[33] He was occasionally raided but never shut down during Prohibition for any length of time. Nobody seemed to care about or pay attention to the gambling that was said to go on upstairs.

In 1926 Ernie Caldwell's band backed a small floor show at the Granada featuring Sid Erdman and the six Spree Girls.[34] Seeing what was happening downtown at the Blackhawk gave Quodbach bigger ideas. He contacted Jules Stein and tried but failed to hire the Coon-Sanders Nighthawks. However, as noted in chapter 2, MCA gladly directed Quodbach's attention to a recently discovered but unknown young band from Canada, Guy Lombardo and his Royal Canadians, then doing fairly well around Cleveland and identified by Stein as having excellent potential. Because Chicago union rules forbade MCA or any other agency to import an out-of-town band, Stein suggested Quodbach visit Cleveland to hear Lombardo and company and hire them directly. He did just that with MCA's help and guidance.[35]

The story was told earlier of Lombardo's quick rise to local fame once a WBBM radio wire was installed. Two years later, when MCA decided it was time for the Canadians to cash in on their newfound celebrity and hit the big-time in New York, Quodbach didn't want to let them go. He had a point because the Lombardo band had turned his little café into a gold mine. But more significant than that, the Lombardo band had markedly changed the dancing style in Chicago by slowing it down from the quick step to a slow fox-trot, and it converted a large number of Chicago and Midwest dancers' preferences in dance bands from hot to sweet. As a result, there emerged over the next decade about forty sound-alike sweet bands, from Art Kassel and Sammy Kaye through Kay Kyser and Ray Pearl to Chuck Foster and Blue Barron.

When Lombardo left in June 1929 for his one-nighter tour en route to the Roosevelt Hotel in New York, MCA installed a couple of local bands to play for the summer: Al Katz and His Kittens and Fred Hamm.[36] MCA then brought in some of its best-drawing bands to play for the Quodbach club during the winter season. Ted Weems was booked for the Granada in October 1929 for the 1929–30 season. Ben Pollack, Paul Whiteman, and others followed over the next few years.

Quodbach boasted that his business hadn't been hurt by the economic downturn in 1931 because he had Whiteman on the bandstand.[37] However, the magical crowd-attracting quality of the club departed with the Royal Canadians. When Whiteman left, Quodbach, contrary to his earlier boast, could no longer justify the high cost of bringing in name bands, so he relied on two fine Chicago-based black bands, those of Tiny Parham and Eddie Mallory, which played most of 1932 at the Granada.[38]

In 1934 fire destroyed the Granada Café but it was declared accidental and, with no insurance, Quodbach was said to have taken a $100,000 loss.[39]

Two years later he followed Lombardo to New York, where he reopened the old Delmonico Club on Fifty-first Street as Coffee Dan's.

If the Granada Café was located off the beaten path, the Jeffery Tavern and Beverly Gardens were even more so. Owned and operated by the Ahearn brothers, the Jeffery Tavern was located at Seventy-ninth Street and Jeffery Boulevard and the Beverly Gardens was at Ninety-first Street and Western Avenue. Both clubs served a white clientele but in the mid-1920s hired black dance bands. Robinson's Syncopators, a Detroit band, played a long engagement at the Beverly Gardens. Hughie Swift and his ten-piece musical aggregation also played at both clubs in that period, broadcasting nightly from the Jeffery Tavern in 1925.[40]

Vernon Roulette's orchestra and the pianist Henry Crowder's Washingtonians were also featured at the clubs. Crowder's crew gained some notoriety when it was selected by MCA to be the road version of Jelly Roll Morton's Red Hot Peppers.[41] Jelly's Red Hot Peppers Victor records were selling very well but his recording band of the same name was made up of highly regarded Chicago musicians, all of whom had local jobs and refused to go on the road tour booked by MCA to capitalize on Jelly's popularity.

The Jeffery Tavern was raided in early 1928 by federal authorities for violation of the Volstead Act, part of the crackdown on twelve Chicago nightspots, but it reopened much later. Corey Lynn, a white bandleader, had a band there in early 1933.[42] A year later, during the Century of Progress, it became a taxi dance hall.[43]

Chicago's North Side was alive with cabaret activity in the 1920s. Like the Loop and the South Side, it was home to a wide range of venues for the average working man and woman as well as for the well-to-do crowd. One of the cabarets that appealed to both types of patrons was the Rainbo Garden, at 4812 North Clark Street. It began as a pedestrian roadhouse but by the late 1910s had gradually evolved into an early North Side dance venue.

Fred C. Mann, a veteran Chicago restaurateur, bought the parcel of property in the late 1910s and changed its name to Rainbo Garden, after the famous Rainbow Division of the U.S. Army in World War I, in which Mann's son served. The "w" was deliberately omitted from the name for no explainable reason. In 1922 Mann built one of the largest show rooms in the country on the site, Mann's Million-Dollar Rainbo Room. It was a sight to behold, equipped with the latest theatrical staging equipment including a revolving combined dance floor and show stage that could present acts both in the Rainbo Room and to the outdoor garden behind the building.[44]

The Rainbo Room was part of a new building erected along Clark Street on a portion of the old outdoor gardens, replacing an older structure. It later became another chameleon among Chicago nightspots because it changed its name so many times. Isham Jones and his orchestra had played at the original Rainbo Garden from 1918 through 1920 and recorded for Brunswick as the Rainbo Garden Orchestra. For the opening of the new, dazzling, gold, blue, and ivory Rainbo Room in October 1922, however, Frank Westphal's orchestra was hired to play for dancing and the floor show. Isham Jones was by this time ensconced at the College Inn in the Loop.

The skillfully produced shows were presented in a room that could seat 2,000. In May 1928, 4,000 people crowded into the Rainbo Room to attend the farewell party of Paul Ash, the Oriental Theater's stage-band leader, an event that severely overloaded the staff's serving capabilities.[45] In 1927, Mann had built a jai alai arena adjoining the Rainbo Room building that could seat more than 1,700 people. It replaced a part of the former outdoor garden and later was used for boxing and wrestling matches in the forties.[46]

The orchestras of Ralph Williams, Al Katz, Charlie Straight, Jack Chapman, Waddy Wadsworth, and Sol Wagner also were featured through 1928, whereupon the Rainbo and several other establishments were closed due to liquor violations and hundreds of entertainers and musicians were put out of work.[47] Mann sold the building the following year but remained on the premises as manager. The place was remodeled by its new owners and reopened in November 1929.

In 1934 the Rainbo Room became the French Casino and featured a show with fifty entertainers from the Folies Bergère in Paris. The Chicago leader Carl Hoff's orchestra did yeoman service as it accompanied the complicated show with a large cast and multiple costume changes. The prominent black bandleader and composer Noble Sissle, for years associated with Eubie Blake, led a second band that played for dancing between shows.[48] It was all timed for the Century of Progress. A little over a year later, the French Casino was out of business, unable to support the expensive show and other overhead costs without the world's fair business.

In 1939 the producer-entrepreneur Mike Todd reopened the room as a theater-restaurant called the Million-Dollar Ballroom and featured top acts such as Gypsy Rose Lee. It too closed in less than a year. Following the war, it was reopened again, this time as a ballroom, and featured Tommy Dorsey, Les

Brown, Stan Kenton, and the Chicago bands of Jay Burkhart, Teddy Phillips, and Arnie Barnett.[49] In the fifties the jai alai arena (which by then was also used as an ice rink on occasion) again hosted boxing and wrestling matches televised over the early national TV networks.[50] In recent years the former Rainbo Room became a roller skating rink but now has been demolished.

Several blocks east of Rainbo Garden things were happening with the old Green Mill outdoor garden run by the brothers Tom and Bill Chamales. They built a permanent two-story building on the east side of the garden at Lawrence and Broadway in 1922 to provide year-round entertainment. The new $150,000 L-shaped building had 128 feet of frontage along Broadway Avenue.[51] A medium-sized show room with dance floor occupied a good part of the second floor. Below were commercial stores.

The show room was fairly intimate, unlike the mammoth Rainbo Room, and more in keeping with the cabaret tradition where patrons sat in close proximity to the performers. A new grand entrance for the garden and the second-floor cabaret was included in the new building and a new outdoor stage was constructed on the north end of the garden. Two years later, however, the Chamales brothers sold the adjacent L-shaped garden property to the Balaban and Katz organization, which erected on the land its new Uptown Theater, said to be the largest (4,307 seats) in the United States at the time it was built.[52]

By the time the Uptown Theater was built, the "new" Green Mill building was leased to other operators. "Machine Gun" Jack McGurn, whose real name was Vincent Gebardi, allegedly was a partner in the enterprise.[53] It was a high-priced show room with a stiff ten-dollar cover charge and catered to a clientele that was well heeled and well dressed. Charlie Elgar's orchestra played there in 1922 accompanying the "Plantation Days" production.

Renamed Montmartre in 1924, the place was enlarged, refurnished, and ballyhooed as a New York–style nightclub.[54] Paul Zimm and his Chicagoans moved onto the newly remodeled bandstand that year. Henry Gendron's orchestra followed in 1925 with Dave Peyton's Club Bagdad Orchestra succeeding Gendron's.[55] Martin Paley, the former manager of the Café de Paris on the South Side and then the manager of the Green Mill, more than likely was responsible for bringing Elgar's and Peyton's orchestras to the club.

Texas Guinan, the sassy, peripatetic dancer, mistress of ceremonies, and cabaret operator who greeted patrons with "Hello, Sucker," leased the club in 1930.[56] But it was shut down by police after a shooting in March of that year. Later reopened, it featured a show called "Green Mill Follies of 1930," which was backed by the Vern Buck orchestra and featured the comedian Joe E. Lewis.

A 1927 incident that attracted nationwide headlines indirectly involved the Green Mill when Joe E. Lewis decided to leave the club and move his one-man act to the Rendezvous cabaret on the Near North Side. The move precipitated a vicious knife attack on the comedian shortly thereafter.[57] Lewis miraculously survived the assault and later resumed his successful career.[58] In 1931 Jack Huff, a roadhouse operator, leased the building and named it the Lincoln Tavern Town Club.[59] After Repeal in the mid-1930s the Green Mill continued under various names but mostly was a dance hall. In later years the space has been rented to a number of commercial tenants. The Green Mill Tavern, located on the first floor, is a latter-day reminder of the glory days of the café upstairs and features a wide assortment of jazz music and other entertainment.

The Rendezvous, 626 West Diversey Parkway near the corner of North Clark Street, was another Chicago café that went through a series of name changes, having at least five names over three decades. Located on the second floor of the Rienzi Hotel, it was first known as Rienzi Gardens. About 1923, Henry Horn, the former manager of Chamale's Green Mill, opened the Rendezvous on the site. Shortly thereafter the café was taken over by George Liederman and Sam Rothschild, the former manager of De l'Abbee Café in the Normandie Hotel.[60] The café's shows and dancing attracted a lively crowd.

Al Copeland's band was one of the earliest into the Rendezvous followed by the popular Charlie Straight and his veteran Chicago orchestra, now well known for its Brunswick recordings.[61] Also on the bandstand at various times during the twenties were the bands of Mike Speciale, Louis Panico, and the Seattle Harmony Kings. Ben Pollack brought his band into the club in 1926, playing at the Rendezvous between his Southmoor Hotel and Blackhawk engagements.

The next year Joe E. Lewis moved his act from the Green Mill to the Rendezvous, resulting in the savage attack on him recounted earlier. By this time John Fogarty was managing the place. George Devron and "Mezz" Mezzrow had bands at the Rendezvous that year.[62] In February 1928 the Rendezvous was shut down by federal agents and later padlocked for one year.[63]

The Rendezvous reopened a year later as the Aladdin and then in the late thirties became the Famous Door. It took on the name Paddock Club in the 1940s but it never achieved the popularity or the notoriety of its predecessors in the twenties. The building was torn down in the late 1980s to clear the valuable parcel of land for a high-rise condominium building.

Meanwhile, farther to the north on Broadway at Grace, the old Marigold Garden continued its dual existence. It was an outdoor beer garden and dance venue in the summer and an indoor cabaret with dancing between shows in winter, an arrangement that lasted into the early 1920s.[64] In 1923, however, Karl Eitel gave up trying to keep the doors of his establishment open without liquor, saying, "It can't be done on ginger ale."[65] The garden reopened under new lessees as a twin ballroom (the old garden area was floored over) and operated from 1924 until 1926, at which time the indoor winter garden was subleased. Thus began a checkered period for the venerable old location.[66]

In 1929 the Eitels leased their North Side Marigold property to other interests, and through the 1930s and 1940s the building was used for multiple purposes. Boxing and wrestling matches were staged frequently in the winter garden building, but in 1930 it was reopened again as a dine-and-dance venue and renamed the Vanity Fair. The Phil Levant and Al Kvale bands accompanied the acts there and also played for dancing. For the next twenty years the building was used almost exclusively for boxing and wrestling matches. The Marigold became a well-known location for these matches, which were televised weekly via the Dumont network in the late 1940s.[67]

Scores of new, usually smaller clubs opened all over the North Side in the 1920s along Clark and Broadway Streets, between Diversey Parkway on the south and Foster Street on the north. The Alamo, later the Via Lago, located in the Alamo Hotel building at 837 West Wilson, several blocks east of Broadway, was typical of the smaller but nicely appointed cafés with small floor shows and dance bands. The Alamo was owned by James Davis, who built the Davis Hotel at 163 East Walton Street, just across the street from the Drake Hotel. Both the Davis Hotel and the Alamo were known for their glass dance floors, the only two in Chicago. The one at the former Davis Hotel, now called the Knickerbocker Hotel, survives to this day.

Al Handler was the longtime bandleader at the Alamo in the 1920s and, coincidentally, also played at the Davis Hotel, underscoring the management link of the two venues. The Handler band recorded for Gennett and Columbia in the mid-1920s and Handler was reported to be a human encyclopedia of tunes.[68] A Jean Goldkette band led by Harold Stokes also played at the Alamo in 1928.[69] After the Alamo was shut down that same year during the big twelve-club raid by federal authorities, it reopened for a time but later was padlocked.[70] It reopened in 1931 as the Via Lago, a Chinese restaurant operated by the same management as that of the Uptown Village, and featured dancing to the music of Earl Hoffman, which was broadcast via station WMAQ.[71]

The Uptown Village was located at 4822 North Broadway, next to the Uptown Theater, just north of Lawrence. It also was known as Uptown Gardens. Barney Richards's orchestra played there in the twenties; Richards later was president of the Chicago Musicians Union local. Earl Hoffman's band, formerly of Chez Pierre, also played at the Uptown Village in 1931, broadcasting via WMAQ nightly.[72] Another North Side place was the Winter Garden at 519 West Diversey Parkway, which was Sam Hare's winter headquarters. (In addition to operating the Dells roadhouse in Morton Grove during the summer, he had another club in Florida.)

In the days before air conditioning, only the large theaters and a few dance halls could afford the expensive refrigeration systems that allowed year-around operation. The cabarets and many of the larger restaurants that featured music and entertainment either shut their doors during the hot summer months or reduced their hours of operation. The summertime was a time for city dwellers to be out of doors enjoying the weather. From an entertainment standpoint it became a time for outdoor beer gardens, amusement parks, and summer dance halls that were open to the cooling evening breezes. For those seeking more excitement in their summer evenings, however, there were the roadhouses.

# 10 Dance Bands in the Roadhouses

COOK County roadhouses, those rural taverns and resorts of varying sizes, took on new significance during Prohibition in the United States, 1920–33. You could get a drink of illicit booze much easier at those distant and often rustic roadside watering holes than in Chicago venues, which were under more intense scrutiny of federal officials. Thanks to increased automobile ownership and a growing number of paved roads, roadhouses—there were more than 250 of them in Cook County by 1929—became easily accessible destinations for summertime excursions.[1]

Most of the larger and better-known roadhouses featured live music and some entertainment. In the smaller venues there often was nothing more than a bare floor upon which patrons could dance to phonograph music. As the decade wore on, however, small to medium-sized combos and dance ensembles became more prevalent. A few other roadhouses were more like posh cabarets in the country, complete with large dance bands and elaborate floor shows, and these establishments provided work for a growing number of bands. The quantity and quality of entertainment in the roadhouses increased significantly after aggressive Prohibition enforcement raids in 1928 shut down a number of major in-town Chicago cabarets and restaurants. Many out-of-work performers and musicians suddenly found employment in the country.[2]

The tradition of roadhouses goes back to the early days of stagecoach travel in the United States and probably dates to the era of roadside taverns in England. These wayside stops along primitive early routes offered refreshment for travelers and draft animals alike and often provided overnight accommodations for those on longer trips. But the big attraction of the modern, Chicago-area roadhouses in the 1920s clearly was the availability of bootleg liquor. Law enforcement in the sparsely populated rural areas and small towns nearby in Cook County was minimal at best. There were similar roadhouses located outside other major American cities during Prohibition.

Gambling and prostitution also frequently were available at some road-houses if you knew where to go or whom to ask.[3] Many of the roadhouses became magnets for people under thirty, some of the younger ones seeking their first taste of alcohol and often becoming inebriated in the process.

The larger, more established roadhouses were located in nicely landscaped settings and had rather elaborately decorated and furnished interiors. They were generally well managed and had lighted parking areas and valet parking to discourage petting parties. Because they also had popular dance bands they charged higher prices than the more modest establishments; as a result their clientele tended to be upscale and generally a bit older.

Roadhouses were usually located along main highways leading out of town, and there were two major clusters in Cook County: to the north and south. Two northern communities, Morton Grove and Wheeling, together had a total of twenty-two roadhouses, according to studies made at the time.[4] Like in-town nightspots, many of these exurban establishments featured dancing and small shows and often served good food. Some of the 1920s roadhouse buildings survive to this day as restaurants and taverns.

Several roadhouses in particular are of interest in this study of dance bands and are representative of the higher-class venues: the Lincoln Tavern and the Dells in Morton Grove, the Villa Venice near Glenview, and Le Chateau in Thornton. All were prominent from the very early 1920s through the early 1930s. The Purple Grackle, just east of Elgin, also drew large crowds from the Chicago area. The two best-known of the Chicago area's many 1920s roadhouses were the Lincoln Tavern and the Dells, sometimes called the New Dells; they were practically neighbors at about 6000 West Dempster Road in Morton Grove, near the intersection of present-day Austin Avenue.

Jack Huff operated the Lincoln Tavern, a large white frame building set back about a hundred feet south of Dempster Road. The place was built to accommodate big crowds, and its large, semicircular parking lot could handle a hundred cars. The focal point of the Lincoln Tavern, however, was its two dining rooms; the larger of them measured two hundred feet by seventy-five feet and had a polished dance floor in the middle.[5] Huff hired the Coon-Sanders band from Kansas City to play during the summer of 1924 at the Lincoln Tavern It was the first major out-of-town name band to play at a roadhouse. As an employer, Huff could circumvent the Chicago musicians union rules, which forbade agents from "importing" out-of-town bands. Huff gets an "A" for his initiative in boarding a train to Kansas City to convince the co-leaders of the Nighthawks that Chicago offered them greater opportunity.

Huff furthered the careers of Coon, Sanders, and the band by introducing them to the Congress Hotel's manager, H. L. Kaufman, who offered the band a contract to play at the Congress beginning that fall.[6] The Nighthawks ended up with a very sweet combination of bookings, thanks to Sam Huff: all summer at the Lincoln Tavern and the following season of 1924–25 at the Congress Hotel.

The Nighthawks broadcast over KYW from the Lincoln Tavern bandstand that summer. MCA's Jules Stein visited the band several times and eventually convinced Coon and Sanders to let him plan a tour of one-night engagements that fall before they began their Congress Hotel engagement. In earlier seasons Huff had employed Charlie Straight's very popular local band to play the summer-long engagements in Morton Grove. It had been a nice fit, too, because Straight and the band played during the winter months at the in-town Rendezvous Café at Diversey and Clark Streets.

The Nighthawks did not return to the Lincoln Tavern following their 1924–25 summer season engagement and this was the end of Huff's relationship with the band. It was financially more lucrative for the band (and for MCA) to stay on the one-nighter circuit as long as it could. Joe Kayser tells of the band's earning up to six thousand dollars a night.[7] However, seeing how successful the Nighthawks had been in drawing crowds to the Lincoln Tavern, Huff continued booking local and name bands.

By this time MCA was representing Huff and, in the summer of 1926, moved Jack Crawford's band into the suburban venue.[8] Crawford was called the "Clown Prince of Jazz" and had been a member of the Paul Biese band. Like Biese, he was a plump saxophone player who, as a leader, had a lot of bounce to the ounce. MCA, noting his talent, almost certainly helped Crawford organize his band following Biese's untimely death in 1925.

The Lincoln Tavern was staging big revues by 1929 with chorus lines of up to forty dancers. The California leader and songwriter Earl Burtnett, who was a big name at the Los Angeles Biltmore Hotel, played an engagement or two at Lincoln Tavern in the early thirties before settling in for a long run at the downtown Drake Hotel. Huff did not renew his lease for the Lincoln Tavern in 1934. The comedian Joe E. Lewis, however, picked up the lease with the intention of operating the club for the summer.[9] Lewis brought in Ben Pollack's popular dance band, put together a floor show, and opened for business. But a month later the club was shut down.

William Skidmore and William Johnson assumed control of the Lincoln Tavern at this point and converted it into a huge gambling house. There had been discrete gambling at the Lincoln Tavern under the management of Sam Huff, but in this case it was open and flagrant.[10] Under Skidmore and Johnson the Lincoln Tavern came to offer one-stop shopping for gambling: roulette, blackjack, slot machines, and dice tables were available. If all that strenuous gambling made you hungry, you could have a meal in the restaurant, a part of the former dining room, which now served as a convenient front for the operation. Gambling was the main show although Ben Pollack's band played there during the summers of 1935 and 1936. Skidmore and Johnson also operated the Bon Aire Country Club in Wheeling.

Across Dempster Road and east of the Lincoln Tavern was the Dells. During the 1920s and early 1930s, the dapper Sam Hare managed the Dells, which had gambling, dancing, good food, and, if they knew you, some good illicit booze. Hare, a veteran cabaret operator, had been boss of the popular Near South Side café called Schiller's on Thirty-first Street and later, during the winter months, of the Winter Garden at 519 West Diversey Parkway. He also had a place in Florida and earlier in his career allegedly ran the Victoria bordello at Armour and Archer Avenues for Jim Colosimo.[11] It can be safely assumed that Sam knew his way around the business.

The Dells originally was the home of the Huscher family, who were among the early settlers of Morton Grove. It was built around the turn of the century in a thickly wooded area about a hundred feet off the road.[12] In 1917 it was leased to a man named Johnson and with extensive remodeling and expansion was converted into a roadhouse. Sid Simon's orchestra played for dancing and there was a small floor show.[13] Sam Hare took over management in 1924. Hare added colored lights along the circular driveway leading into the wooded property from Dempster Road and redecorated the interior.[14] Down Dempster Road to the east, Hare installed a large electrically lit billboard announcing the Dells attractions. A huge parking area surrounded the building. Inside, the large, richly appointed dining area could hold 850 people or more and, as at the Lincoln Tavern across the road, the dance floor was right in the center of the room.

Noticing the large crowds at the nearby Lincoln Tavern when the Coon-Sanders Nighthawks band from Kansas City played there, Hare figured he ought to book name bands as well. Music certainly had worked well for him as a crowd builder when he managed Schiller's Café in the 1910s. He re-decorated the roadhouse and for the summer of 1926, his third at the Dells, Hare hired the Abe Lyman band, which he advertised widely in the Chicago newspapers and in lights on Dempster Road.[15] Two months earlier Lyman and his California band had concluded a very successful engagement at the downtown College Inn of the Sherman Hotel.

At the Dells, Lyman's band was paid a weekly guarantee of $2,500 that was collected from the cover charges paid by the customers, ranging from fifty cents per person on week nights to two dollars on weekends. Any cover charges exceeding the guarantee were shared 50-50 with management. With his expensive contract, Lyman was the only attraction at the Dells that summer but drew good crowds because of the radio buildup he had received previously at the College Inn.[16]

Following his success with Abe Lyman in the summer of 1926, Hare wanted another name band for the following year. He now looked favorably at the Coon-Sanders band, by then comfortably ensconced during the winter season at the Blackhawk Restaurant downtown. Hare contacted MCA and made a deal to hire the Nighthawks to play for his floor show and for dancing during the next several summers.[17]

He also brought in other MCA name bands such as Ted Lewis and star attractions such as Sophie Tucker when the Coon-Sanders band left for its annual end-of-summer road trips. To fill in between name bands, Huff often booked local Chicago bands such as Joe Kayser, then also being booked by MCA.[18] In 1934 Carlos Molina's orchestra entertained the Dells patrons during the second season of the Century of Progress, but not for long because the roadhouse was shut down over a liquor license wrangle.[19]

The Dells attracted a tonier crowd than the Lincoln Tavern. The patrons were among the city's "movers and shakers," affluent and politically influential and out for an evening of gambling, dining, and dancing in what could be called for those times a swanky setting. Hare was an interesting and seasoned veteran of the entertainment business in the Chicago area and his ability to deal with people of both high and low station was one of his greatest attributes.

Hare occasionally had trouble with his illegal liquor suppliers, which often resulted in business disruptions. The premises were broken up on at least one occasion and the place was bombed in May 1929 after Hare reported being threatened several times by members of one of the outfits fighting over liquor distribution rights in the territory. A fire later that summer severely damaged the building but it was repaired for the following year's season.[20]

In the summer of 1933 an Englishman named John "Jake the Barber" Factor allegedly was kidnapped from a location just east of the Dells after leaving the roadhouse.[21] The following May, the Cook County State's Attorney barred the club from reopening and asked the state liquor control commission to revoke the establishment's liquor license (by this time it was again legal to sell liquor). Later in the summer of 1934 a suspicious fire destroyed the Dells. The destruction of the former posh suburban watering hole symbolized the end of an era.[22]

The Triangle Café in west suburban Forest Park was not technically a roadhouse but it was far enough removed from the city to miss some of the close scrutiny by federal Prohibition authorities. Mickey Rafferty operated the place, which wasn't nearly as palatial as either the Dells or the Lincoln Tavern but had a big clientele. Gambling was the big thing at Rafferty's but he also employed a small band for dancing, and during Prohibition getting a drink of illegal liquor apparently was quite doable.[23]

The musicians for a while were mostly young and of the jazz persuasion working under a nominal leader, Floyd Town. The prominent black theater leader Erskine Tate had a band at the Triangle by the early 1930s and, like the other groups, broadcast regularly over Rafferty's radio station WKFI each evening at 10 P.M.[24] The repeal of Prohibition in 1933 ended the roadhouse phase of the Triangle's existence.

The Villa Venice was far too luxurious to be called a roadhouse. It was more like a posh country club or sprawling country estate. Extravagant floor shows and gambling were the attractions. The place had a very colorful history. Operating only from May through September, it began as "The House That Jack Built" on a lonely stretch of Milwaukee Avenue where it crossed the Des Plaines River on the border between what is now Northbrook and Glenview.

The House That Jack Built actually was built by Harry Wuerzinger. Wuerzinger and his partner, A. E. Frost, broke ground and erected the building in the summer of 1914, but the structure quickly was encumbered by building contractors' liens.[25] The property subsequently went through several changes in management. The jazz scholar Lawrence Gushee says the Beifield family, whose members were prominently connected with both the White City Amusement Park on the far South Side and the downtown Sherman Hotel, operated the property during the summer of 1917.[26] Bert Kelly is identified as the manager of the roadhouse about that time and also led a band there.[27]

In 1921 the showman Albert Bouché began operating the House That Jack Built and converted it into a Mediterranean-style villa that became known as the Villa Venice Theater Restaurant.[28] During the winter months Bouché also managed the downtown Moulin Rouge, where he produced lavish shows.[29] In 1922 Bouché took ownership of the three-story, stucco-and-wood structure and its surrounding ten wooded acres along the Des Plaines River, which backed up to a Cook County Forest Preserve. It was a twin to another restaurant of the same name that Bouché and his brother Hugo ran in Miami, Florida, during the winter.

All patrons arrived at the Villa Venice by car because of the remote location and entered the grounds through a large, lighted archway. To carry out his Venetian theme, Bouché created beautifully manicured grounds and installed an adjoining boat landing along the riverfront where patrons could take rides in gondolas during the warm summer evenings. Colorful Venetian lanterns cast a romantic glow along the river route.

Bouché was said to be a master showman. He staged lavish French-themed shows on the raised floor in the middle of the expansive 100-by-75-foot dining room of the Villa Venice during the 1920s.[30] Entertainers and sumptuously costumed, semi-nude chorus girls performed in revues, and Bouché always featured top-notch local bands, many of them from the South Side. During the summers from 1923 to 1926 and again for part of 1928, Jimmy Wade, who apparently had several bands working at various venues, put a band into the Villa Venice following his winter job downtown at the Moulin Rouge.[31] Clarence Jones, the staff pianist at WBBM and a theater orchestra leader (at the Owl, Metropolitan, and Vendome theaters), and the violinist Eddie South alternately led these Wade organizations at various times during the seasons of 1927 and 1928.[32] The band of Charlie Kerr, a white Philadelphia leader, followed for the 1929 season.[33] Eddie Mallory's band was hired for the summer of 1932 after it closed its winter engagement at the Granada Café on the South Side.[34]

The Chicago trumpeter Frankie Quartell, a member of the popular Fio-Rito-Russo orchestra at the Edgewater Beach Hotel during the early 1920s, took a band into the Villa during the mid-1930s where it remained for several seasons. Then, in 1939, Papa Bouché sent Quartell and forty chorus girls and performers to Havana, Cuba, to staff the show at his new Villa Venice there. Quartell organized a new band of Havana musicians.[35] For the suburban Chicago Villa that year, Bouché coaxed Isham Jones out of retirement to organize a band, one of Jones's last professional engagements in the area.

Bouché continued to manage the Villa Venice until 1956 and then sold it to resolve financial difficulties. The Meo family managed the Villa for a time. By then there were no shows and the Villa was just a very big restaurant. The bandleader Dick Sarlo, whose show-oriented quartet was playing weekends at the Congress Hotel downtown, furnished the week-night entertainment and music for dancing.

Leo Olsen took over the operation from the Meos in 1959 and began catering for parties and special events. Three years later, perhaps in an attempt to recapture some of the glory of the Villa Venice during the twenties, Olsen hired several big-name entertainers. First on the list was Eddie Fisher, who played the Villa for one week. Sammy Davis Jr. followed Fisher, also for a week.[36] Then Frank Sinatra, Dean Martin, and Sammy Davis Jr. appeared together for about eleven days.

Dick Sarlo's quartet continued during the month of star attractions and did the warmup for Fisher, Davis, Sinatra, and Martin. But to support these name performers, all of whom were accustomed to the extravagant production facilities of Las Vegas, Olsen hired a forty-piece orchestra led by the veteran Chicago leader and conductor Henry Brandon, who had directed the Chicago Theater stage band four years earlier.

The cost for the shows and expanded orchestra was said to be about $100,000 for the four weeks, but the place did standing-room-only business. When Sinatra, Martin, and Davis concluded their engagement, the Villa Venice seemed on the verge of filling its stage with more star attractions and reclaiming some of its past glory.[37] However, it was destroyed by fire in November 1967, ending a forty-six-year-run in the northern suburbs that was highlighted by hip-flasks, chorus lines, handsomely dressed patrons, star attractions, gondola rides on the Des Plaines River, and, certainly, good dance music. Allgauer's Restaurant and the Northbrook Hilton Hotel now occupy the old Villa Venice property, which is still handsomely landscaped.

East of the Villa Venice on the southeast corner of Lake Avenue and Waukegan Road in Glenview, the veteran Chicago café entrepreneur Al Tierney operated the Garden of Allah. It was described as a big and classy operation, the interior of which, as the name suggests, followed a Middle Eastern theme. Henri Lishon's band appeared there in 1928 backing the three-act cabaret show.[38]

A mile to the south the smaller White House/Coconut Grove had dancing and small shows.[39] The promoter, booker, and leader Husk O'Hare and his brother George assumed management of the Coconut Grove in the late thirties and Husk's band played at the nightspot. An explosion leveled the Coconut Grove some time later.[40]

The Blue Heron in Glenview and the Lighthouse west of Evanston used black Chicago bands for the shows and dancing. Archie Anderson led a seven-piece band at the Blue Heron in 1926, followed by Ralph Brown's band.[41] Tom Johnson's small orchestra accompanied a three-act show at the Lighthouse in 1926 with Bud Whalen, a veteran singer and master of ceremonies, on hand to direct the proceedings.[42] Sammy Stewart's orchestra, so popular at the Sunset Café and other South Side Chicago venues, moved into the Lighthouse for the summer of 1928.[43]

Out in the far northwest corner of Cook County along Route 20, just east of Elgin, was the Purple Grackle, owned for a time by Charles Erbstein, the prominent Chicago attorney who operated the early pioneer radio station WTAS. Erbstein's elaborate home, Villa Olivia, was located near the Grackle.[44]

Quite a few bands from Chicago played at the Grackle and broadcast via WTAS. Other bands went directly to the WTAS studio, located on Erbstein's property, to broadcast because Erbstein did not honor what were then called silent Mondays. In the early 1920s, silent nights were selected by radio stations in different cities to remain silent (not broadcast) so local residents could hear radio stations from other U.S. cities (a big deal in the days of crystal sets). Monday was selected by Chicago broadcasters to remain off the air, but Erbstein did not comply. Jules Herbuveaux told of taking his Paradise Ballroom band to play in Elgin on Monday nights. "Every Monday night we would go out to Charlie Erbstein's place, the Villa Olivia [to broadcast] ... and we got a tremendous amount of mail," he said.[45] Fred Hamm, Husk O'Hare, Mezz Mezzrow, and Walt Loftus were four other Chicago bands to play and broadcast from either the Grackle or the station.[46]

Like the communities to the north, the towns in southern Cook County in which many of these establishments were located generally were unincorporated and law enforcement was spotty at best. Le Chateau was situated at the intersection of Ridge Road and Leland Avenue in what is present-day Lansing. Like many of its counterparts, it was nicely appointed. It had a large dance area, a six-piece white band, and a floor show consisting of four female vocalists who, as was the custom of the day, went table-to-table, singing for tips.[47]

Le Chateau served setups—bottles of ginger ale or club soda with ice—that patrons presumably mixed with liquor they brought along in flasks. Amusingly, the setup bottles carried a warning from the management stating that intoxicating liquor was not allowed on the premises. It was a sham, of course, but the management could always point to their "good-faith effort" if the Prohibition patrol showed up.

In Burnham, two of the better-known venues in the town were the Coney Island on 138th Place and the Arrowhead Inn.[48] Both places boasted a four-to-six-piece band and entertainers, usually female vocalists who sang a few numbers and then did the customary table-to-table routine.

Other fairly well known southern Cook County roadhouses included the Martinique Inn in Indiana Harbor; the Roadside House, on Archer Road on the way to Joliet;[49] Dutch's, on Ridge Road in Thornton; the Glenwood Inn, on Dyer Road in Glenwood; and the Equator, also on Ridge Road but in nearby Lansing.[50] Others were the Club Princeton at the intersection of

175th and Halsted Streets and the Nickson House, located at 175th and the Dixie Highway in present-day Homewood.

Of these, the Club Princeton, Dutch's, and the Nickson House were the bigger, more elaborate establishments. The Princeton had a seven-piece instrumental group on the bandstand and the Nickson House featured a five-piece all-girl ensemble.[51] Dutch's was a nicely decorated, two-story frame house set back from Ridge Road. It featured a four-to-five-piece band domiciled on a bandstand under a striped canopy. Small bands and the requisite female vocalists seemed to rule in most of these venues. A few places provided young hostesses to dance with single male patrons.

The roadhouses in Cook County lost their raison d'être in 1933 with the repeal of Prohibition. Many of them just closed their doors but some obtained liquor licenses and continued to operate. A few remain standing today as legitimate bars and restaurants, now enveloped by the metropolitan sprawl. The roadhouses came and went quickly but left their mark on the entertainment habits of Chicagoans. They provided an exciting and adventurous thirteen-year interlude for many. Automobiles and paved roads provided new mobility and allowed folks inexpensive access to relatively high quality dance music and entertainment.[52] The excitement of sneaking drinks of illegal alcoholic beverages and indulging in a little uninhibited behavior in a relatively loose environment, to be sure, provided a dimension of risk and excitement even beyond that in the city cabarets and must have been an added lure. In many ways the roadhouses set the stage for a new era of music and entertainment to follow in the 1930s and 1940s.

# 11   "Rah, Rah, Rajah"

THE stage-band policy, which offered a new type of variety show presented in movie houses between films, was introduced in Chicago in the mid-1920s and profoundly influenced dance bands and especially their leaders. Stage-band presentations differed from regular vaudeville shows and the earlier live talent performances in movie theaters in two important ways. First, the former theater pit orchestra was moved onto the stage, where it became a stage band; the acts were then introduced by the leader and presented in front of the band. Often an orchestra of reduced size remained in the pit to accompany the films, which were still silent in those days. Second, using newly designed staging equipment and elevators, the stage band and the acts could enter the stage from below as well as from the wings and could perform at stage level or on elevated platforms.

The new presentation policy put the bandleader in charge of the show and recast him as a combined interlocutor, master of ceremonies, and director, unfamiliar territory for most theater conductors before the mid-1920s. The stage-band leaders would become role models for dance-band leaders, and the stage bands would set new standards of performance and showmanship for the dance bands.

The new live entertainment policy was adopted quickly by Chicago theaters and ultimately became popular in other cities in the Midwest and East. Theater owners liked the new policy because it was a moneymaker. The stage shows were the theatrical equivalents of the floor-show revues being presented in cabarets of the day, but on a much grander scale. They were built around a theme like the revues but could be more elaborate and at the same time more cost effective because they were presented to larger audiences.

Paul Ash and a few early stage-band leaders became instant celebrities. Many aspiring stage-band leaders "went to school" at Ash's shows at the McVickers Theater and later at the Oriental Theater, studying his every move and carefully noting the performance of the stage band. Some bandleaders sought help from drama coaches to make them more appealing "frontmen" in their hoped-for new role. Others just didn't have the disposition or personality to make the change. It also became apparent to dance venue proprietors that good dance-band leaders, like the new breed of stage-band leaders, had to be able to "sell" the band to the people, not just wave a baton.

The stage-band policy also indirectly helped establish the format for the early variety and comedy shows being broadcast on radio about that time. Not only did the personalities or acts appearing on the radio show perform in front of the studio orchestra; the orchestra leader often had a speaking part. Don Bestor, Guy Lombardo, Phil Harris, Ray Noble, Ted Weems, Skinnay Ennis, and many other early leaders played the straight man or foil for comedians such as Jack Benny, George Burns and Gracie Allen, and Bob Hope. These radio programs also helped accelerate the metamorphosis of the bandleader from "silent baton waver" to "speaking personality" and often master of ceremonies.

Balaban and Katz (B&K), the giant Chicago-based movie theater chain, introduced the stage-band policy to Chicago in 1925 at its newly acquired McVickers Theater on Madison Street after experimenting with the idea for several years at its Tivoli Theater on the South Side.[1] Paul Ash, the new master of ceremonies and band leader at the McVickers, provided the continuity for the show and kept the carefully organized presentations running smoothly. The McVickers's first show established the format in Chicago for all later shows in which the costumes, music, and scenery were designed around a special theme and changed weekly. Many of the shows, like "Rah, Rah, Rajah," had an Asian theme and Ash acquired his tagline, "the Rajah of Jazz," from the show's title.

Jack Partington, a theatrical producer at San Francisco's Granada Theater, was the genius who created the policy about 1921 by turning the static, single-level stage into dynamic, multilevel performing platforms using special elevators and other devices.[2] Partington invented some of the mechanical devices or supervised their application or adaptation to fulfill his vision of the new stage presentations. The orchestra often rose dramatically out of the orchestra pit on an elevator invented by Partington, then rolled back onto the stage on a specially designed platform. This added a vertical dimension of presentation never before possible. Acts too could ascend to stage level on built-in stage elevators or be taken off the same way. The idea added dynamism, variety, and visual appeal to the show and allowed for quick, smooth changes of acts and scenes without performers having to enter or exit exclusively from the wings.

The stage-band leader for this new concept had to be someone with charm and individuality, someone with a sense of showmanship who could "talk," that is, effectively introduce the acts and provide some continuity chatter. That someone turned out to be Paul Ash, the Granada Theater pit-orchestra conductor.[3] As the first to be cast in the role of a stage-band leader, he became the model for all future stage-band leaders. More than that, after coming to Chicago, Ash became one of the biggest box-office earners in show business and one of the most popular and probably the highest-paid bandleader in the United States.

Ash did more than just wave a baton and act as master of ceremonies; he jumped around, he wiggled his derriere, and he danced in front of the band as he directed it. He had personality plus and, as a master of ceremonies, he was able to bring an unaffected friendliness to the proceedings, which he laced with humor and jokes.[4] In short, he captivated his audiences and was especially popular with the ladies.

Theater-orchestra leaders who were able to act as masters of ceremony were a scarce commodity in the mid-1920. Managers hiring stage-band leaders, even if those leaders were musically well qualified, had to give some candidates lessons in elocution and voice projection and polish up their conducting skills to prepare them for the job. In short, bandleaders had to master many of the theatrical techniques required for the more visual and vocal demands of the stage. As a result, stage-band leaders set a new level of expectation for all bandleaders. Even those leading dance bands occasionally got some "finishing" to make them more appealing frontmen. Good leaders had to be able to sell the band to the people.[5]

It was appropriate that Balaban and Katz would introduce the new stage-band policy to Chicago audiences. Fifteen or more years earlier they had inaugurated the idea of presenting vaudeville acts between films at their Circle and Central Park Theaters on the West Side. In addition, the chain in the early 1920s was in the midst of building several large, elaborate new movie theaters for which they were becoming famous. These luxurious and expensively appointed houses were called "atmospheric" theaters because they were designed to resemble Oriental palaces, medieval castles, formal gardens, and other exotic settings. Everything about the new atmospheric theaters was big—the lobbies, the grand staircases, and the seating capacities. What was considered a first-class house in 1912—a theater that seated 1,200 or more—had by 1928 come to mean a theater seating in excess of 3,000 people.[6] There were thirteen Chicago theaters in this class by then.

The Balaban and Katz managers were intrigued by Paul Ash and the new stage-band policy in San Francisco because they had been testing a similar stage-show policy since 1921 at their huge new Tivoli Theater, located on Chicago's South Side near the Sixty-third Street and Cottage Grove Avenue commercial center.[7] A. J. Balaban and Sam Katz already had been booking dance bands for the stage of their Central Park Theater on West Roosevelt Road. The theater was fairly small compared to the giant houses built after 1920. The Central Park management produced "jazz nights" sporadically during the 1920s at the theater.[8] Local Chicago dance bands such as those led by the trumpet players Ralph Williams and Louis Panico were two mid-1920s attractions. Panico was famous for "Wabash Blues," a tune he recorded on the Brunswick label as a member of the Isham Jones orchestra in 1921. Roy Bargy led an orchestra that played on the stage of the big new Chicago Theater on State Street and later at the Tivoli.

As part of the B&K Tivoli experiment, the conductor Al Short in 1922 hired the Pinky Aarseth dance orchestra as his permanent stage band. The Aarseth orchestra had been at liberty since the new Driscoll's Danceland on the West Side closed after less than a year. The trial presentations at the 3,400-seat Tivoli were modest compared to the Granada Theater's offerings with Paul Ash in San Francisco. The Tivoli experiment lacked both a charismatic master of ceremonies and some of Jack Partington's mechanical aids that had sparked the California productions.

Satisfied they were on the right track, Balaban and Katz hired Ash away from the Granada in 1925 to replicate the new stage-band policy for their B&K theaters.[9] Things would never be the same again in Chicago. Very soon, the new policy caught the public's fancy and spread to movie houses in most major cities around the country. Although the idea for the stage-band presentation with all its elaborate mechanical assists is rightfully credited to Jack Partington, it was regularly referred to as the "Paul Ash policy."[10] Others also made claims that the stage band was their idea. Stanley Brown, the manager of Milwaukee's Strand Theater, wrote a letter to the editor of *Variety* saying that Joie Lichter's Strand orchestra had been doing something similar since 1921 but never claimed credit.[11]

Partington was held in high esteem by senior B&K management and was later hired by Sam Katz, then in New York running the new Paramount Publix Pictures Corporation chain created when B&K merged with Paramount–Famous Players.[12] Partington became one of several producers packaging road shows for the chain. Later he moved on to senior positions with other production firms.

Paul Ash made his much-publicized debut in Chicago on May 11, 1925, at the newly acquired McVickers Theater, a former Paramount–Famous Players vaudeville and movie presentation house at 25 West Madison Street. The all-new twelve-piece Ash band replaced that of H. Leopold Spitalny, who had joined B&K when the theater chain assumed control of the McVickers Theater. Additional musicians played in the pit for the silent movies. Leaders and musicians alike flocked to the McVickers to observe Ash in action and to get ideas. The whole concept was new; they had never before seen a band remain on stage for the whole show, supporting the acts, and they had never seen anyone like Ash.

Overnight Ash became a matinee idol at the McVickers, but in March 1926, B&K moved Ash and his band—often billed as "his merry, musical maniacs"—two blocks north to the chain's recently completed Oriental Theater at 20 West Randolph Street, which was designed by Rapp and Rapp. The first production at the new theater was "Insultin' the Sultan." B&K's publicity agents hinted in their press handouts that the Oriental had been specially built to feature Paul Ash and the stage-band policy, which probably was press agent hyperbole.[13] The theater was part of the twenty-two-story New Masonic Temple building that had been under construction since before Ash arrived in town. A building of that magnitude simply could not have been designed and built in less than a year. More likely the theater's stage was custom fitted with the special elevators and other new stage equipment required for the stage-band shows as the theater was being completed. Press agents most likely dreamed up the rest, but it made a good story.

The theater's interior was a wild conglomeration of eclectic Oriental decor clichés in keeping with the atmospheric theater style of the times. But it is doubtful the audience paid much attention to the decor for it was Ash they came to see. The lines awaiting the Oriental's shows each day snaked down Randolph Street and around the corner. Ash was signed to a five-year contract said to be worth $1 million, a lot of money for the late 1920s, and B&K reportedly insured Ash for $750,000.[14] Both figures were probably inflated by 1920s press agents. But even if the numbers were the products of an overly creative publicity department, Ash still was the highest-paid bandleader in Chicago and maybe in the country, and clearly B&K was doing something to protect its top moneymaking attraction.

There are many stories about Paul Ash, Chicago's personality kid with the marcelled red hair. The tales most often told had to do with Ash's poor memory.[15] He forgot names of the acts he was to introduce, and the titles of tunes the band was to play often eluded him. But the audience seemed to care not at all. His popularity influenced radio station WGN to begin weekly broadcasts of the Ash performances directly from the stage of the Oriental in May 1928.[16] Ash narrated the proceedings on stage for the benefit of radio listeners. KYW had previously broadcast Paul Ash shows from the stage of the McVickers in 1925, adding to the local celebrity status for some of the performers and bandsmen, not to mention for Ash himself.

He remained in Chicago for about three years and made nearly 4,500 combined appearances in the McVickers and Oriental theaters.[17] At the McVickers, Ash brought in more than $30,000 a week at the box office. But at the bigger Oriental in 1926, weekly ticket sales were nearly $50,000 and he received thousands of letters from admiring fans, mostly women. By comparison, the McVickers began losing money the day Ash and company left. It reportedly cost $20,000 a week just to keep the McVickers doors open for business.[18] After Ash's departure it ran a weekly deficit of $11,000.

Publix Theaters, which had become the parent of B&K, decided to move Ash to its New York Paramount Theater in 1928. Before he left town, he took time off from his M.C. duties at the Oriental just to attend the farewell parties given him. Four thousand well-wishers, including Mayor William "Big Bill" Thompson, participated in the largest gathering, held at Mann's Million-Dollar Rainbo Garden.[19] Undoubtedly included in the large crowd, which the Rainbo had trouble feeding, were some of the 2,400 members of the "Greater Paul Ash Every Week Club."[20]

A veritable parade of leaders moved in and out of the Oriental following Ash's departure. The popular Mark Fisher, from the Senate Theater, and Al Kvale and Lou Kosloff, alumni of the original Ash band of Merry Makers, were just a few of them. J. Walter Davidson conducted the pit orchestra during this period.[21] The good times for the Oriental, however, came to an end by 1930 and it went dark briefly in the next few years, the deepest part of the Depression.

It reopened later in the 1930s, and stage shows again were very popular during the 1940s. Carl Sands, a pianist, directed what by the late 1940s became the Oriental house band. Sherman Hayes succeeded Sands and was the last stage-band leader at the theater.

B&K's Chicago Theater, on State near Lake, and the giant State and Lake Theater, across the street at 190 North State Street, both featured the new stage-band policy beginning in the late 1920s. The State and Lake, originally named the Great States Theater, was built in 1917 to showcase Orpheum circuit vaudeville acts and was taken over later by B&K. The Chicago Theater, however, designed by Rapp and Rapp and completed in 1921, was built by B&K and became the chain's headquarters.

During the 1930s the State and Lake featured Verne Buck's orchestra. At the Chicago, the violinist Lou Adrian was assistant conductor and, later, conductor of the pit orchestra off and on from the 1920s through the early 1940s. Nate Finstone, Joseph Cherniavsky, the composer-conductor Jules Buffano (later Jimmy Durante's accompanist), and H. Leopold Spitalny were other Chicago Theater conductors. Then in 1944 Lou Breese, with years of experience as a show conductor, left the Chez Paree and moved to the stage of the Chicago Theater to direct the house stage band; he was followed by Louis Basil, who had come from the East, and, finally, by the Chicagoan Henry Brandon.

For years during the 1920s and 1930s the Chicago Theater pit orchestra presented classical and semiclassical concerts each Sunday at noon, called the Symphonic Hour.[22] The performances, which featured familiar works from the opera or operetta stages, often with guest singers and dancers, were always very popular with the public and allowed the conductors and musicians temporarily to break out of the popular music milieu and demonstrate their talents in serious music.

As big as Paul Ash's weekly grosses were at the Oriental, they never surpassed those of the 3,250-seat Chicago Theater.[23] And as big as the Chicago was, it was outclassed in seating capacity by the giant Uptown Theater at Lawrence and Broadway, which could accommodate 4,325 patrons. At the time it was built in 1925, the Uptown was claimed to be the largest movie house in the United States. But it never exceeded the Chicago at the box office.

As the stage-band policy became the rage in theaters not only in Chicago but all over the country, the stage-band leaders became matinee idols and often made personal appearances. Joe Kayser, who was popular with the North Side dancing crowds at the Arcadia and Merry Garden ballrooms, was hired by the managers of the Diversey Theater, on Clark near Diversey, to lead the stage band at the giant new house.[24] Kayser later moved to the Karzas Brothers–owned State Theater in nearby Hammond, Indiana, in the same role.

Soon other Chicago dance-band leaders such as Al Morey, Buddy Fisher, and Armin Hand were leading stage bands and presiding as masters of ceremony for stage shows in theaters all over the city. The West Side's Paradise and the North Side's NorShore, Riviera, Howard, Harding, Sheridan, Pantheon, North Center, and Belmont theaters were other outlying neighborhood houses featuring stage orchestras. It was a new fad. B&K even hired several out-of-town leaders such as the New York saxophonist Benny Krueger to lead its new stage band at the giant Tivoli Theater following Al Short's departure in 1925 for the nearby Capitol Theater, at Seventy-ninth and Halsted. Short later moved to the newly built Piccadilly Theater in Hyde Park. Lubliner and Trinz hired Art Kahn for their Senate Theater on West Madison Street, where he became especially popular.

On the greater South Side, the aforementioned Tivoli at Sixty-third and Cottage Grove, the Avalon at Seventy-ninth and Stony Island, the Stratford, and the Capitol were the major theaters with stage-show entertainment. Two giant theaters near the intersection of Forty-seventh Street and South Parkway (now Dr. Martin Luther King Jr. Drive) serving the black audiences in the area were the Regal and the Metropolitan. Both had fully embraced the stage-band policy by 1928.

Many fine musicians peopled the B&K theater-pit orchestras around town. Victor Young, David Rose, Marvin Saxbe, Volly De Faut, Bill Davison, Walter Steindl, Julie Styne (later a Broadway composer), and Ulderico Marcelli were just a few of them. Victor Young, a violinist, later became chief arranger for the B&K chain, working for his old boss Louis Lipstone, who by 1929 had become the vice president and general musical director of B&K. Lipstone later moved to Hollywood, where he became music director of Paramount Pictures and later sent for Victor Young.

It was Lipstone, along with the visionary B&K management, who was credited with introducing large orchestras into America's theaters. B&K had orchestras ranging in size from twenty-five to seventy-five pieces in its Chicago theaters, which was unprecedented in show business until then.[25] It was estimated that the city's silent-movie theaters employed two thousand pit musicians.[26] More than a few of the musicians were from Poland, Russia, Italy, and elsewhere. B&K also had the largest group of highly paid orchestra conductors in the world.

The Paul Ash stage-band policy lasted about five years. Two powerful events brought it and the era of large pit orchestras to a close: the arrival of talking motion pictures and the Great Depression. Theater-pit orchestras no longer were needed to play musical accompaniment for the talking movies because films now had their own soundtracks. For a while, the talking movies were a big-enough lure to become the featured attractions themselves, and stage entertainment seemed less necessary.

The Depression began cutting into box-office receipts by the early 1930s. What vestiges of locally produced stage shows were left in a few major downtown theaters and key neighborhood houses were replaced with touring packaged shows. Later even these packaged shows were eliminated. Balaban and Katz continued to produce a few stage shows for their key theaters, but the productions were scaled-down versions that hardly resembled the original shows of the mid-twenties. By then the pit and stage orchestras also had been reduced in size; the total number of full-time theater musicians working in Chicago by the mid-1930s had dropped to 125.[27]

As the full impact of the Depression began being felt by theater musicians and leaders, some of the latter formed dance bands, the market for which had not been hit as hard economically. In most cases MCA or other booking agencies assisted leaders such as Frankie Master, Benny Meroff, Mark Fisher, Buddy Fisher, and others in the organizing process. Joe Kayser and Art Kahn simply resumed their old careers and again hit the road.

The Chicago Theater ended its stage presentation policy in 1955 with a show built around the popular Chicago radio disk jockeys Eddie Hubbard and Jim Lounsbury and featuring the popular vocal group the Hilltoppers and the singer Nick Noble.[28] The Oriental and State and Lake theaters had taken the step several years earlier. That left the two South Side theaters—the Tivoli and the Regal—still featuring live talent on their stages. The Tivoli, the first of Chicago's super theaters, called it quits in February 1962. The Regal, buoyed primarily by the success of a once-monthly blues show, held out until 1968.

It was Balaban and Katz that started it all in Chicago in 1925 at the McVickers, and it was Balaban and Katz that brought down the curtain on the stage-show policy thirty-seven years later at the Tivoli, but it was an era that will long be remembered. Not only did it bring enjoyment and entertainment to millions of people, but it launched the careers of thousands of performers who went on to fame and fortune in television and the movies.

Although Paul Ash closed at the Oriental Theater in May 1928 and headed for New York City, he was still under contract to the Paramount Publix Pictures Corporation and returned to Chicago many times to fulfill engagements. But in 1930 he left for good to direct short film subjects in New York and later became head of the Roxy Theater orchestra.[29] By then, however, times had changed and the stage shows had been subsumed by the sound movies. As a result, Ash never achieved the fame or success in New York that he had enjoyed in Chicago.

In Chicago, Ash had become not only a local institution but also a box-office phenomenon. During his three-year stay at the McVickers and Oriental theaters he made 4,500 appearances, according to a 1928 article in *Variety,* the show business weekly. The article said he "played to 14,700,000 paid admissions, equaling about $6,000,000 at the box office."[30] Until that time there had been no one like him. Equally important, though, is the way Ash and his many stage-band disciples influenced the dance-band leaders of the day and elevated the expectations of proprietors and fans alike. Static, stiff-legged, long-faced leaders simply wielding a baton were no longer acceptable to either dancers or venue managers at ballrooms or in hotel dining rooms. The successful dance bands from that point forward not only played good music but were visually interesting units able to entertain dancers and diners; and they were led by lively, animated, and personable leaders who could handle being a master of ceremonies with aplomb and skill. In the 1930s and 1940s, the Kay Kyser and Dick Jurgens bands were two of the best examples of fine musical organizations that also were highly entertaining attractions.

Prior to the stage-band era, some of the earlier dance bands had appeared as acts on the vaudeville stage and had developed entertaining routines, but the routines seldom were used outside the theaters and they were rarely used in a ballroom setting. That all changed with the stage-band policy. More and more dance bands, popular through their radio broadcasts and recordings, began appearing on theater stages, often as one of the acts of the stage-band presentations. Although Paul Ash was never a dance-band leader, he left a rich legacy to those who were, and he set high performing standards that changed significantly the dance bands and their leaders.

# 12 The Economic Challenge of the Thirties

TWO major events in 1933 reshaped the landscape of the music business in Chicago: the repeal of Prohibition and the opening of the Century of Progress world's fair. The United States was then deep into a fourth year of economic depression with millions of people—including thousands of musicians—out of work. But repeal and the world's fair would bring much-needed employment to many in the city.

Bars reopened immediately after repeal, and restaurants, cabarets (many now being called nightclubs), and other entertainment establishments were reinvigorated by the thousands of people who sought their first legal drink after a thirteen-year drought. An increasing number of local entrepreneurs considered the business environment right for opening new nightclubs or show rooms, a far less risky investment now that selling and consuming alcoholic beverages was legal. Two of the best-known examples of these new clubs were the Chez Paree and the Empire Room of the Palmer House. Ironically, they became two of the most elegant and long-lived show rooms in the nation.

While the parade of new nightclubs and other nighttime venues meant employment for musicians and dance bands in the next decade, the Century of Progress meant jobs that year. The fair couldn't have been more welcome to Chicago musicians. Spread along the Lake Michigan shoreline just south of the central city, the fairgrounds had a main entrance at Twelfth Street. The exposition's art-deco and moderne buildings held exhibits of new technology, products, and crafts from many different countries. Most important to the musicians, it provided additional work in the many restaurants, clubs, and "villages" erected along the fair's Midway. Most major European, Latin American, and Asian nations had pavilions at the fair and many cafés, restaurants, and clubs on the Midway reflected, at least thematically, the entertainment from those countries. The talent in most cases, however, was American. In addition, nightlife outside the fair picked up considerably as thousands of visitors who descended upon the city sought additional entertainment at night.

From an economic point of view the fair couldn't have come along at a better time; Chicago, like the rest of the nation, was mired in the depths of the Depression. The music and entertainment industry was particularly hard hit not just by the Depression but also by the cutbacks of theater orchestras resulting from the introduction of sound movies and by the intensive federal crack-down on Volstead Act violations beginning in 1927. The fair now put a fire under the musical pot.

Fifteen cafés and restaurants within the fairgrounds provided musical entertainment, not including marching bands and musical groups used in public expositions and other ceremonial events. Paul Ash, Phil Levant, Austin Mack, and others led bands at such diverse venues as Old Heidelberg, the Spanish Village, and Hollywood at the Fair.[1] The big attraction at the fair, however, was Sally Rand, the nude fan dancer appearing in Ernie Young's Streets of Paris show. More than seventy thousand fair-goers saw her perform in the first thirty days.[2]

Rand's real name was Helen Gould Beck and she had danced in the Ernie Young Marigold Gardens revues during the early 1920s. In 1933, the first year of the fair, Rand did her artistic feathered-fan dance in front of Joe Kayser's band at the Streets of Paris. The band got a completely different view of Rand than the public did because the fans covered only that part of her nude body facing the audience. The following year she was featured in Ernie Young's "1934 World's Fair Revue" at the Italian Village. Bob Pacelli's band got the scenic view this time.[3]

Social critics of the day were up in arms over nudity and what they termed obscene or lewd dancing in the various cabaret shows along the Midway. Sally Rand was at the eye of the storm because she wore nothing behind her fans, which she dropped briefly at the conclusion of her dance. The various court proceedings and other actions seeking to rein in nudity and exotic dancing at the fair, all given coverage by Chicago newspapers, only increased attendance at the fair in general and at the cabaret shows in particular, especially those featuring dancing.[4] There were incidents of what the Juvenile Protective Association termed "suggestive dancing." In the report the association prepared on conditions at the Century of Progress, the JPA claimed the show presented at the Canadian Club contained "suggestive dancing" because the dancers lifted their costumes during their dance, exposing black briefs.[5]

Outside the fair it seemed like most other Chicago musicians were working somewhere. In addition to the Chicago bands, several out-of-town dance bands were hired especially for the period of the fair. Vincent Lopez was at the Congress and Drake hotels, Buddy Rogers appeared for a while at the College Inn of the Sherman Hotel, and Clyde Lucas and his California Dons performed at the Morrison Hotel. Eddy Duchin at the Congress Hotel, Hal Kemp at the Blackhawk, and Anson Weeks's West Coast band at the Aragon completed the lineup of non-Chicago bands.

The Century of Progress and the repeal of Prohibition combined to create a mood of optimism in Chicago in spite of the hardships created by the deepening economic depression. Repeal triggered a renewal in the recently dormant dine-and-dance entertainment market and several new venues opened rather quickly.

Mike Fritzel, the veteran Chicago bar and cabaret operator of the 1910s and 1920s, had survived the raucous Prohibition years in spite of having his various establishments raided, closed down, and involved in legal actions with the federal government. Unbowed, he launched yet another venture in late 1932, just before Prohibition ended. The new Chez Paree would be his biggest and classiest enterprise by far.

The 17,500-square-foot venue was located on the site of the former Chez Pierre at the southwest corner of Fairbanks Court and Ontario Streets.[6] Fritzel and his partner, Joe Jacobson, clearly were gambling on the fact that Prohibition would soon end. To identify the Chez Paree as a new club, Fritzel moved the entrance around the corner, from Ontario Street to Fairbanks Court. Ben Pollack's band played from the elevated stand for the opening and backed an elaborate inaugural floor show, which featured the veteran performer Sophie Tucker.[7] Very quickly the Chez became a premier nightclub with some of the biggest shows in the city and featuring big names in the entertainment world.

Following the Century of Progress in 1933, Vincent Lopez and his New York band went over to the Chez from the Congress Hotel and stayed for the season. After that a parade of bands played at the club, including Ben Bernie, now resident in Chicago, and the out-of-town bands of Phil Harris, Abe Lyman, and Paul Whiteman among others. But the dance-band rotation at Chez Paree settled down in the thirties and forties to three long-term house bands that handled the important role of accompanying the shows: the bands of Henry Busse (1934–38), Lou Breese (1938–44), and Gay Claridge (1944–47).[8] As early as 1933 a second relief band, usually a rhumba combo, played for dancing between the shows.

The Chez Paree became the preeminent nightclub in Chicago and, according to a *Chicago Tribune* article about Fritzel, "one of the half-dozen best known clubs in the country."[9] Some of the headliners featured on the Chez stage included Jimmy Durante, Harry Richman, Carmen Miranda, Judy Garland, the Andrew Sisters, Helen Morgan, George Jessel, Sammy Davis, and the dance team Veloz and Yolanda.[10] Three acts set attendance records: Ted Lewis, Joe E. Lewis, and Dean Martin and Jerry Lewis.

Fritzel and Jacobson continued to run the Chez Paree until 1949 when they sold out to the building owner, Jay Schatz, and several partners. The new owners continued the headliner presentations until the Chez closed in 1960. Cecil "Cee" Davidson, Brian Farnon, Marty Gould, and Phil Levant were among the orchestras accompanying the shows after the Mike Fritzel period.

Fritzel and Jacobson in 1947 took a lease on the defunct Copacabana night-club at 201 North State and turned it into a restaurant named, appropriately enough, Fritzel's. Jacobson bought Fritzel's interest in 1953 and two years later Fritzel purchased the Tradewinds Restaurant at 865 North Rush Street.[11] In addition, he and Jacobson also owned an interest in Don the Beachcomber, a Polynesian restaurant.

Fritzel was the son of a Nebraska cowboy. He had arrived in Chicago just before the turn of the century to begin his exciting life in the city. He was a barkeep, a saloon owner, a café proprietor, and, finally, an architect of one of the most prestigious nightclubs in the world. His odyssey as a proprietor was not without tribulations. But through it all he prevailed, establishing a reputation as one of the smartest and most successful nightclub operators in the country. He died in 1956 at the age of seventy-five. Coincidentally, his career of more than fifty years as a Chicago nightlife entrepreneur spans the years addressed in this study.

The venerable Colosimo's, the legendary Chicago restaurant and cabaret, opened in 1914 at Wabash and Twenty-second Streets and continued to thrive during Prohibition in spite of the usual ups-and-downs caused by government crackdowns on illegal liquor. Repeal rejuvenated the nightspot and Colosimo's remained in business into the 1940s. The place was in the hands of Big Jim Colosimo until his murder in 1920, whereupon management of it fell to his partner, Mike "The Greek" Potson (real name Mihail Bodoglou), during the 1920s.[12] The place was closed down for a year in 1926 for the usual liquor violations.[13] Potson owned half interest in the club with Colosimo and also owned the building. He bought Colosimo's interest from Jim's heirs following Big Jim's death. Potson acquired another partner along the way when Al Capone is alleged to have "bought" an interest.[14] Potson was said to have been close to Capone's alleged gambling chief, Jake Guzik.

The small but posh club on South Wabash, decorated in rose and gold, mostly had small bands of about five to seven musicians and a four-to-five-act floor show. Peter de Quarto's "Jaysee" (for Jim Colosimo?) orchestra held the assignment to accompany the acts and play for dancing at Colosimo's for most of the 1920s, followed by Bob Tinsley's band in the 1930s. However, the club did bring in bigger musical units as the main attractions, such as Ada Leonard's sixteen-piece all-girl orchestra in 1946.[15]

Even though the old neighborhood was a bit shabby and the club was located more than a mile south of the Loop, Chicago's main entertainment center, Colosimo's continued to be a place to go to see a floor show and order a plate of spaghetti. The floor shows were entertaining, usually consisting of a dance team, a comedian, and at least one singer in addition to the band for dancing. There was always gambling in a back room and they had the best spaghetti sauce in town, according to some aficionados. The club was ideally located for the crowds attending the nearby Century of Progress in the summers of 1933 and 1934. Many out-of-town curiosity seekers wanted to visit the infamous Colosimo's, so closely linked with the lore of the Chicago bootleggers of the 1920s. It was a late-night club where things didn't start happening until midnight, and it was a popular stop for the after-theater crowd. During the 1920s it briefly was a favorite watering hole for the college crowd.

During World War II, groups of service men and women, in town for one night or a weekend in the early 1940s, kept business brisk. But with the end of the war and a change in entertainment patterns, trade at Colosimo's, as at many other amusement attractions in the city, fell off considerably. Potson sold out in 1945.[16] New owners tried to breathe new life into the Chicago legend, but the place later closed. In 1952, a small group of investors again tried to resurrect the club but the city denied a license after investigating the principals' backgrounds.[17]

Just across the Chicago River from the Loop, at 400 North Wabash Avenue, was Harry's New York Bar, also called Harry's New Yorker, a diminutive name for a rather large club. Paul Mares, the New Orleans Rhythm Kings cornetist, fronted a band in the second-floor bar in the mid-1930s.[18] The Chicagoan Floyd Town's band came in during the late thirties and remained a fixture there. Both Mares and Town featured some outstanding jazz players in their combos.

The distinct jazz bias of the music purveyed in Harry's Bar was a precursor to the so-called Dixieland revival in Chicago during the 1940s through the 1950s. Austin Mack, an early Chicago leader and later an accompanist for Joe E. Lewis, was the intermission pianist at Harry's for a time during the thirties following his world's fair engagement at the Irish Village.[19] The veteran keyboard artist and arranger Elmer Schoebel also did a stint there. So that the music could be enjoyed during the day as well as in the evening, Harry's had tea dancing in the main room in the mid-thirties with Joe Buckley's combo. In 1941 the Arne Barnett orchestra was on the bandstand at Harry's and, like most of the other bands that played there, was frequently heard late at night over Chicago radio stations.

In the mid-1940s, Harry's became the Rio Cabana, a flashy nightclub featuring big productions and large dance bands. The longtime resident conductor of the house orchestra during this period was the veteran Chicago theater bandleader Cecil "Cee" Davidson. Later the Silver Frolics succeeded the Rio Cabana at the 400 North Wabash address. The Silver Frolics, originally located on the West Side at Madison and Crawford (later Pulaski Road), moved into the building and featured girlie shows. It continued to operate well into the 1950s when the building was razed and replaced by a multistory parking garage to accommodate the autos of visitors and employees of the *Chicago Sun-Times*, just across the street.

The Colony Club, at 744 North Rush Street, was a smaller, more intimate club that, in the 1930s, often presented well-known entertainers late in the evening. Sophie Tucker, following her habit of doubling between two engagements while in Chicago, did a "supper" show there in 1938 after appearing earlier in the evening at the Auditorium Theater in her show "Leave It to Me." Backing the Colony Club shows over time were the combos of Earl Hoffman and the accordionist Don Orlando. In the late 1930s, in the midst of the rhumba craze, the Colony brought in the Jose Manzanares Latin band to furnish rhumba music for the patrons.[20] Another Near North Side nightspot, Club Paramount at 162 East Huron Street, featured a few acts and dancing, with Maurie Stein's combo providing the music. Sally Rand, who would be such a hot attraction at the Century of Progress the following year, spent 1932 perfecting her fan dance at Club Paramount.[21]

On the South Side, Prohibition enforcement raids during the late 1920s and the early years of the Depression put a lot of clubs out of business. The Granada Café at Sixty-eighth and Cottage Grove and the Grand Terrace on South Parkway were two exceptions. The Granada lasted only a while longer, however, before being destroyed by a fire in 1934, whereas the Grand Terrace kept its doors open through the 1930s, moving to a new location in 1937.

Some of the older establishments on the North Side such as the Marigold Gardens and the Green Mill also continued doing business through the 1930s but often under other names. As noted earlier, the Marigold Gardens property was leased to others and the building was used for several different purposes. Although boxing and wrestling matches were often staged in the winter garden building, the venue was reopened as a nightclub called the Vanity Fair. Phil

Levant's band spent the 1930 and 1931 seasons there accompanying the acts and playing for dancing. Al Kvale, so popular as a theater-stage bandleader, played at the Vanity Fair during the 1930s.

By the early 1950s, wrestling matches were being televised nationwide from the Marigold by the budding TV networks, which were hungry for programming opportunities much as radio had been twenty years earlier.[22] After going through a series of transformations, including being used as a supermarket for a time, the former Marigold Gardens building today is owned by Faith Tabernacle, a house of worship.

The Winona Gardens, on the North Side at 5150 North Broadway Avenue, was an unpretentious restaurant and bar when Frank Snyder and his Rhythm Kings were hired to play there in 1936.[23] Located on the southwest corner of Winona and Broadway, the place quickly became a hangout for visiting and in-town musicians alike wanting to hear Snyder's brand of small-group jazz. Snyder was an original member of the New Orleans Rhythm Kings at Friar's Inn in the early 1920s and was one of the Chicago musicians who kept the jazz lamp lit during the 1930s and beyond.

The Winona Gardens and Snyder continued their musical relationship through the late 1930s. With the popular 5100 Club less than a block to the south, the neighborhood around Winona Gardens became an extension of the busy Lawrence and Broadway music and entertainment nexus three blocks farther south, where the Aragon Ballroom, the Uptown and Riviera theaters, and the Green Mill Café all were located.

The Green Mill Café had a checkered history as a show room following the 1920s. Its small dance floor not withstanding, it was used periodically as a ballroom. During the 1930s it closed and reopened under a succession of owners and lessees. Frank Snyder's Dixieland band, well known for its long stay at the nearby Winona Gardens, was one of the attractions in December 1939.[24] In the 1940s the place was remodeled and renamed the Paradise Ballroom, although the original Paradise Ballroom was still in operation on the West Side. The building still stands and is rented out to merchants on the first floor, including a bar carrying the old Green Mill name, which features small jazz groups. Some offices and businesses occupy the second floor, in the former premises of the old Green Mill Garden cabaret.

A somewhat newer venue was the Ivanhoe restaurant and nightclub, an early version of today's popular "theme" clubs in Chicago. It was located at 3000 North Clark Street and opened in 1920 by Harold Jansen.[25] Modeled after a medieval castle, it featured two levels of activity. On the main floor was a restaurant and show room. The basement was called the Catacombs and was constructed to look like a "castle dungeon" with twisting, poorly lit passageways that frequently led to scary surprises in darkened corners. Featured there over the years were numerous small orchestras including those of Earl Hoffman, Don Chiesta, George Snurpus, and Barney Richards.

## The Chinese Restaurants

Restaurants serving chop suey and Chinese food became a fad in Chicago from the late 1920s through the early 1940s and many of the larger ones also featured afternoon and evening dancing and floor shows. The biggest were the Oriental Gardens, the Canton Tea Garden, the Beachview Gardens Café, the Golden Lily, and the Golden Pumpkin. Local dance bands worked steadily in all these venues.

The Canton Tea Garden opened in 1929 at 404 South Wabash Avenue. Louis Panico, the cornetist known for work on the Isham Jones orchestra's recording of "Wabash Blues" (Brunswick, 1921), spent the first six seasons at the new restaurant playing for dancing. The band later returned several times until 1938.[26] The Panico band and others were often heard broadcasting via KYW and over the NBC and CBS networks. Jack Russell's and Dan Russo's Chicago bands also were regulars at the Canton Tea Garden. When Panico left the Canton in 1938 he moved to another major downtown Chinese restaurant, the Oriental Gardens. Like many other Chicago venues, the Canton Tea Garden featured a celebrity night once each week.

Opened in early 1931, the Oriental Gardens was located on the second floor of a new building at 23–29 West Randolph Street in the heart of the entertainment district.[27] The new five-story building was built by the John R. Thompson Company, then a major national restaurant chain. The Oriental Gardens was operated by Chin Wai, who also owned the Rialto Gardens, another Chinese restaurant, one block west on Randolph. The Don Pedro, Dan Russo, Henry Gendron, and Al Turk bands played for dancing at the Oriental Gardens at various times through the 1930s, broadcasting frequently.

Less well known was the Bamboo Inn, located along the north side of Randolph Street, west of State Street on the lower level. It was opened in the 1920s in the former premises of Lamb's Café but the entrance was moved from Clark Street to Randolph Street.[28] Steve Leonardo's small band was one of several groups that provided dance music in the early to mid-1930s.

On the North Side there was Maroni's Beachview Gardens, located on the second floor at 804 West Wilson Avenue, just west of Clarendon. Harold Leonard and his Red Jacket orchestra, a Benson group, played there as early as 1923. But in 1929, following the breakup of the FioRito-Russo Oriole Terrace Orchestra, Dan Russo took his version of the Orioles into the restaurant. Russo and the band spent the season playing for dancing at the Beachview Gardens.[29] While there, Russo and company broadcast regularly via WIBO (Russo owned part of the station with FioRito), and on Fridays evenings they were on the air with a two-hour "celebrity show." The Friday-night show attracted many performers such as Sophie Tucker and the bandleader Mark fisher, an alumnus of the FioRito-Russo Oriole Terrace Orchestra from its days at the Edgewater Beach Hotel.

Over the next few years John Tobin's band filled the bandstand at the Beachview Gardens. Then, in December 1931, six gunmen brazenly tried to rob the restaurant just after one o'clock in the morning. Verne Buck and his band, then playing there, had concluded their regular WIBO broadcast just five minutes before the incident occurred.[30] Nine band members, two managers, and all the patrons were held at gunpoint during the robbery attempt. A policeman who intervened was shot and later died, and a young woman was wounded.

Farther to the north, Howard Street was the dividing line between Chicago on the South and Evanston on the north. Because Evanston and other towns on the North Shore remained dry following the repeal of Prohibition, the bars and clubs along the south side of Howard Street were the closest places to get a drink. One of the most popular destinations where patrons could drink, eat Chinese food, and dance was Benjamin Joe's Limehouse, a second-floor establishment at 1563 West Howard Street within walking distance of the Howard Street Elevated station. The bands of Barney Richards and Al Handler were regulars at the Limehouse during the 1930s.[31] Later, Woody Woodruff's band played more than a decade at the restaurant.

West Madison Street had been a popular entertainment area in the 1910s and 1920s and continued to attract amusement seekers through the 1940s. Located along the street or nearby were the Senate Theater, Graemere Hotel, and Princess Ballroom. Farther west were the Keyman's Club, the Paradise and Byrd ballrooms, the Marbro and Paradise theaters, and numerous restaurants and clubs, such as the aforementioned Silver Frolics.

One of the most popular restaurants was the Golden Pumpkin, owned by Joe Enge and located at 3825 West Madison, just west of the intersection of Madison Street and Homan Avenue. The Golden Pumpkin occupied the premises of the former Driscoll's Danceland and operated from 1927 through the early 1930s. It was one of the largest restaurants in Chicago and could accommodate up to a thousand diners.

From its opening the Golden Pumpkin was an MCA client, and Henry Gendron's band was one of the first booked into the venue.[32] Austin Mack's ensemble, late of the Midnight Frolics, moved to the Pumpkin the following year and began playing for the small, four-act floor show and for dancing.[33] Following Mack was an attractive lady bass player named Thelma Terry and her orchestra.[34] Terry, whose real name was Thelma Combes, got her start as the singer-bassist in Howard Osborne's band a few years earlier at the Vanity Fair (once the Marigold Gardens). Jack Chapman's orchestra, a former Benson organization that for years played at the posh downtown Drake Hotel, moved on to Joe Enge's bandstand in the early 1930s, playing nightly not only for the diners but for WGN radio listeners.[35] The economic slowdown deeply affected business, however, and the restaurant eventually closed.

The Via Lago, Uptown Village, and the Oriole Gardens—all on the North Side—also were Chinese restaurants by virtue of the type of food they served. But by 1941, the combination of dance music and chop suey had run its course. While Chinese restaurants continue to be popular in Chicago, their counterparts that offered dining, dancing, and a floor show in the 1920s and 1930s became anachronisms. They were another fad that came and went in the panoply of leisure-time pursuits and amusements.

Public dancing in the 1930s seemed to defy the economic conditions of the early Depression years and ballrooms continued to operate. Major city venues like the Trianon, Aragon, and Paradise and the suburban Melody Mill and Oh Henry remained open with few interruptions. That is not to say all Chicago ballrooms made a lot of money in the decade. Perhaps it was the low price of admission that attracted the dancers. Another explanation was that dancing acted as a palliative that promoted feelings of well being and provided dancers a brief escape from reality.[36]

Three of the biggest ballrooms did have an economic upset or two and many others struggled at times. In 1939 the Karzas organization, operators of the Trianon and Aragon, ran into economic difficulties and had to reorganize the financial end of their businesses.[37] The giant White City dance hall at Sixty-third Street and South Parkway, already a bit shaky following the opening of the nearby Trianon ten years earlier, reduced its dancing schedule due to poor business in the early thirties, and by 1933 it fell behind on its city taxes. Creditors filed a bankruptcy plea the same year; however, dancing resumed at the White City briefly later in the decade.[38]

The repeal of Prohibition and the opening of the Century of Progress world's fair were welcome events in an otherwise gloomy economic period during the early 1930s, but when the fair closed in 1934 much of the economic euphoria it fostered evaporated. A number of new nightclubs opened their doors during the thirties but there wasn't much else to buoy up optimism in the entertainment sector. Many of the pricier hotel show rooms struggled for survival in the wake of the world's fair. Hotel occupancy rates dropped dramatically as fewer business travelers visited the city. The hotels' more affluent clientele or those not greatly affected by the economic hard times were not enough to stave off economic trouble. Some hotels closed their show rooms for short periods or longer. Others filed for bankruptcy or went into receivership. Better times were coming in the 1940s, but no one could know that the next decade was the beginning of the end for the dance bands.

# 13 The Last Hurrah

BUSINESS looked promising for the dance bands as the 1940s dawned. The buildup for World War II in Europe, which the United States would enter in 1941, had brought with it some modest economic prosperity. This in turn put money in the public's pockets, some of which was spent for entertainment and dancing. While the entertainment business in general boomed during the war years, it became clear by the late 1940s, as the country returned to peace, that the interest in dancing and dance bands was still strong but beginning to fade. The signs were numerous; the public's growing interest in the new broadcast technology called television, the dramatic increases in labor and other costs brought on by the war, major changes in demographics, and shifts in popular music tastes were just a few of them. The American Federation of Musicians launched two long work bans against the record companies, in 1942–43 and again in 1948, during which union musicians made no records. The bans not only were unpopular with the public but deeply affected sales of recorded instrumental music from that point forward. Other branches of the entertainment business were affected as well. The 1940s proved clearly to be dancing's last hurrah.

But none of these things were apparent at the end of the 1930s. The dance band business seemed to be recovering after a few less-than-spectacular years during the depths of the Great Depression although some dance bands, especially the better-known sweet bands like those of Guy Lombardo and Wayne King, had some of their best years during the Depression.[1]

The swing bands during the late 1930s added robustness to the dance band industry as it entered the new decade. Four hundred or more theaters in the United States featured entertainment and dance bands. Hotels alone were said to be spending ten million dollars a year for bands and entertainers, and the number of job opportunities for dance bands to play on radio, in nightclubs, and in other venues was said to be greater than at any time in the industry's history.[2]

The bands kept getting bigger in size. The standard nine-man dance orchestra of the 1920s had swollen in numbers through the later thirties and continued to grow into the forties. Bands now had four or five saxophones, up to five or six brass, and a standard four-piece rhythm section of piano, string bass, drums, and guitar. Some leaders added string sections for the first time.

After the United States entered World War II, war production and military activity went into high gear and the economy expanded enormously. The tempo of the entertainment business picked up noticeably. In spite of the popularity of large dance bands, there was a growing demand for combos—from a duo to five or six pieces—to play in the increasing number of smaller clubs and cocktail lounges, a new name for bars. A wartime cabaret tax on dancing and certain forms of entertainment forced many club and cocktail lounge operators to remove their dance floors rather than add the additional tax to patrons' tabs.[3] In these venues, combos and small bands (singers were considered entertainment) now began performing for entertainment rather than dancing, a significant change in focus from previous decades.

The cabaret tax did not apply to ballrooms; instead those venues had their own 20 percent tax, which was added to the admission price. Business during the war was never better. The Aragon and Trianon ballrooms were open seven nights a week to accommodate the dramatic increase in business from the service men and women, thousands of whom were stationed at Great Lakes Naval Training Center and at Fort Sheridan north of Chicago. The city's smaller ballrooms plus the Melody Mill and Oh Henry ballrooms to the west and southwest also expanded their operating schedules for the increased crowds. It clearly must have seemed to the ballroom operators like the 1920s again.

The Loop buzzed with activity. Although two major South Michigan Avenue hotels, the Stevens and the Congress, were commandeered as military housing for service men and women taking training in the city in 1942, the hostelries were returned to civilian hands the following year. The downtown hotel bars and, to a lesser extent, the hotel show rooms had enjoyed the extra business from this military presence, which was welcome after some bad years in the Depression. Many major hotel show rooms had gone dark in the early and mid-thirties.

Some of the Chicago dance bands of the 1920s that had formed the backbone of MCA's catalog of bands in the following decade continued to be active in Chicago and environs into the 1940s. With a few exceptions, many had become the unheralded day-to-day workhorses of the agency. Art Kassel and Charlie Agnew, when not traveling in the Midwest territory, played long annual engagements in Chicago, Kassel at the Bismarck and Agnew at the Edgewater Beach and Stevens hotels. Don Bestor had relocated to the East Coast by the early thirties to play for a season on the Jack Benny radio show and became a steady income producer for many hotels and restaurants, if not a big name in the business. Frankie Masters was by the end of the thirties playing at the Essex House, the Roosevelt, and the Taft hotels in New York City and producing hit records.

Wayne King, the waltz king whose orchestra had outgrown the mammoth Aragon Ballroom by the mid-thirties, was playing at major hotels throughout the country when not on theater stages or cashing in on the one-nighter trail. By 1935 on the strength of its three-times-a-week Lady Esther network radio broadcasts and Victor recordings, the band was said to be earning between ten and fourteen thousand dollars per week.[4]

In the meantime, MCA brought several popular West Coast dance bands to Chicago in the 1930s to fill the bandstands of its ever-expanding number of contract locations. Anson Weeks, Earl Burtnett, Dick Jurgens, Carl Ravazza, Ray Herbeck, and Griff Williams all became favorites in the Chicago and Midwest territory. Burtnett and Jurgens played long engagements in the Drake Hotel and in the city's ballrooms and restaurants. Williams settled into the Palmer House's Empire Room in the early 1940s after a successful engagement at the Congress Hotel. In fact, the Williams band was contracted to stay at the Palmer House for the duration of the war, but Williams enlisted in the navy before the war's end, breaking up the band. With these bands and many others during the late thirties and forties, Chicago's hotels were in clover. Weeks, Burtnett, Jurgens, and Williams all moved their headquarters to Chicago to capitalize on their growing popularity in the Midwest.

During the late thirties, Ted Weems and his band had been alternating at the Karzas Brothers' Trianon Ballroom with Kay Kyser, whose newfound popularity at the Blackhawk Restaurant and his *Kollege of Musical Knowledge* radio show quickly made him a national name band. Weems and his musicians, another early Chicago-based band from the 1920s, gained a good share of fame through their weekly NBC network show, *Beat the Band,* which conveniently emanated from the Chicago studios in the Merchandise Mart. Weems also had become a national touring band for MCA and a steady income earner.

As the 1940s dawned, the bands of Lawrence Welk and Don Reid assumed the house-band chores at the Trianon as Kyser moved on to New York and Hollywood and Weems disbanded to enlist in the merchant marine. The Welk and Reid bands drew big crowds to the Trianon during the war years as did their counterparts at the Aragon, George Olsen and Henry King.

A few of the 1920s Chicago bands had dropped out along the way or lost their musical appeal. Charlie Straight, one of MCA's earliest 1920s leaders, had been dropped by the agency by 1930, as had Al Katz. Dan Russo, so famous in Chicago when he and the pianist Ted FioRito were co-leaders of the Oriole Terrace Orchestra at the Edgewater Beach Hotel and the Aragon, continued to play major Chicago engagements and tour the Midwest with a smaller band until 1937.

The bars and small clubs along Randolph and Clark Streets and throughout the city, however, cashed in on the wartime business. Small combos dominated the entertainment in these clubs. While limited dancing was allowed at first, club managers took out their dance floors after the federal cabaret tax on dancing became law. Booking agencies such as Frederick Brothers and the McConkey agency specialized in providing small combos and acts to these clubs and others throughout the Midwest and East.

There was a parallel demand for solo pianists and organists by 1940, by which time the Hammond electric organ had become popular. Many restaurants and cocktail lounges hired organists or pianists where before they didn't have any musical entertainment. Some musicians felt that the Hammond organ put many of the smaller bands out of business because of the variety of sounds and volume it produced. Whether the electric organ resulted in a net gain or loss of work for musicians will never be known.

The explosion of small-group music in Chicago from the late 1930s to the mid-1950s was significant. There was so much combo and solo work for musicians in Chicago during this period that many sidemen left dance bands to join the small ensembles. For musicians who had been working in traveling bands, local small groups provided a more stable life, and the informality and lack of structure in combos gave many sidemen a freedom of expression not possible in the big bands.

Music and entertainment activity in the downtown area was never brisker than during the World War II years, 1941–45. Most of the dancing in the Loop and environs, however, was in the big hotels and a few small ballrooms. Music for listening, on the other hand, was another subject. Patrons seated at a bar or in adjacent booths now expected to be entertained, not just serenaded by the musicians, so the combos began improving their showmanship and adding lively, often humorous routines to their musical repertoires.

A string of bars and nightclubs (the latter term applied to almost any venue presenting music and entertainment) opened along Randolph Street. The street had been a magnet for entertainment since the 1920s and before, anchored on the west by the Bismarck and Sherman hotels and by the Blackhawk Restaurant on the east at Wabash. Also lined up along Randolph were the giant Palace, United Artists, Garrick, Woods, and Oriental theaters. On Dearborn just north of Randolph were the Selwyn and Harris legitimate theaters and on State Street, north and south of Randolph, were the Chicago, Roosevelt, and State and Lake theaters. All of this entertainment concentrated within five blocks by the 1940s made Randolph Street the show business mecca for the city and the Midwest.

In the two blocks of Randolph just west of State Street were located the Preview (7 West), Latin Quarter (23–29 West), Band Box (36 West), Brass Rail (52 West), Hollywood Lounge (87 West), and the Garrick (100 West). The Latin Quarter was the biggest of these venues (it could accommodate several hundred patrons) and featured full-blown floor shows with name entertainers and a nine-piece orchestra. Ralph Berger opened his second-floor nightclub in the early 1940s when business from service men and women and civilians was booming. The club occupied the space that previously had been the Oriental Gardens Chinese restaurant during the 1930s.

The Latin Quarter competed with the Chez Paree in attracting top name entertainers and bands. In 1944 Ted Lewis brought to the room his show and band, which then featured the jazzmen Muggsy Spanier, Georg Brunis, and Tony Parenti.[5] The following year the veteran Chicago saxophonist Buddy Shaw succeeded Irwin Kostal, an arranger and pianist, as leader of the nine-piece house band that backed the acts. Shaw recalls that the first performer to appear there during his time as leader was the popular cabaret entertainer Harry Richman.[6] Following in close order were attractions such as Martha Rae, the Ritz Brothers, the pianist Dorothy Donnegan, the young comedians Joey Bishop and Buddy Lester, and the former child movie star Jane Withers.

Several large dance bands appeared at the Latin Quarter, the Rhumba Casino, and the Oriental Ballroom atop the Oriental Theater building in the early 1940s, but few others played in the Loop outside of the hotels and the Blackhawk. Most of the smaller clubs featured combos for listening. In 1945, however, the Band Box began featuring such big bands as Boyd Raeburn, Jess Stacy, Joe Sanders, Lionel Hampton, and George Winslow, although small jazz combos headed by Art Tatum and Jay McShann were the usual fare.[7] The Brass Rail and the Preview Lounge also leaned heavily toward jazz combos, mostly fronted by well-known players like Red Norvo, Charlie Ventura, Roy Eldridge, and Jack Teagarden. Small units headed by the local jazzmen Porky Panico, Art Hodes, and Eddie Wiggins also were featured, often as second attractions.

Joe Sherman's Garrick and Hollywood lounges had a similar format with the hot violinist Stuff Smith; Red Allen; Walter Fuller, formerly of the Earl Hines band; and the Chicago drummer and trumpeter Phil Dooley leading combos. A block or so farther west on Randolph was the Dome Lounge, on the southeast corner of the Sherman Hotel, which featured many small combos and solo pianists over the years. Jules Herbuveaux heard the Art Van Damme quartet at the Dome and in his capacity as program director for NBC Chicago hired the group for the network, an engagement that lasted fifteen years.

The Capitol Lounge just north of Randolph on State Street showcased popular attractions ranging from the singer-drummer-leader Harry Cool to the violinist Eddie South. Located across an alley just south of the Chicago Theater, the lounge attracted a lot of after-theater business. In the block north of the Capitol Lounge, on the northwest corner of State and Lake Streets, was Sam Beer's Three Deuces, a downtown music institution since 1927.[8] It derived its name from its address, 222 North State Street. Local and out-of-town musicians were welcomed at the club and it very quickly became a hangout for them because of the frequent jam sessions held there late at night.

During the thirties, the jazz musicians Roy Eldridge, Wingy Manone, Zutty Singleton, and Art Tatum led small combos in the downstairs show room. A smaller room upstairs featured mostly pianists, vocalists, and small groups on a postage-stamp-sized bandstand behind the bar. Art Tatum, when not fronting a group downstairs, frequently was at the piano in the upstairs room. In the mid-thirties the downstairs room became the Off-Beat Club. A fire in 1940 destroyed the building housing the clubs and put the bands of Baby Dodds and Stuff Smith then playing there out on the street.[9] The remains of the building were torn down and replaced by a new building in 1941, the first floor of which became home of the Rhumba Casino.[10]

Latin dance music, a fad during the late 1930s and early 1940s, was the feature at the new place. Eddie LeBaron's and Arne Barnett's bands appeared there along with Don Pedro's combo in 1941 and 1942. The club later became the Shangri-La Restaurant, owned by Frankie Harmon, nephew of Paddy Harmon, who operated the Dreamland and Arcadia ballrooms in the 1920s and who built the Chicago Stadium. The Shangri-La was razed in 1981 to make room for a new hotel.

While jazz music is not within the purview of this study, a few of the larger clubs that featured the music are noteworthy here. The small-combo trend accelerated in the late 1940s as the Dixieland jazz revival came into full bloom in Chicago. Many dance-band musicians left the road and gravitated into the clubs where they could express their individual talents in the traditional jazz band environment.

There were a number of major jazz clubs in or near the Loop. Jazz Ltd. was located in an old brownstone on Grand Avenue, just east of State Street, and seated only eighty-one people. The Blue Note, at 56 West Madison Street, was much larger. Both opened in 1947 and had basement locations, but the similarities ended there. Jazz Ltd., operated by Bill and Ruth Reinhardt, was one of the earliest clubs to cash in on the Dixieland jazz revival. Featured was a house band of rotating personnel including some of the big names in traditional jazz such as Sidney Bechet and Muggsy Spanier. Bill Reinhardt, a clarinet player as well as the co-owner of the establishment, was the only permanent member of the band.[11]

The Blue Note had a more eclectic jazz format than Jazz Ltd. and featured everything from Dixieland through contemporary performers to some of the more modern jazz artists like Dave Brubeck. Even though the confines were a bit tight, Frank Holzfeind managed to shoehorn the big bands of Duke Ellington, Count Basie, and Stan Kenton into his basement club.[12] The Blue Note moved to 3 North Clark Street in 1953. The second-floor quarters were much roomier and could easily accommodate big bands such as those of Ellington and Chico O'Farrell. The Blue Note closed in 1960, however, primarily because the bands, big and small, became too expensive.

Jazz Ltd., on the other hand, lasted until 1972 and had moved to a new location farther east on Grand Avenue.[13] It was the longest-lived jazz club in Chicago up to that time. More than six hundred traditional jazz musicians rotated through the Jazz Ltd. bands in its twenty-five year history.

There were numerous other jazz clubs sprinkled along North Clark Street just north of the Chicago River, such as the Liberty Inn, the Hi-Note, the New Apex Club, and, on State Street, the Airliner. All of these clubs featured combos, mostly jazz groups, in which many dance-band musicians found employment. Another big center of small traditional or Dixieland jazz clubs was on the North Side in Uptown, that area around the intersection of Lawrence and Broadway Avenues. Most notable and the longer lasting of these jazz venues were the 1111 Club, at 1111 West Bryn Mawr Avenue, and Rupneck's, a few blocks to the north on Thorndale. The Normandy Lounge in the Aragon building, just east of Broadway on Lawrence, and Helsing's Vod'vil Lounge, to the southeast in the 4300 block of North Sheridan Road, were two other mainstays during the late 1940s and early 1950s.

Another club of interest in the Uptown area was the 5100 Club, located at that address on North Broadway Avenue. The 5100 Club had been operating since the late 1930s and featured variety acts and small dance bands of some note, such as those of Horace Henderson and Mark Fisher, the latter the stage bandleader from the twenties and thirties.[14] But the person who put the 5100 Club on the map was a comedian by the name of Danny Thomas. As his reputation as an entertainer grew, the 5100 Club became a "must" stop on the rounds of the city night-clubbers. Thomas became the successful star of his own television show and later a successful producer of other TV shows.

A number of clubs in the South Side black district attracted a sizable white audience during the 1940s. The venerable Club DeLisa on South State Street, owned by the DeLisa brothers, who were white, and the recycled Swingland, now called Rhumboogie, were both holdovers from the mid-1930s, as was the Grand Terrace Café, which was reviewed earlier. New on the scene was the El Grotto, in the Pershing Hotel basement; the Sutherland Lounge, just off the Sutherland Hotel lobby; and the Bee Hive, a Dixieland club and later a modern jazz venue, near the University of Chicago campus.

The three DeLisa brothers—Michael, James, and Louis—founded one of the city's best known and longest lived nightclubs in Chicago, Club DeLisa, in 1935.[15] The club's first modest venue was in a second-floor room on State Street just south of Fifty-fifth Street. Only black bands and acts were featured at DeLisa. Hal Draper led a band there called the Arcadians, which played for dancing and accompanied the small floor shows. Although the club flourished, it was burned out of its first location and, in two moves, ended up across the street at 5521 South State in a building built especially for the DeLisa brothers.[16]

As the club's reputation grew, bigger and better-known dance bands were brought in to provide the music. Between 1935 and the early 1940s, the bands of Albert Ammons, Jesse Miller, Del Bright, Junie Cobb, Ray Nance, Fletcher Henderson, Tommy Powell (with the Hi Dee Ho Boys), and the drummer Red Saunders played for dancing and the show.[17] Saunders practically became an institution at Club DeLisa, playing there from 1938 to 1946.[18] The club closed in the 1950s like many others as times and tastes in entertainment changed.

In the early 1940s the heavyweight boxing champion Joe Louis, just reaching his peak in popularity, and Marshall Miles bought an interest in Swingland, 343 East Garfield Boulevard, from Charlie Glenn and changed the name to the Rhumboogie.[19]

Floyd Campbell, by now a very popular bandleader and entertainer on the South Side, led the first band at the newly renamed club. Marl Young, a talented pianist, tenor saxist, and arranger, did musical arrangements for the shows and rehearsed the entertainers. Following Campbell's group were the Jeter-Pillars band and those of Milt Larkin, Slam Stewart, Marl Young, and Slim Gaillard. Sarah Vaughn also appeared there as a young singer. The club closed in 1947 allegedly for being delinquent in paying taxes.

To the north along Thirty-fifth Street, the bandleader Earl Hines left the Grand Terrace Café in 1940, breaking up his show band in the process. He formed a new, more modern-sounding unit and went back on the road. About 1944 he took the new band into the basement club of the Pershing Hotel, just a block south of the Sixty-third and Cottage Grove intersection. The club was renamed El Grotto and a few years later Hines became the club's co-proprietor.[20] When Hines and the band hit the road, other South Side groups came in to back the fairly elaborate floor shows. The bands of Sonny Thompson and Walter Dyett were two of them. Singers like Johnny Hartman and June Davis plus a chorus line were featured in the shows. Between shows a combo played for dancing. One of the off-night relief bands to play El Grotto was that of the white bandleader Jay Burkhart, which was one of the most musically progressive groups of the day. Too much red ink on the club's books finally drove Hines to liquidate his interest, and the El Grotto closed in 1947.[21]

Sol Tananbaum's Bee Hive was located at 1503 East Fifty-fifth Street, near the University of Chicago campus in Hyde Park, during the late 1940s and early 1950s. It drew a large share of its audience from the college students. The Bee Hive featured many Dixieland groups, such as those led by Doc Evans, Miff Mole, and Booker T. Washington.[22] The Slim Gaillard group was a popular attraction at the Bee Hive and the bassist Slam Stewart's band also occasionally was booked for engagements there. Both bands had been popular previously at the Rhumboogie. The intermission pianists were Don Ewell or the boogie-woogie artist Jimmy Yancey, both in longtime residence at the Bee Hive. The club later installed a more progressive jazz policy featuring Lester Young, Max Roach, Clifford Brown, Sonny Stitt, Ira Sullivan, Charlie Parker, and others.

Entertainment in the late 1940s and early 1950s wasn't all small combos and Dixieland bands playing in cocktail lounges and small nightclubs. As Chicago's population began moving into the northern, western, and southern suburbs after World War II, a number of large new clubs opened in the 1950s to serve their entertainment needs. In the southern suburbs were the Condessa del Mar in Alsip, Field's Supper Club and Tony DeSantis's Martinique Restaurant in Oak Lawn, the Sabre Room, and Ray Columb's on Eighty-seventh Street. The Condessa del Mar and Field's both had large floor shows with nationally known celebrities and large dance bands.

Tony DeSantis's Martinique Restaurant, at 9750 South Western Avenue in Oak Lawn, favored the sweet bands of Art Kassel, Jimmy Featherstone, Freddie Nagel, Ray Pearl, and Gay Claridge. Opened in the late 1940s, DeSantis's place kept the dance-band policy going until 1971; Gay Claridge was the last band to play in the restaurant. In the meantime, however, DeSantis started producing plays, first in a tent alongside the restaurant, later inside a specially built theater called Drury Lane.[23] Successful in this venture, he later opened several other theaters in different parts of the city, and one of them still operates today.

Frank Mangam and his wife, Helen, opened Mangam's Chateau in an old roadhouse in southwest suburban Lyons in 1945.[24] The couple staged rather grandiose shows in the large club using mostly second-tier celebrities or entertainers from an earlier era, such as Sally Rand and the Duncan Sisters. A chorus line of twelve complemented the large dance band and featured acts at the Chateau. In an effort to recapture the halcyon days of the thirties, the club, under new management by the 1970s, hired the Victor Lombardo orchestra to play for dancing, but the time for big shows—even smaller "tab" versions of Broadway shows—was over and the club eventually closed. The club probably outlasted the decline in live shows by about ten years.

The Sky Club in west suburban Elmwood Park was another popular venue in the 1930s through the early fifties. It was a medium-sized club located near the intersection of North and Harlem Avenues and very much along the lines of earlier roadhouses. Small floor shows and dancing were presented during the 1930s and 1940s. Buddy DeVito, Jay Burkhart and Carl Schreiber, Lee Bennett's orchestra, and traveling bands played at the club occasionally during this period. During the late 1940s, the management brought in Georg Brunis and a Dixieland combo in an attempt to capitalize on the Dixie revival. A few other Dixie groups followed Brunis, but presenting live music was a short-lived effort at the Sky Club. The club reverted to presenting a few dance bands but closed after a fire.

The era had run its course, and entrepreneurs, bookers, and bandleaders could see the work drying up. It was a difficult pill to swallow because dance bands had prospered just a few years earlier, during World War II. Traveling dance bands alone brought in about $145 million per year between 1941 and 1945, according to James C. Petrillo, the president of the American Federation of Musicians, and that didn't count the dance bands playing in semipermanent locations or the jobbing bands that played incidental engagements.[25] But traveling bands also had to deal with wartime rationing of gasoline and tires, higher-priced and often sold-out hotels, higher musicians' salaries brought on by wartime prosperity and competition from other bands, and the loss of musicians to the draft. Leaders also had to keep their old vehicles patched up and running, often at great expense, because no civilian automobiles, trucks, or buses were manufactured during the war.

Following the war there was an immediate surge in dancing and dance-band activity as the returning soldiers and sailors tried to make up for lost time away from home. Driven by this demand for entertainment, it seemed like old times again. The Aragon and Trianon continued to do land-office business.[26] People flocked downtown to the Chicago, Oriental, and State and Lake movie theaters to see the movies and stage shows. With business particularly good in the music bars and clubs along Randolph Street and in the North and South Side entertainment hubs, the postwar entertainment and music business maintained a healthy glow. If there were economic storm clouds on the horizon, nobody paid much attention.

Business in the city's five largest ballrooms—the Aragon, Trianon, Paradise, Melody Mill, and Oh Henry—began to slow down by the early 1950s. The establishments still employed dance bands on a regular schedule but the dancers weren't clicking through the turnstiles like before. The segregated Trianon ultimately closed in 1954 amid pressures from the black population demanding entry. Melody Mill and Oh Henry, however, continued to prosper moderately because the great migration of families to the suburbs was bringing dancers into the west and southwest areas they served. Only the Willowbrook, successor to the Oh Henry, and the newer Glendora remain open today and rely mostly on catering parties. The others succumbed to the change in entertainment habits by the 1960s.

Many 1920s Chicago dance bands such as those led by Joe Sanders and Charlie Agnew, which were so important to MCA in the early years of the business, often were relegated to second-class status in the rapidly changing music world by 1940. As a result they missed the later big-earning days for bands. Younger, more contemporary groups recruited by the New York and Los Angeles offices replaced them at the top of the batting order at MCA and other agencies.

Times and the style of music changed in the thirties but many of the Chicago bands did not change, severely limiting their salability. Once again history shined its light on the harsh truth that dance bands were a business; the marketplace bestowed success on those bands that could best adapt to change.

Ralph Williams and Mark Fisher, big local names as bandleaders in the 1920s and to a lesser extent in the 1930s, had faded into near obscurity. They ended their careers playing clubs as singles by the late forties. Charlie Straight, another popular leader, by the late 1930s played only occasional nights and on weekends. Straight was killed tragically in 1940 while working in his new day job with the Metropolitan Sanitary District.[27] Al Turk, the longtime bandleader at the Princess Ballroom, and Dan Russo, who with Ted FioRito was so popular at the Edgewater Beach Hotel in the 1920s and later, had retired by 1940. Other bandleaders left the music business during the 1930s and took other jobs ranging from postmen to building contractors.

By 1946, the 20 percent wartime cabaret tax was proving to be a drag on the music business. It was supposed to expire in June 1947 but, to the surprise and disappointment of club operators, Congress renewed the tax just before its scheduled expiration. Some nightclub and hotel dining room operators reported business declined as much as 50 percent because of the tax. The College Inn actually closed down in 1948 partly to protest the tax.[28] Local 10's reduction of the musicians' work week in 1951 from six to five days, but at the same pay, put additional economic pressure on club operators.[29] To compensate for the increased cost of a relief band to play on the sixth night, some operators dropped one or more musicians from the payroll or, in more extreme cases, terminated entire bands or combos.

By the mid-1950s the dance bands were nearing the end of the line. Many traveling dance bands had decided to call it quits by then; the costs were making it a losing proposition for leaders and operators alike. Ballrooms, now struggling to stay afloat with decreasing attendance and increasing band costs, were either closing or hiring local bands. A few top name bands carried on into the 1960s, some under new leaders, but they were the last of the breed.

The much-heralded dance-band or big-band era lasted only about thirty-five years—from 1920 to 1955. It was just a moment in the sweep of history, but it was an exciting period in the annals of American entertainment. The dance bands were a product of the dancing craze sweeping the nation in general and Chicago in particular. Their rise in popularity coincided with the emergence of three technologies: phonograph recording, commercial radio broadcasting, and talking motion pictures. Few other segments of the late nineteenth- and early twentieth-century entertainment industry, with the possible exception of motion pictures, have been so well documented—both aurally and visually.

This confluence of bands and the growing popularity of phonograph records and radio broadcasting, in particular, and, to a lesser extent, talking motion pictures created a synergy that resulted in the birth of the enormous dance-band industry. Phonograph records helped sustain the dance bands' popularity but it was radio broadcasting that became the dance bands' great ally. The partnership, albeit strained at times, was mutually beneficial and continued into the 1950s.

The musicians union recording bans in 1942–43 and again in 1948 hit the dance-band industry hard.[30] These bans on making records were unpopular with the public, but they were a part of James Petrillo's ongoing opposition to mechanical music, which he claimed deprived musicians of work. No band recordings were made of currently popular tunes during the bans, leaving the field open to popular singers who didn't have to belong to the musicians union. It was an unprecedented opportunity for the vocalists to capture the public's attention and they took full advantage of it. By the late 1940s, vocalists became the new darlings of show business. Frank Sinatra, Perry Como, and Dinah Shore—just a few of the beneficiaries of this new interest in vocalists—now had their own radio shows. Seeing where the profits were, the record companies began heavily promoting the vocalists at the expense of dance bands.[31] Not surprisingly, the dance bands had one of their worst years in 1949, the year after the second recording moratorium was ended.[32]

If radio helped create the success of dance bands, it was television that helped seal their fate. With the exception of Lawrence Welk's orchestra, the dance bands never did very well on the highly visual new medium after a few successful shows in the early 1950s. Several popular radio shows such as Kay Kyser's *Kollege of Musical Knowledge* moved to television but never captured the same excitement and popularity of the radio version. Watching a dance band perform on television just wasn't lively enough for people who now were becoming conditioned to more visual and active entertainment. Lawrence Welk's format of presenting what amounted to a stage show of variety acts—singers, dancers, and other performers—seemed to meet the new performance standards without sacrificing the nostalgia of dance bands, a capability no other band seemed to have.

It was all of these issues and probably a few others that finally overpowered the dance bands. The low point for the dance bands may have been in 1949 but it took another decade for the industry to go through its death throes. If a date and event can be said to mark officially the point when the industry came to an end it probably would be in 1962 when MCA, the company that had practically invented the modern dance-band business, dissolved its talent agency. By then bands produced only a small share of the company's income. MCA, always forward-looking and constantly reinventing itself with the times, by then had major holdings in motion pictures, records, television production, and other lucrative ventures, some outside the entertainment field. Ultimately it became as successful with these new businesses as it had been with dance bands thirty years earlier.

The dance band business had been a giant star that lighted up the entertainment sky in the United States for nearly four decades. Many of the millions of dancers and listeners who lived during that era as well as the leaders, musicians, and others in the industry thought the music would never end. But it did end. For future generations interested in learning about twentieth-century popular music, however, abundant evidence of the past glamorous days of the dance bands awaits discovery.

# Appendix A

Maps of Important Chicago Dance Venues, 1900–1950

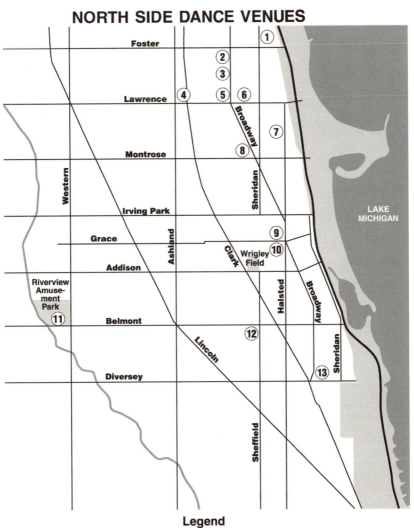

## NORTH SIDE DANCE VENUES

### Legend

1. Edgewater Beach Hotel
2. Winona Gardens
3. 5100 Club
4. Rainbo Gardens
5. Green Mill Gardens
6. Aragon Ballroom
7. Alamo (Via Lago) Café
8. Arcadia Ballroom
9. Vogue Ballroom
10. Marigold Gardens
11. Riverview Ballroom
12. Merry Garden Ballroom
13. Rendezvous Café

# DOWNTOWN DANCE VENUES

Lake

Randolph

Washington

Madison

Monroe

Adams

Jackson

VanBuren

Chicago River

Wacker

Wells

LaSalle

Clark

Dearborn

State

Wabash

Michigan

Grant Park

Art Institute

1 Three Deuces
2 Chicago Theater
3 Sherman Hotel
4 Garrick Lounge
5 Lamb's (Bamboo Inn)
6 Brass Rail
7 Band Box
8 Capitol Lounge
9 Bismarck Hotel
10 Palace Theater
11 Hollywood Lounge
12 Latin Quarter
13 Preview Lounge
14 Blackhawk Restaurant

## Legend

15 LaSalle Hotel
16 Blue Note #2
17 Blue Note #1
18 Morrison Hotel
19 Palmer House
20 Friar's Inn
21 Royal Frolics
22 Normandie Hotel
23 Congress Hotel
24 Blackstone Hotel
25 Stevens (Conrad Hilton) Hotel
26 Freiberg's (Midnight Frolics)
27 Colosimo's

Cermak    22nd Street

# WEST SIDE DANCE VENUES

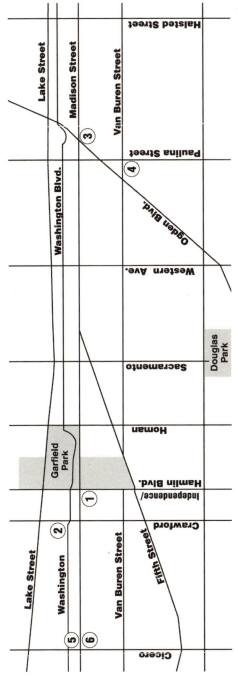

## Legend

1. Driscoll's Danceland (Golden Pumpkin)
2. Paradise Ballroom
3. Princess Ballroom
4. Dreamland Ballroom
5. Byrd Ballroom
6. Keyman's Club

# SOUTH SIDE DANCE VENUES

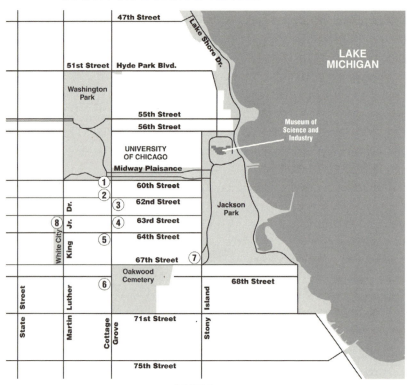

## Legend

1. Midway Gardens Ballroom
2. Merry Garden Ballroom
3. Trianon Ballroom
4. Tivoli Theater
5. Pershing Hotel
6. Granada Café
7. Southmoor Hotel
8. White City Ballroom

# Appendix B

## Major Chicago Dance Venues and the Bands That Played There

The venues are listed alphabetically; the bands are generally listed in the order in which they played at a venue.

*Alamo Café (Via Lago), 837 W. Wilson Ave.*
Al Handler, Jean Goldkette (Harold Stokes), Earl Hoffman

*Aragon Ballroom, 1106 W. Lawrence Ave.*
FioRito-Russo Oriole Terrace Orchestra, Al Morey, Wayne King, Orville Knapp, Anson Weeks, Freddy Martin, Griff Williams, Dick Jurgens, Eddie Howard, Henry King, Billy Bishop, George Olsen, Teddy Phillips, most name bands and sweet orchestras

*Arcadia Ballroom, 4444 N. Broadway Ave.*
Al Copeland, George Mallen, Sol Wagner, Joe Kayser, Charles Elgar, Clifford "Klarinet" King, Walter Barnes's Royal Creoleans, Leon Bloom

*Beverly Gardens, Ninety-first St. and Western Ave.*
Robinson's Syncopators, Hughie Swift, Vernon Roulette, Henry Crowder's Washingtonians, Clarence Black, Corey Lynn

*Bismarck Hotel, 171 W. Randolph St.*
The Flamingo Orchestra, Cope Harvey, Art Kassel, Eddie Varzos, Phil Levant, Pinky Aarseth, Leonard Keller, Jimmy Joy, Sherman Hayes, Don Reid, Benny Strong

*Blackhawk Restaurant, 139 N. Wabash Ave.*
Paul Biese, Frank Westphal, Charlie Straight, Ralph Williams, Ralph Ginsburg, Coon-Sanders Kansas City Nighthawks, George Konchar, Ben Pollack, Herbie Kay, Earl Burtnett, Hal Kemp, Kay Kyser, Bob Crosby, Red Norvo, Jack Teagarden, Johnny "Scat" Davis, Chico Marx, Carl Ravazza, Ted FioRito, Les Brown, Harry Cool, Art Kassel, Eddie Howard, Gay Claridge, Henry Brandon, many other name bands

*Blue Fountain Room (LaSalle Hotel), 10 N. LaSalle St.*
Jean Goldkette, Carl Rupp, George Nachstadter, Gus Edwards, Jack Chapman, Doc Davis, Lew Diamond, Husk O'Hare, George Devron, Del Coon, Bob Mc-Grew, Buddy Fisher, Little Jack Little, Stuff Smith Sextet, Milt Herth Trio, Charlie Agnew, others

*Booster's Club (Morrison Hotel), 79 W. Madison St.*
Bert Kelly

*Boulevard Room (Stevens, later Conrad Hilton, Hotel), 720 S. Michigan Ave.*
Jack Chapman, Armand Hand, Paul Ash, Roy Bargy, Dave Peyton, Husk O'Hare, Doc Davis, Ralph Foote, Frankie Masters, Little Jackie Heller, George Devron, Carlos Molina, Harry James, Duke Ellington, Bernie Cummins, George Olsen, Chuck Foster, Griff Williams, Orrin Tucker, Don McGrane, Benny Strong, Gay Claridge, Norm Krone, Frank Bettencourt

*Brilliant Ballroom (also Playdium), 3825 W. Madison St.*
Arnold Johnson

*Buttery (Ambassador West Hotel), 1300 N. State St.*
Romeo Meltz

*Byrd Ballroom, 4728 W. Madison St.*
Carl Schreiber

*Camellia House (Drake Hotel), 140 E. Walton St.*
Jimmy Blade, Bill Snyder, Dick Judson, Victor Lombardo

*Castle Gardens, Quincy and State St.*
Husk O'Hare, Joe "King" Oliver, Jelly Roll Morton

*Chateau (Andy Anderson's; later, Vogue Ballroom), 3810 N. Broadway Ave.*
Gordon Birch, Gay Claridge, Carl Sands, others

*Chevy Chase Country Club, Milwaukee Ave. near Lake-Cook Road, Wheeling*
Henri Lishon, Freddy Martin, Teddy Lee, Jack Morgan, Don Glasser/Lois Costello, Buddy Pressner, Mitch Smalley, Sammy Marino, others

*Chez Pierre, 247 E. Ontario St.*
Earl Hoffman

*College Inn (Sherman Hotel), 112 W. Randolph St.*
Rigo and his Gypsy Orchestra, Walter Blaufus, Paul Biese, Bert Kelly, Isham Jones, Vincent Rose, Maurie Sherman, Abe Lyman, Ray Miller, Ted Lewis, Red Nichols, Ben Bernie, Coon-Sanders, George Olsen, Al Trace, Frankie Masters, Buddy Rogers, Bill Snyder, Peter Palmer, others

*College Inn Porterhouse (Sherman Hotel), 112 W. Randolph St.*
Frank York

*Colosimo's, 2126 S. Wabash Ave.*
Peter DeQuarto, Jimmy Meo, Bernie Fisher, Ada Leonard, others

*Columbia Ballroom, 1527 N. Clark St.*
Harry Plattenberg's "McGuire's Ice Cream Kings," Sig Meyer, Jimmy Bell, others

*Congress Hotel, 520 S. Michigan Ave.*
Paul Whiteman's Collegians, Coon-Sanders Kansas City Nighthawks, Abe Lyman, Husk O'Hare, George Mallen, Ben Bernie, Fletcher Henderson. Henry King, Vincent Lopez, Eddie Duchin, Jack Russell, Harry Sosnick, Phil Levant, George Devron, Benny Goodman, Duke Ellington, Casa Loma Orchestra, Ben Pollack, Will Back, Wayne Muir, Dick Sarlo

*Drake Hotel, 140 E. Walton St.*
Jack Chapman, Bobbie Meeker, Whitey Berquist

*Dreamland (Casino), 1701 W. Van Buren St.*
Frank Cavallo, Charles Elgar, Charles Cooke (Doc Cook), Clifford "Klarinet" King, Henry Marshall, Jerome DonPasqual

*Driscoll's Danceland, 3825 W. Madison St.*
Pinky Aarseth

*El Grotto (Pershing Hotel), 6400 S. Cottage Grove Ave.*
Earl Hines, Eddie South, Walter Dyett, Charlie Parker

*Embassy Ballroom, 3940 W. Fullerton Ave.*
Freddy Mills, Dan Belloc, Mitch Smalley, Gay Claridge, Tony Barren, Teddy Lee, others

*Empire Room (Palmer House), 17 E. Monroe St.*
Shep Fields, George Hamilton, Orrin Tucker, Tommy Dorsey, Guy Lombardo, Hal Kemp, Ray Noble, Griff Williams, Eddie O'Neal, Henry King, Carmen Cavallaro, Dick LaSalle, Ben Arden, Frankie Masters, Norm Krone, Norm Ladd, others

*5100 Club, 5100 N. Broadway Ave.*
Mark Fisher, Horace Henderson

*French Casino (former Rainbo Garden), 4812 N. Clark St.*
Carl Hoff, Noble Sissle

*Friar's Inn, 343 S. Wabash Ave.*
Pinky Aarseth, New Orleans Rhythm Kings, Merritt Brunies, Wingy Manone, Bill Paley

*Fritzel's (Arsonia Café), 1654 W. Madison St.*
Pinky Aarseth, Manuel Perez, Tom Brown, others

*Gold Coast Room (Drake Hotel), 140 E. Walton St.*
Paul Whiteman, Vincent Lopez, Horace Heidt, Clyde Lucas, Dick Jurgens, Wayne King, Jack Hylton, others

*Graemere Hotel, 113 N. Homan Ave.*
Don Pedro, Joe Vera

*Granada Café, 6800 S. Cottage Grove Ave.*
Ernie Caldwell, Guy Lombardo, Al Katz and his Kittens, Fred Hamm, Ted Weems, Ben Pollack, Paul Whiteman, Tiny Parham, Eddie Mallory

*Grand Auto Inn (Al Tierney's), 338 E. Thirty-fifth St.*
Clint Brush, other Bert Kelly groups

*Grand Terrace, 3955 South Parkway (first location)*
Earl Hines, Erskine Tate, Carroll Dickerson, Fletcher Henderson, Count Basie

*Grand Terrace, 313 E. Thirty-fifth St. (second location)*
Earl Hines, Louis Armstrong, Fletcher Henderson, Andy Kirk, Walter Fuller, Lionel Hampton

*Green Mill Gardens, 4806 N. Broadway Ave.*
Patricola, Bert Kelly, Henry Theiss, Arnold Johnson, Tommy Rogers, Charlie Elgar, Melody Boys, Vern Buck

*Jeffery Tavern, Seventy-ninth St. and Jeffery Blvd.*
Hughie Swift, Vernon Roulette

*Kelly's Stables, 431 N. Rush St.*
Johnny Dodds, Alcide "Yellow" Nunez, Freddie Keppard, other small jazz combos

*Madura's Danceland, 114th St. and Indianapolis Blvd., Hammond*
Howard Smith, Bernie Young, Joe Gerken, Joe Ohromis, Elmer Kaiser, Johnny Kay, Tiny Hill, Mickey Prindl, others

*Marigold (former Bismarck) Gardens, 817 W. Grace St.*
Paul Biese, Fred Hamm, Verne Buck, Isham Jones, Ralph Foote, Herb Carlin, others

*Marine Dining Room (Edgewater Beach Hotel), 5349 N. Sheridan Rd.*
Paul Biese, FioRito-Russo Oriole Terrace Orchestra, Joe Gallicchio, George Devron, Charlie Agnew, Harry Sosnick, Phil Spitalny, Paul Whiteman, Mark Fisher, Bernie Cummins, Anson Weeks, Dusty Rhoades, Del Courtney, Bill Snyder, Henry Brandon, Orrin Tucker, Gay Claridge, Wayne King, Jack Cavan, other name orchestras

*Mayfair Room (Blackstone Hotel), 636 S. Michigan Ave.*
Al Kavelin, Neil Bondshu, Dick LaSalle, Jan Garber, other bands

*Melody Mill, 2401 S. Des Plaines Ave., North Riverside*
Jack Russell, Tiny Hill, Ray Pearl, Larry Fotine, Ralph Marterie, Ernie Rudy, Larry Faith, Jimmy Palmer, most name and sweet bands

*Merry Garden (South Side), 6040 S. Cottage Grove Avenue*
Cope Harvey

*Merry Garden (North Side), 3136 N. Sheffield Ave.*
Verne Buck, Rex Maupin, Jess Hawkins, Hal Hiatt, Jack Russell, Joe Kayser, Johnny Maitland, Jimmy Bell, Walter Barnes, Charlie Agnew, Gay Claridge, Ace Brigode, Tiny Parham, others

*Midnight Frolics, 18 E. Twenty-second St.*
Jules Buffano, Austin Mack, Aarseth and Cope's Eleven Owls, Charlie Straight, Ralph Williams, Charley Kaley, Charlie Agnew, Henri Lishon

*Midway Dancing Gardens, 6000 S. Cottage Grove Ave.*
Cope Harvey, Art Kassel, Memphis Melody Boys (Elmer Schoebel), Floyd Town, Ralph Williams, Mel Stitzel

*Midway Gardens (outdoor pavilion), 6000 S. Cottage Grove Ave.*
Ted Lewis, Walter Ford, George Mallen

*Milford Ballroom, 3311 N. Milwaukee Ave.*
Hal Munro, Gay Claridge, Mitch Smalley, Don McClain, Tony Barren, Teddy Lee, others

*Montmartre, 4806 N. Broadway Ave.*
Paul Zimm, Henry Gendron, Dave Peyton

*Moulin Rouge (Royal Frolics), 416 S. Wabash Ave.*
Clarence M. Jones, Jimmy Wade, Eddie Richmond, Henri Lishon, Mark Fisher, Al Turk

*Municipal Pier (Navy Pier), Grand Ave. at the Lake*
Charles Elgar, Doc Cook, Clifford "Klarinet" King, Jerome Don Pasqual, Joe Kayser

*North American Restaurant, 36 S. State St.*
Patricola, James Henschel, various musical organizations appeared there as acts

*Oh Henry Ballroom, 8900 S. Archer Rd., Willow Springs*
Kenny's Red Peppers, Art Kassel, Ben Bernie, Clyde McCoy, Emil Flindt, Ray Herbeck, Ray Pearl, Arvin Dale (Don Reid), George Winslow, Mickey Prindl, George Winslow, Tommy Reed, Tommy Carlyn, Russ Carlyle, most sweet bands

*Oriental Ballroom, 32 W. Randolph St.*
Herbie Mintz, Dave Peyton

*Oriole Gardens, Broadway Ave. at Devon Ave.*
Don Bestor

*Pan American Room (LaSalle Hotel), 10 N. LaSalle St.*
Jose Cortez, Ralph Morrison

*Panther Room (Sherman Hotel), 112 W. Randolph St.*
Gene Krupa, Woody Herman, Duke Ellington, most every swing band

*Paradise Ballroom, 128 N. Crawford Ave. (Pulaski Rd.)*
Gordon Pouliet, Jules Herbuveaux, Herb Carlin, Louis Panico, Eddie Neibauer's Seattle Harmony Kings, Bill Davison, Charlie Agnew, Ray Parsons, Henry Gendron, Boyd Raeburn, Emil Flindt

*Pershing Hotel (also Club Bagdad), 6400 S. Cottage Grove Ave.*
Dave Peyton, Walter Ford, Doc Rudder, Bernie Cummins, Charlie Pierce, Johnny Maitland, Jimmy Dale, others

*Playdium, 1701 W. Van Buren St.*
Joe Kayser

*Princess Ballroom, 1519 W. Madison St.*
Al Turk, Mike Parsons, Jules Goldberg's Princess Serenaders

*Pump Room (Ambassador East Hotel), 1301 N. State St.*
Fabian Andre, Lou Holden, Jerry Shelton, John Kirby, Emil Petti, Dave LeWinter, Chauncey Gray, Stanley Paul, Romeo Meltz

*Rainbo Ballroom, 4812 N. Clark St.*
Tommy Dorsey, Johnny Scat Davis, Bobby Sherwood, Les Brown, Stan Kenton, Jay Burkhart, Teddy Phillips, Arnie Barnett

*Rainbo Garden, 4812 N. Clark St.*
Isham Jones, Frank Westphal, Ralph Williams, Al Katz and His Kittens, Charlie Straight, Jack Chapman, Waddy Wadsworth, Sol Wagner, others

*Rendezvous Café, 626 W. Diversey Pkwy.*
Al Copeland, Charlie Straight, Mike Speciale, Louis Panico, Seattle Harmony Kings, Ben Pollack, George Devron, Mezz Mezzrow

*Riverview Ballroom, 2528 W. Belmont Ave.*
Ralph Foote, Tomasco, Doc Cook, Frank Schmidt's Million Dollar Orchestra, Elmer Kaiser

*Sheraton Chicago Hotel, 505 N. Michigan Ave.*
Hal Munro, Joe Vera, Gary Claridge, Johnny Raftis, Hal Munro, Mickey Prindl

*Silver Slipper, 184 W. Randolph St.*
Sol Wagner

*Southmoor Hotel, 6646 S. Stony Island Ave.*
Ben Pollack, Art Kassel, Hughie Swift, Ralph Williams, Dick McPartland, George Foster

*Terrace Garden (Morrison Hotel), 79 W. Madison St.*
John Wickliffe's Ginger Band, Austin Mack's Century Serenaders, Roy Bargy, Al Eldridge, Don Bestor, Art S. With, Ralph Williams, Herbie Mintz, Gus Edwards, George Devron, Don Pedro, Jack Russell, Clyde Lucas, Stan Myers, Ted FioRito, Lou Breese, others

*Trianon Ballroom, 6201 S. Cottage Grove Ave.*
Paul Whiteman, Roy Bargy, Dell Lampe, Art Kassel, Abe Lyman, Husk O'Hare, Harold Stokes, Joe Kayser, Eddie Neibauer's Seattle Harmony Kings, Walter Vaughn, Johnny Mulaney, Hal Kemp, Ted Weems, Arnold Johnson, Jan Garber, Kay Kyser, Bill Carlsen, Don Reid, Lawrence Welk, most every sweet band in the country

*Uptown Village, 4822 N. Broadway Ave.*
Barney Richards, Earl Hoffman

*Vanity Fair, 817 W. Grace St.*
Phil Levant, Al Kvale

*Victorian Room (Palmer House), 17 E. Monroe St.*
Louis Alberti, Jules Herbuveaux

*White City, Sixty-third Street at South Parkway (Dr. Martin Luther King Jr. Dr.)*
Eli Courlander, Bert Kelly, Sig Meyer, Davy Jones II and his Pirates, Jimmy McPartland's Wolverines, Cope Harvey, Doc Cook, Clarence Moore, Verne Buck

*Winona Gardens, 5150 N. Broadway Ave.*
Frank Snyder

# Appendix C

## Benson Bands and Orchestras

The following is a partial alphabetical list of the bands and orchestras booked by the Benson Organization, 1924 and before.

Ashley Ballou, Roy Bargy, the Benson Band (Ferdinand Steindel, director), the Benson Orchestra of Chicago, Don Bestor, Paul Biese, Jack Chapman, Al Copeland, Doc Davis, Lew Diamond, Gus C. Edwards, Ralph Foote, Walter Ford and his Tent Orchestra, Jules Goldberg, Ike Goldsmith's Vaudeville Dance Orchestra, Fred Hamm, Leroy Hanson, Clarence Jones, Isham Jones, Harold Leonard, Jerome Levy, Austin Mack, Jean Mack, George Mallen, Irving Margraf, Johnny Mulaney, Dave O'Malley, Carl Rupp, Guy Schrigley, Henry Selinger, E. E. Sheetz, Maurie Sherman, Sisson Society Syncopators (A. Shynman, director), the Spanish Serenaders, Charlie Straight, Fred Travers, Waddy Wadsworth, Sol Wagner, Frank Westphal, Ralph Williams, Art S. With

Compiled from the Benson Organization 1923 catalog, *Conn Musical Truth* 13, no. 32 (April 1923), and the author's files.

# Appendix D

## Chicago Ballroom Floor Dimensions

| Ballroom | Location | Size of Dance Floor (in square feet) |
|---|---|---|
| Aragon | 1106 W. Lawrence Ave. | 21,036 |
| Arcadia | 4444 N. Broadway Ave. | 15,000 est. |
| Casino Moderne | 63rd St. east of Drexel Blvd. | 8,100 |
| Chateau (later Vogue) | 3810 N. Broadway Ave. | 6,600 |
| Danceland (later Brilliant, then Golden Pumpkin) | 3825 W. Madison St. | 13,593 |
| Granada | 68th & Cottage Grove Ave. | 6,200 |
| Melody Mill | 2401 S. Des Plaines Ave., North Riverside, Ill. | 15,000 |
| Merry Garden | 3136 N. Sheffield Ave. | 14,355 |
| Midway Gardens | 6000 S. Cottage Grove Ave. | 21,600 |
| Oh Henry (later Willowbrook) | 8900 S. Archer Rd., Willow Springs, Ill. | 5,000 |
| Paradise | 128 N. Pulaski Rd. (Crawford Ave.) | 25,500 |
| Park Casino (earlier Driscoll's Danceland) | 3825 W. Madison St. | 13,593 |
| Pershing Hotel | 6400 S. Cottage Grove Ave. | 7,175 |
| Princess | 1519 W. Madison St. | 8,500 |
| Rainbo Garden | 4812 N. Clark St. | 6,400 |
| Savoy | 4735 S. Dr. Martin Luther King Jr. Dr. | 12,500 |

| Ballroom | Location | Size of Dance Floor (in square feet) |
|---|---|---|
| Trianon | 6201 S. Cottage Grove Ave. | 29,580 |
| White City | 63rd St. & Dr. Martin Luther King Jr. Dr. | 33,800 |

Compiled by Charles A. Sengstock Jr., based on information from Todd, Byron, and Viernow, *Chicago Recreation Survey, 1937,* and other sources.

# Notes

## Introduction

1. "Here's What It's All About," Blackhawk Restaurant flyer, ca. 1990s.
2. Petrillo, "Dance Biz Needs New Blood."
3. Nye, "Saturday Night at the Paradise Ballroom," 14–16; Kenney, *Chicago Jazz,* 62–63.
4. Castle and Duncan, *Castles in the Air,* 66, 85, 91–92, 118.
5. Ibid., 118.
6. Nye, "Saturday Night at the Paradise Ballroom."
7. Leiter, *The Musicians and Petrillo,* 47–48.
8. Wendt and Kogan, *Lords of the Levee,* 276.
9. White City booklet, ca. 1907, John Steiner Collection, Chicago Jazz Archive, University of Chicago.
10. Rode, "The Concert Band in Chicago," 25.
11. Dedmon, *Fabulous Chicago,* 119, 182 (regarding the Field birthday); "Hand's Death Shows Sacrifice" (regarding Mrs. Potter Palmer).
12. "Hundreds Pay Final Tributes."
13. "Musicians Balk on Strike."
14. Lombardo and Altschul, *Auld Acquaintance,* 55.
15. Arlen, "No. 1 Band Builder."
16. Lombardo and Altschul, *Auld Acquaintance,* 85.

## Chapter 1: Edgar Benson and the Early Chicago Booking Agents

1. On the many cabarets and dance halls, see Sudhalter, *Lost Chords,* 89.
2. *Marigold Gardens Benson Revue,* program, 1922, 7, photocopy in author's collection.
3. Rode, "The Concert Band in Chicago," 25–26.
4. U.S. Bureau of the Census, *Fourteenth Census (1920) of the U.S.*
5. *Marigold Gardens Benson Revue,* 12.
6. Joe Kayser, conversation with author, Chicago, April 6, 1974.
7. *Variety,* March 3, 1922, 8.
8. Benson Organization catalog, 1923, 1, author's collection.
9. Wittels, "Star-Spangled Octopus," 44.
10. Joe Kayser, conversation with author, Chicago, April 6, 1974.
11. Kenney, *Chicago Jazz,* 84.
12. "Quigley-Benson Tieup."
13. Mills, "Leaders and Publishers."

14. Secon, "Remotes Good Programming?"
15. Ad, *Chicago Defender,* November 15, 1913; Nome, "The Race and Music."
16. Bergreen, *Louis Armstrong,* 186.
17. Joe Kayser, conversation with author, Chicago, April 30, 1974.
18. "Harvey Roll Lengthy."
19. "The Most Popular Attractions."
20. Sudhalter, *Lost Chords,* 24; Holbrook, "Mister Jazz Himself," part 1, 145.
21. "Cabarets," December 1, 1916.
22. Ibid., January 5, 1917, 13.
23. Lait, "Night Life of the World," 60.
24. "Bert Kelly."
25. Rust, *The American Dance Band Discography,* vol. 1, 169.
26. Joe Kayser, interview by author, Chicago, March 2, 1979; ad for Arnold Johnson orchestra, *Variety,* May 27, 1925, 39.
27. Pollack, "Ten Years of Good Bands and Bad Breaks."
28. Identified from Husk O'Hare band photos, author's collection.
29. Pollack, "Ten Years of Good Bands and Bad Breaks."
30. Stearns, "The History of Swing."
31. Flyer on Castle Gardens letterhead, ca. 1924, George O'Hare Collection.
32. Montgomery, "'New' Jelly Roll Morton Piano Roll."
33. Allen and Rust, *King Joe Oliver,* rev. ed., 15–16.

## Chapter 2: Jules Stein and James Petrillo

1. McDougal, *The Last Mogul,* 14.
2. "10% of Everything"; Schumach, "Hollywood's Music Mogul," 98.
3. "Chicago's Music Corp. Going after Local Biz."
4. Joe Kayser, conversation with author, Chicago, July 12, 1974.
5. McDougal, *The Last Mogul,* 16.
6. Moldea, *Dark Victory,* 14–15.
7. Wittels, "Star-Spangled Octopus," 44.
8. McDougal, *The Last Mogul,* 13; Allen and Rust, *King Joe Oliver,* rev. ed., 38–41.
9. Ad, *Intermezzo,* September 1925, 39.
10. "Routes Department"; "MCA Notes."
11. Edmiston, *The Coon-Sanders Nighthawks,* 117.
12. Ibid.
13. Joe Kayser, conversation with author, Chicago, July 12, 1974.
14. "Chicago's Music Corp. Going after Local Biz."
15. Ad, *Intermezzo,* September 1925, 39.
16. Ad for Ernie Young Agency, *Variety,* August 19, 1921, 17.
17. Ibid., March 1, 1923, 16, 53, and April 22, 1925, 38; "Ernie Young's Fla. Revue."
18. "Paul Biese, 38, Dies Suddenly after Operation."
19. "Harold Thiell," Death Records, Chicago Federation of Musicians, Special Collections, Music Information Center, Chicago Public Library.

20. Joe Kayser, tape-recorded interview by author, Chicago, September 5, 1975. Unless noted otherwise, all interview tapes are in the possession of the author.

21. "Chi Eatery Adopts Dance Policy."

22. Don Roth, tape-recorded interview by author, Wheeling, Ill., November 20, 1989.

23. Edmiston, *The Coon-Sanders Nighthawks*, 190–91.

24. "Orchestras Will Play over Ballroom Circuit by March."

25. Lombardo and Altshul, *Auld Acquaintance*, 57.

26. "Guy Lombardo," Death Records, Chicago Federation of Musicians.

27. "30% Law Modified."

28. "MCA's N.Y. Offices and Music College"; McDougal, *The Last Mogul*, 28.

29. Rose, *The Agency*, 90.

30. McDougal, *The Last Mogul*, 39–40.

31. Kenney, *Chicago Jazz*, 85.

32. "Benson Losing Out in Chicago"; "Benson Losing Hold on Chicago"; "Benson No Longer Is Monopolizing Chi Music"; "Chicago Music Corp. Going after Local Biz."

33. "Chicago Dance Hall Pays $3,000 for Band"; Kenney, *Chicago Jazz*, 84, 85.

34. Rust, *The American Dance Band Discography*, vol. 1, 887.

35. Isham Jones ads, *Variety*, March 25, 1925, 43–50.

36. "Here and There."

37. Joe Kayser, conversation with author, Chicago, April 6, 1974.

38. "Edgar A. Benson."

39. Moldea, *Dark Victory*, 33.

40. "MCA Guarantees $50,000 a Year to Columbia."

41. Eberly, *Music in the Air*, 361.

42. McDougal, *The Last Mogul*, ix.

43. Ibid., 300.

44. Ibid., 484, 508.

45. Leiter, *The Musicians and Petrillo*, 50, 51.

46. Ibid., 49.

47. Joe Kayser, conversation with author, Chicago, April 6, 1974.

48. "Musicians Balk on Strike."

## Chapter 3: How Radio Made Stars of the Dance Bands

1. U.S. Department of Commerce, "R 104 Households with Radio Sets," *Historical Statistics of the United States*, 793.

2. "Chicago Leads with Most Radio Stations."

3. Leiter, *The Musicians and Petrillo*, 47–48; "250 Café Artists—200 Musicians Losing Jobs."

4. Jules Herbuveaux, tape-recorded interview by author, Lake Forest, Ill., September 11, 1976.

5. Fink, *WGN*, 10.

6. Wittels, "Star-Spangled Octopus," 44.

7. Jules Herbuveaux, tape-recorded interview by author, September 11, 1976.

8. Ghrist, *Valley Voices,* 15.

9. Lombardo and Altshul, *Auld Acquaintance,* 60, 61.

10. Joe Kayser, conversations with author, July 28, 1966, April 6, 1974.

11. Fink, *WGN,* 10.

12. Johnson, "Those Happy-Go-Lucky Sounds," 9.

13. Leiter, *The Musicians and Petrillo,* 50.

14. Ibid., 144.

15. Chuck Foster, conversation with author, Los Angeles, June 17, 1970.

16. Schaden, *WBBM Radio,* 22.

17. Evans, *"Prairie Farmer" and WLS,* 175.

18. Arlen, "No. 1 Band Builder."

19. McDougal, *The Last Mogul,* 68.

20. Fink, *WGN,* 17, 28.

21. "$120–$150 Weekly 2-Year Scale Tops N.Y. Pay."

22. DeLong, *Pops,* 156, 158.

23. "Lombardo's $150,000 Dates."

24. McDougal, *The Last Mogul,* 70.

25. Schaden, *WBBM Radio,* 25.

26. Shaughnessy, *Les Paul,* 103–5, 110.

27. "Records."

28. Gunther, *The House That Roone Built,* 34.

29. The information about the dance bands' rigidity comes from Eberly, *Music in the Air,* 75.

## Chapter 4: Ice Rinks, Beer Gardens, and Other Early Chicago Dance Halls

1. Lait, "Night Life of the World," 5.

2. "Desertion of Chicago's 'Loop' Traced to Dance Places."

3. Kenney, *Chicago Jazz,* 62–63; Nye, "Saturday Night at the Paradise Ballroom," 14–15.

4. B. Murray, "Dance Hall versus Ballroom."

5. Banks, "The World's Most Beautiful Ballrooms," 206; Kenney, *Chicago Jazz,* 64–65.

6. Banks, "The World's Most Beautiful Ballrooms," 206; Kenney, *Chicago Jazz,* 64–65.

7. "Roadhouse Survey of Cook County," 1, 3, 11.

8. Kenney, *Chicago Jazz,* 71; "Isham Jones."

9. Cutler, *Chicago,* 55.

10. Bond, "Park Queen Perishes in Fire."

11. Ibid.

12. Kettering, "Last Call for Landmarks."

13. White City ad, *Chicago Tribune,* December 31, 1932.

14. Bond, "Park Queen Perishes in Fire."

15. Kruty, "Pleasure Garden on the Midway," 6, 8.

16. Ibid., 26.

17. Kruty, *Frank Lloyd Wright and Midway Gardens,* 47; Todd, Byron, and Viernow, *Chicago Recreation Survey, 1937,* 138.

18. *Billboard,* October 19, 1929.

19. Ad, *Riverview News,* March 27, 1920.

20. Kruty, *Frank Lloyd Wright and Midway Gardens,* 112–18; Paul Kruty, correspondence with author, June 29, 2001.

21. "$1,000,000 Dance Hall Takes Dancing out of Fad Class."

22. Chase, "World's Famous Midway Gardens to Be Reopened."

23. W. Leonard, "Tower Ticker," September 25, 1951.

24. Kogan, "Dreamland Fades."

25. W. Leonard, "Tower Ticker," October 3, 1951.

26. Kogan, "Dreamland Fades."

27. Peyton, "The Musical Bunch," March 1, 1924.

28. Hayner and McNamee, *The Stadium,* 1.

29. Joe Kayser, conversation with author, Chicago, April 30, 1974.

30. Wiedrich, "Colorful Arena Once Site of Beer Garden."

31. "Close Marigold Gardens Doors."

32. "The Marigold Follies."

33. *Marigold Gardens Benson Revue,* 6.

34. Ad, "'Green Mill' Sunken Gardens Announcement of Opening," *Chicago Tribune,* June 26, 1914.

35. "Cabarets," November 24, 1916; "Patricola."

36. Joe Kayser, tape-recorded interview by author, Chicago, March 2, 1979.

37. Holbrook, "Mister Jazz Himself," part 2, 97.

38. "Dance Hall Invades No. Side Society."

39. Bowman, "The Fast Life and Hard Times."

40. "Dance Hall Invades No. Side Society."

41. Conn, *Musical Truth.*

42. Bowman, "The Fast Life and Hard Times."

43. Joe Kayser, conversation with author, Chicago, May 12, 1976.

44. Ibid.

45. Kayser, "Birth of the One-Nighter."

46. Peyton, "The Musical Bunch," September 22, 1928, May 4, 1929.

47. "Old Arcadia Hall Leased by Elevated Lines."

48. Bowman, "The Fast Life and Hard Times."

49. Kogan, "Dreamland Fades."

50. *Riverview News,* September 4, 1920.

51. Peyton, "The Musical Bunch," May 14, 1927.

52. *Riverview News,* September 4, 1920, January 29, 1921.

53. Ibid., March 27, 1920.

54. Ibid., January 29, 1921.

55. The information about Cook's departure comes from Peyton, "The Musical Bunch," March 1, 1924.

56. Conn, *Musical Truth.*

57. Todd, Byron, and Viernow, *Chicago Recreation Survey, 1937,* 138.

58. Mark Berresford, liner notes to *Chicago Rhythm, Al Turk/Charlie Straight/Gene Green,* Jazz Oracle Phonograph Co., Toronto, 1998, 5.

59. Todd, Byron, and Viernow, *Chicago Recreation Survey, 1937,* 138.

60. Information given on Pla-Mor Café postcard, Curt Teich Postcard Archives, Lake County (Ill.) Discovery Museum.

61. Kogan, "Dreamland Fades."

62. Jules Herbuveaux, tape-recorded interview by author, Lake Forest, Ill., September 11, 1976.

63. "Desertion of Chicago's 'Loop' Traced to Dance Places."

64. Jules Herbuveaux, conversation with author, Lake Forest, Ill., April 16, 1983.

65. Conn, *Musical Truth.*

66. "Fire Levels Ballroom; Routs 100 Families."

## Chapter 5: The Trianon, the Aragon, and the Modern Ballroom Era

1. Banks, "The World's Most Beautiful Ballroom," 206.

2. Ibid., 206, 207.

3. "Chicago Dance Hall Pays $3,000 for Band."

4. Information derived partly from photos of Lampe at Trianon ballroom, author's collection.

5. Information derived from photo of J. B. Lampe with four leaders, author's collection.

6. "23 Years—1934–1957: A Roundup," 13.

7. "Garber Pays $47,000 to Get Out of Contract."

8. Jackman, "Old Memories to Fall with the Trianon."

9. Banks, "The World's Most Beautiful Ballrooms," 209.

10. Dante, "From Big Time to Happiness," 7.

11. "Bright Spots around Town."

12. Dante, "From Big Time to Happiness," 7.

13. Ibid.

14. *Chicago Daily News,* October 19, 1926.

15. Dante, "From Big Time to Happiness," 7.

16. "Chicago Dance Hall Pays $3,000 for Band."

17. Dante, "From Big Time to Happiness," 7.

18. "Ballroom's Year Contract Mutually Dissolved in Chi."

19. "King to End 9 Year Reign at Aragon."

20. Hoefer, "How Radio Helped to Build Big Bands," 52.

21. Ads, *Chicago Tribune,* October 4, 6, 13, 20, 27, 1935.

22. "Knapp and His 'Band of Tomorrow' in Denver."

23. Ibid.

24. "Knapp Crashes to Death in Own Plane."

25. "Karzas Fired Band That Couldn't Play Waltzes."

26. "Last Waltz at Aragon"; "Dancers Bid Farewell to Aragon."

27. "Joe Kayser and His Boys a Tremendous Success."

28. Joe Kayser Band's Merry Garden payroll, November 22, 1928, author's collection.

29. Miller, *Esquire's 1946 Jazz Book,* 35.

30. Bond, "Wreckers Quiet Merry Garden."

31. *Down Beat,* November 1934.

32. Gault, *Ballroom Echoes,* 182, 183.

33. Daunoras, "Willowbrook Founder-Owner to Celebrate His 91st Birthday."

34. Gault, *Ballroom Echoes,* 177; idem, "Dancing and Gayly [*sic*] Romancing," 6.

35. Ibid.

36. Brotman, "Last Dance Is Over for the Melody Mill."

37. Scott, "Pride of Wheeling Gets New Life."

38. Ibid.

## Chapter 6: Early Downtown Chicago Hotels Join the Dance Party

1. Ad, *Billboard,* December 3, 1938.

2. *Book of Chicagoans,* 1917.

3. "College Inn Starts Fifth Decade."

4. W. Leonard, "The Death of a Loop Hotel"; idem, "New College Inn Opens."

5. "Cabarets," December 1, 1916, January 5, 1917.

6. Rust, *The American Dance Band Discography,* vol. 1, 171.

7. "Benson Losing Out in Chicago."

8. Evans, *"Prairie Farmer" and WLS,* 161, 163.

9. McCarthy, *The Dance Band Era,* 71.

10. *Chicago Defender,* July 15, 1922.

11. "College Inn."

12. "Benson Losing Hold on Chicago."

13. "College Inn."

14. Ibid.

15. "Coon-Sanders Original Nighthawks Orchestra," 286, 287.

16. "No Jam in Chicago without O.K. Sez Petrillo"; *Down Beat,* July 1938, photo of band.

17. "College Inn Starts Fifth Decade."

18. "America's Most Hep Band Buyer."

19. "College Inn Starts Fifth Decade."

20. Bowman, "When Ernie Byfield [*sic*] Played Genial Host."

21. W. Leonard, "The Death of a Loop Hotel"; Enstad, "Sherman House Demolition to Start."

22. Kinsley, "Stevens Paints Rosy Business Vision."

23. Sawyers, "The Night Chicago Suffered."

24. Conn, *Musical Truth.*

25. *Chicago Daily News,* March 13, July 3, October 2, October 23, 1926, September 5, 1927; ad, *Chicago Tribune,* May 27, 1928, sec. 1, p. 4.

26. *Down Beat,* October 1936, 13; ibid., April 1939.

27. Sawyers, "The Night Chicago Suffered"; Nagelberg, "Brundage Sells 96% Holding in LaSalle Hotel."

28. Ad, *Variety,* May 2, 1928, 67.

29. *Chicago Herald,* January 20, 1916, 11.

30. Peyton, "The Musical Bunch," May 7, 1927.

31. "Benson Losing Out in Chicago"; "Benson Losing Hold on Chicago."

32. Joe Kayser, conversation with author, Chicago, April 6, 1974.

33. "Clyde Lucas Booked for Longer Stay."

34. Fitzpatrick, "Morrison Hotel to Ring Down Curtain on Gaudy Era."

35. "Hotel Mgrs. Adopt 'There'll Be Some Changes Made.'"

36. "New Bands 'Take Off' in the Windy City."

37. Gavin, "1st National Buys Control of Morrison," sec. F, p. 7.

38. Gold, "'Check in on a Bit of Chicagoana."

39. Edmiston, *The Coon-Sanders Nighthawks,* 127.

40. "Lyman in Chicago."

41. "Cherniavsky Warms Refrigerator Room."

42. Firestone, *Swing, Swing, Swing,* 150, 154, 155.

43. "Second Rhythm Concert Delights Local 'Cats' and '400.'"

44. Jules Herbuveaux, tape-recorded interview by author, Lake Forest, Ill., September 11, 1976.

45. "Hotel Mgrs. Adopt 'There'll Be Some Changes Made.'"

46. "Army to School Radio Experts in Two Seized Hotels."

47. Dick Sarlo, tape-recorded interview by author, Addison, Ill., November 5, 1998.

48. Carroll, "An Eye on You."

49. *Chicago Tribune,* October 23, 1935.

50. "Chicago Band Briefs," April 15, 1944.

51. "Where the Bands Are Playing," November 15, 1942; Harris, "Chicago Band Briefs."

52. Handley, "The Next Magnificent Mile(s)"; ads, *Chicago Tribune,* August 5, 2001, sec. 16, p. 7, May 9, 2004, sec. 5, p. 15.

53. "Cabarets," April 5, 1918.

## Chapter 7: The Beat Goes On

1. Bard-Hall, "For Nearly 125 Years."

2. Jules Herbuveaux, tape-recorded interview by author, Lake Forest, Ill., September 11, 1976.

3. W. Leonard, "Final Act at Empire Room."

4. "Veloz and Yolanda Use Shep Fields Orchestra"; "Veloz and Yolanda Annex 'Spike' Hamilton Ork."

5. Ad, *Down Beat,* November 1934, 8.

6. Dawn, "Griff Williams, Raye and Naldi Lead New Empire Room Revue."

7. Ibid.

8. "Duration Contract for Williams at Empire Room."

9. Bard-Hall, "For Nearly 125 Years."

10. Lesner, "Requiem for the Empire Room."

11. W. Leonard, "Final Act at Empire Room."

12. Kart, "Singer Polly Podewell—a Jewel for $3."

13. Fuller, "Wirtz Acquires Eitel Bismarck Hotel Stock."

14. "Kassel in Bismarck."

15. Reich, "Grand Hotel."

16. Kinsley, "Stevens Paints Rosy Business Vision."

17. *Chicago Daily News*, May 2, 1927.

18. "Army to School Radio Experts in Two Seized Hotels."

19. "Ellington Band for Stevens in Chicago Soon"; "Key Band Spots."

20. Ibata, "Renovated Hilton."

21. W. Leonard, "After 20 Years, Boulevard Room Ice Revues End."

22. "Local Group Buys Drake Hotel"; "The Four Most Valuable Parcels of Land."

23. Fink, *WGN*, 10, 16, 55.

24. "New Silver Forest Room Has 'It.'"

25. *Down Beat*, February 1936; Hoefer, "How Radio Helped to Build Big Band," 52.

26. "Jimmy Blade Rites Planned."

27. W. Leonard, "Lombardo Brings Back the Old Days."

28. "Local Group Buys Drake Hotel."

29. "Chicago Band Briefs," March 11, 4; *Down Beat*, October 6, 1950.

30. W. Leonard, "Too Much Pomp at Pump Room."

31. Rust, *The American Dance Band Discography*, vol. 1, 173.

32. Dante, "From Big Time to Happiness," 7.

33. DeLong, *Pops*, 156, 158, 164.

34. "Don't Know Whether Spitalny In or Out."

35. Langer, "Edgewater Beach Memories," 16, 18.

36. "Chicago Band Briefs," April 1, 1945, 4.

37. Greb, "Edgewater Ends Reign."

38. Ad, *Variety*, October 6, 1926, 12.

39. Shapiro and Hentoff, *Hear Me Talkin' to Ya*, 133; *Chicago Defender*, November 26, 1927, April 7, 1928.

40. "Chi Hotel Builds Jungle for Krupa's Wild Rhythm."

41. *Chicago Defender*, November 19, 1927; "The Pershing Palace."

42. "David A. Solovy."

43. Charles Walton, tape-recorded interviews by author, Chicago, September 2, December 15, 1997.

44. Dance, *World of Earl Hines*, 96, 98, 99.

45. Bowman, "When Ernie Byfield [*sic*] Played Genial Host."

46. "Army to School Radio Experts in Two Seized Hotels"; "Business from Fair Helps Stevens Hotel Pay Off Back Taxes."

47. Carroll, "An Eye on You."

48. Bard-Hall, "For Nearly 125 Years."

49. Jules Herbuveaux, tape-recorded interview by author, Lake Forest, Ill., September 11, 1976.

50. Ad, *Billboard*, December 3, 1938.

## Chapter 8: Dance Bands Thrive in Chicago's Cabarets and Restaurants

1. Duis, *The Saloon*, 293–94; Erenberg, "Ain't We Got Fun," 18.

2. "Mystery Girl."

3. "Cabaret Life as It Exists in City Today."

4. On the North American Restaurant, see Lait, "Night Life of the World."

5. Erenberg, "Ain't We Got Fun," 19.

6. Ibid.

7. Longstreet, *Chicago*, 18–25, 22–23, 116.

8. Lait, "Night Life of the World."

9. "Cabarets," November 5, 1915.

10. Balaban, *Continuous Performance*, 59.

11. "Cabarets," April 5, 1918.

12. "Taylor Tried; Benson Got In."

13. "Cabarets," November 12, 1915.

14. "Taylor Tried; Benson Got In."

15. Wood, "A Half Century of the Culinary Arts," 16.

16. "License Denied for Reopening of Colosimo's."

17. Wood, "A Half Century of the Culinary Arts," 22–23.

18. "License Denied for Reopening of Colosimo's."

19. Ibid.; Burns, "U.S. Padlocks Colosimo's for Dry Violations."

20. Starr, "45 Years of Night Life."

21. Lait and Mortimer, *Chicago Confidential*, 212, 218.

22. Starr, "45 Years of Night Life."

23. "Cabarets, Friar's Inn."

24. Coller, "More on Jack Pettis."

25. "Cabarets," October 20, 1916.

26. Ibid., January 7, 1916.

27. Holbrook, "Mister Jazz Himself," part 2, 95.

28. Erenberg, "Ain't We Got Fun," 18, 19.

29. Lait, "Chicago by Night."

30. "The Marigold Follies."

31. Don Roth, tape-recorded interview by author, Wheeling, Ill., November 20, 1989; Don Roth, conversations with author, Wheeling, Ill., February 11 and June 3, 1991.

32. "Chi Eatery Adopts Dance Policy."

33. "12 Cafés Face U.S. Padlocks."

34. "Hal Kemp."

35. Don Roth, tape-recorded interview by author, November 20, 1989.

36. Wittels, "Star-Spangled Octopus," 47.

37. Don Roth, conversation with author, June 3, 1991; McDougal, *The Last Mogul*, 68.

38. "Fran Coughlin, Noted Radio Writer, Dies."

39. "Kyser Signs Contract for Lucky Strike Program."

40. Ibid.

41. Chilton, *Stomp Off, Let's Go*, 13, 14.

42. Don Roth, conversations with author, October 17, June 3, 1991; Don Roth, tape-recorded interview by author, November 20, 1989.

43. Don Roth, tape-recorded interview by author, November 20, 1989.

44. "Here's What It's All About," Blackhawk Restaurant flyer, ca. 1990s.

45. Don Roth, conversation with author, October 17, 1991.

46. Herrmann, "Blackhawk Goes."
47. "Mike Fritzel, 75, Nightclub Owner, Dies"; Starr, "45 Years of Night Life."
48. "Cabaret Bills," *Variety*, January 21, 1916, 8; Lait, "Night Life of the World, Chicago."
49. "Long Hours but Kicks A-Plenty at Friar's Inn."
50. "Friar's Inn."
51. Shapiro and Hentoff, *Hear Me Talkin' to Ya*, 132; "Friar's."
52. Starr, "45 Years of Night Life."
53. Chase, "Mike Fritzel Leases Former Chez Pierre Café."

## Chapter 9: The Bands Earn Respect

1. Holbrook, "Mister Jazz Himself," part 1, 145.
2. "The Cabaret."
3. Klatzko, "Johnny Dodds."
4. Van Vorst, "The Chicago Bosses."
5. *Chicago Defender*, September 16, 1922.
6. Ibid., February 2, 1924.
7. Ibid., June 16, 1928.
8. "Cabaret Reviews, Moulin Rouge," 34.
9. Wendt and Kogan, *Lords of the Levee*, 329, 340.
10. DeMaris, *Captive City*, 138.
11. "Lishon Has Smart Band at Club Royal."
12. "Find Night Club Girls Cheating on State Dole."
13. Ad for Mandarin Inn, *Chicago Post*, February 23, 1915; "Wong: Restaurateur Wanted Mall along Argyle."
14. "16,000 Beer Flats in Chicago Grab Customers."
15. Information derived from photo of Earl Hoffman band, *Billboard*, November 1, 1924, 12.
16. "12 Cafés Face U.S. Padlocks."
17. "Town Club."
18. "The Pershing Palace"; *Chicago Defender*, November 19, 1927.
19. "Frolics (Chicago)."
20. Kobler, *The Life and World of Al Capone*, 230.
21. "Frolics (Chicago)."
22. Ibid.
23. "Blanket Raid Covers Chi Cafés."
24. "Lishon Has Smart Band at Club Royal."
25. "Ike Bloom's Deauville Popular in Chicago."
26. Dance, *World of Earl Hines*, 57–58.
27. Ibid., 62–63.
28. The information about Dickerson comes from "Grand Terrace Café Closed"; otherwise, see "Basie Makes Chi Debut."
29. Dance, *World of Earl Hines*, 297.
30. Ibid., 154.
31. "16,000 Beer Flats in Chicago Grab Customers."

32. "Granada" (1928).

33. "Granada Café Destroyed by $100,000 Fire."

34. "Granada" (1926).

35. Joe Kayser, conversation with author, Chicago, July 28, 1966; Lombardo and Altschul, *Auld Acquaintance,* 56, 57.

36. *Billboard,* July 7, 1928.

37. Lord, "Around Chicago."

38. Barnes, "Hitting the High Notes."

39. "No Incendiary Clues in Granada Café Fire."

40. Peyton, "The Musical Bunch," December 4, 1926.

41. Henry Crowder to Dave Peyton; Kramer, "Jelly Roll in Chicago (1927)," part 2, 19.

42. *Chicago Herald Examiner,* January 1, 1933.

43. "Century of Progress, 1934," 5.

44. Lyden and Jakus, *Landmarks and Legends of Uptown,* 39; "Blanket Raid Covers Chi Cafés."

45. "4,000 People of Chi Greet Ash at Farewell Dinner."

46. "Old Rainbo Gardens Will Get New Look."

47. "Rainbo Closed; 11 More Cafés Face Padlocks"; "250 Café Artists—200 Musicians Losing Jobs."

48. Melcher, "At the World's Fair."

49. "Rainbo Clicks with a Swing-Name Ork Policy."

50. "Old Rainbo Gardens Will Get New Look."

51. Chase, "World's Famous Midway Gardens to Be Reopened."

52. Chase, "Famed Uptown Nightspot of 'Dry Era' Sold"; Heise, *Chaos, Creativity, and Culture,* 63.

53. Cohn, *The Joker Is Wild,* 4–7.

54. Ad, *Variety,* June 25, 1924, 43.

55. Peyton, "The Musical Bunch," January 21, 1928.

56. Sawyers, "Whooping It Up."

57. Ebisch, "Whatever Happened to the Green Mill Gardens?" 20.

58. Cohn, *The Joker Is Wild,* 17–18.

59. Drury, *Dining in Chicago,* 260.

60. "Rendezvous."

61. Ibid.

62. Mezzrow and Wolfe, *Really the Blues,* 126.

63. "U.S. Puts Lock on Rendezvous, Jeffery Tavern."

64. Forbes, "Marigold Room Is Dowager of City's Cabarets."

65. Wiedrich, "Colorful Arena Once Site of Beer Garden."

66. "Marigold Ends Career as Café; Turns to Dance."

67. Mastro, "57 TV Stations to Carry Bouts from Marigold."

68. "Al Handler Knows Tunes from Way Back When."

69. "Cabaret Bills," May 23, 1928, 64.

70. "12 Cafés Face U.S. Padlocks."

71. Lord, "Around Chicago."

72. Ibid.

## Chapter 10: Dance Bands in the Roadhouses

1. "Roadhouse Survey of Cook County," 1, 11.
2. "250 Café Artists—200 Musicians Losing Jobs."
3. "Commercialized Prostitution in Morton Grove," 2.
4. "Roadhouse Survey of Cook County," 11.
5. Ibid., A-1, 1–2.
6. Edmiston, *The Coon-Sanders Nighthawks*, 127.
7. Joe Kayser, conversation with author, Chicago, August 26, 1966.
8. "Cabaret Bills," August 18, 1926, 38.
9. Cohn, *The Joker Is Wild*, 128.
10. *Morton Grove, 1895–1995*, 35.
11. Wendt and Kogan, *Lords of the Levee*, 283.
12. *Morton Grove, 1895–1995*, 34.
13. The Dells advertising card, ca. 1920, author's collection.
14. "The Dells."
15. Ibid.
16. "College Inn, Chi."
17. Edmiston, *The Coon-Sanders Nighthawks*, 215, 217.
18. The Dells table tent card, ca. 1926, author's collection.
19. Melcher, "At the World's Fair."
20. "Fire Destroys the Dells; Arson Is Suspected."
21. "'That's the Man.'"
22. *Morton Grove, 1895–1995*, 34.
23. Ghrist, *Valley Voices*, 187.
24. Barnes, "Hitting the High Notes."
25. House That Jack Built documents, Cook County Recorders Office, book 42-12, book 57A.
26. Lawrence Gushee, conversation with author, Urbana, Ill., April 10, 2001.
27. Lait, "Night Life of the World."
28. Cappo, "Villa Venice's Years of Glory Die in Flames."
29. Ad, *Variety*, January 27, 1922.
30. "Roadhouse Survey of Cook County," A-140, 1.
31. "Cabaret Bills," May 30, 1928, 56.
32. *Chicago Defender*, August 4, 1928.
33. Tom Hilliard, tape-recorded interview by author, Chicago, March 15, 2001.
34. *Chicago Defender*, July 9, 1932,
35. "Chi Hotel Builds Jungle for Krupa's Wild Rhythm."
36. Dick Sarlo, tape-recorded interview by author, Addison, Ill., November 5, 1998.
37. Cappo, "Villa Venice's Years of Glory Die in Flames."
38. "Roadhouse Survey of Cook County," A-94, 1–3.
39. "No Jam in Chicago without O.K. Sez Petrillo."
40. "Anderson O'Hare Memorial May 3."
41. *Chicago Defender*, August 21, September 4, 1926.
42. "Cabaret Bills," June 9, 1926, 46.

43. *Chicago Defender,* May 19, 1928.

44. Ghrist, *Valley Voices,* 11.

45. Jules Herbuveaux, tape-recorded interview by author, Lake Forest, Ill., September 11, 1976.

46. Mezzrow and Wolfe, *Really the Blues,* 137.

47. "Roadhouse Survey of Cook County," 7–9.

48. Mezzrow and Wolfe, *Really the Blues,* 57–58.

49. Ibid., 57–60, 64, 66–72.

50. "Roadhouse Survey of Cook County," 10–14.

51. Ibid.

52. Kenney, *Chicago Jazz,* 158–59.

## Chapter 11: "Rah, Rah, Rajah"

1. Balaban, *Continuous Performance,* 60–62.

2. Hall, *The Best Remaining Seats,* 210–13.

3. Ibid., 212, 213.

4. Ibid., 213.

5. "Leader 50% of Band, Says Op."

6. Sengstock, *Jazz Music in Chicago's Early South-Side Theaters,* 27.

7. Balaban, *Continuous Performance,* 60, 61.

8. Ibid., 58.

9. Ibid., 60, 61.

10. "The Paul Ash Record."

11. Letter to the editor, *Variety,* November 18, 1925, 43.

12. Hall, *The Best Remaining Seats,* 214.

13. "Paul Ash, 67, Theater Band Pioneer, Dies."

14. Ibid.

15. DeMichael, *Red Norvo,* 12.

16. "Paul Ash to Do His Stuff for WGN Fans."

17. "The Paul Ash Record"; *Variety,* August 18, 1926, 44.

18. "McVickers Theater."

19. "4,000 People of Chi Greet Ash at Farewell Dinner."

20. "Paul Ash Back to Bid Good-By to Old Friends."

21. Ads, *Variety,* February 27, 1929, 25.

22. Balaban, *Continuous Performance,* 57–58.

23. Ibid., 62.

24. Joe Kayser, conversation with author, Chicago, July 12, 1974.

25. "Chicago Orchestra News."

26. Leiter, *The Musicians and Petrillo,* 47–48.

27. Ibid.

28. Katz, "Return Engagement for Stage Shows," 15.

29. "Paul Ash, 67, Theater Band Pioneer, Dies."

30. "The Paul Ash Record."

## Chapter 12: The Economic Challenge of the Thirties

1. Melcher, "At the World's Fair," 12; Lewin, "Music Is First at 1934 Century of Progress," 1, 5.

2. Cahan and Jacobs, "Fair Ladies," 74, 111.

3. Melcher, "At the World's Fair," 12.

4. Cohan and Jacobs, "Fair Ladies," 111.

5. "Century of Progress, 1934," 2.

6. Chase, "Mike Fritzel Leases Former Chez Pierre Café."

7. Starr, "45 Years of Night Life"; Cushman, "Chicago's Chez Led the Way."

8. Cushman, "Chicago's Chez Led the Way."

9. Starr, "45 Years of Night Life."

10. Cushman, "Chicago's Chez Led the Way."

11. "Mike Fritzel, 75, Nightclub Owner, Dies."

12. Thompson, "Potson Parole Recalls Reign at Colosimo's."

13. Burns, "U.S. Padlocks Colosimo's for Dry Violations."

14. Thompson, "Potson Parole Recalls Reign at Colosimo's."

15. "Ah, Fair Ada."

16. "$1-a-Shot Gin Sale Profits Told by Potson"; Thompson, "Potson Parole Recalls Reign at Colosimo's."

17. "License Denied for Reopening of Colosimo's."

18. Paul E. Miller and George Hoefer, "Chicago Jazz History," in Miller, *Esquire's 1946 Jazz Book,* 36.

19. Melcher, "At the World's Fair," 12; Cohn, *The Joker Is Wild,* 154.

20. "Chi Hotel Builds Jungle for Krupa's Wild Rhythm."

21. "Sally Rand Dies at 75; Leaves Many Fans Behind."

22. Mastro, "57 TV Stations to Carry Bouts from Marigold."

23. Coller, "Frank Snyder," 8; "Swing Fans Flock to Hear Frank Snyder."

24. "Where the Bands Are Playing," December 15, 1939.

25. Gonzalez, "Owner of Ivanhoe Theater."

26. "Critics in the Dog House."

27. Chase, "Plan $150,000 Chinese Café on the Rialto."

28. Drury, *Dining in Chicago,* 130–31.

29. *Billboard,* November 30, 1929.

30. "Girl Wounded by Robbers in Crowded Café."

31. "Al Handler Knows Tunes from Way Back When."

32. "News about Town."

33. "Cabaret Bills," April 11, 1928, 56.

34. Miller and Hoefer, "Chicago Jazz History," 35.

35. Lord, "Around Chicago."

36. Greene, "Friendly Entertainers," 185–86.

37. Banks, "The World's Most Beautiful Ballrooms," 212.

38. Bond, "Park Queen Perishes in Fire."

## Chapter 13: The Last Hurrah

1. Greene, "Friendly Entertainers," 186.

2. Ad, "1939, The Year for Live Talent," *Billboard,* December 3, 1938.

3. Sippel, "Music Affected by New Tax Measure."

4. Wolters, "Radio Station News."

5. The information about the band members comes from a photo in "Three from the Lewis Band," *Down Beat,* August 15, 1944.

6. Buddy Shaw, tape-recorded interview by author, Northbrook, Ill., August 29, 2000.

7. "Chicago Band Briefs," November 15, 1945.

8. "Beers to Enlarge 3 Deuces in the Fall."

9. "Stuff Smith's Band Suffers $4,000 Loss."

10. "Grabbing a Breath of Air."

11. W. Leonard, "Tower Ticker."

12. Caine, "Blue Note Memories," 32.

13. Choice, "'Music Americana' Homeless."

14. The information about Horace Henderson comes from Travis, *An Autobiography of Black Jazz,* 406.

15. "James DeLisa; Owned Nightclub."

16. Charles Walton, tape-recorded interview by author, Chicago, September 2, 1997.

17. Travis, *An Autobiography of Black Jazz,* 128.

18. "Red Saunders Garrick's Star."

19. Charles Walton, tape-recorded interviews by author, Chicago, September 1, November 11, 1998.

20. Dance, *World of Earl Hines,* 96, 98.

21. Ibid., 99.

22. Tracy, "Chicago Musicians, Ops Resent Five-Day Week."

23. Christiansen, "There's No Business Like Tony's Business."

24. W. Leonard, "King-Sized Memories of Mangam's Glory Year."

25. Petrillo, "Dance Biz Needs New Blood."

26. Banks, "The World's Most Beautiful Ballrooms," 212.

27. "Four from Gary Killed as Train Strikes Auto."

28. "College Inn to End 38-Year Run July 5."

29. Tracy, "Chicago Musicians, Ops Resent Five-Day Week."

30. Leiter, *The Musicians and Petrillo,* 132–41.

31. Herman, "Why I Own Discery: Big Fish, Little Pond."

32. Petrillo, "Dance Biz Needs New Blood."

# Bibliography

Addams, Jane. *Twenty Years at Hull-House.* New York: Buccaneer Books, 1994.

"Ah, Fair Ada." *Down Beat,* July 15, 1946, 4.

"Al Handler Knows Tunes from Way Back When." *Down Beat,* February 1935, 8.

Allen, Walter C., and Brian A. L. Rust. *King Joe Oliver.* London: Jazz Book Club, 1957.

———. *King Joe Oliver.* Revised by Laurie Wright. Essex, Eng.: Storyville Publications, 1987.

"America's Most Hep Band Buyer." *Down Beat,* August 1, 1940, 4.

"Anderson O'Hare Memorial May 3." *Chicago Tribune,* April 24, 1970, 51.

Andries, Dorothy. "Pump Room Closes; Lucia Remembers." *Northbrook (Ill.) Star,* February 12, 1976, 6.

Arlen, David. "No. 1 Band Builder, WGN Chicago, with Vast Midwest Listening Audience, Gets Ratings." *Billboard,* October 7, 1942, 67.

"Army to School Radio Experts in Two Seized Hotels." *Chicago Tribune,* July 11, 1942, sec. F, p. 2.

"'Bad Man,' Killer of Two in Café, Is Third to Die." *Chicago Tribune,* December 9, 1923.

Balaban, Carrie. *Continuous Performance.* New York: A. J. Balaban Foundation, 1964.

"Ballroom's Year Contract Mutually Dissolved in Chi." *Variety,* January 5, 1927, 48.

Banks, Nancy. "The World's Most Beautiful Ballrooms." *Chicago History,* Fall–Winter 1973, 206–15.

Bard-Hall, Susan. "For Nearly 125 Years, the Palmer House Has Built Its Own Empire." *Chicago Tribune,* September 10, 1945, sec. 16, pp. 1, 4.

Barnes, Walter. "Hitting the High Notes with Walter Barnes." *Chicago Defender,* January 2, 1932, 7, January 9, 1932, 7.

Basie, William, and Albert Murray. *Good Morning Blues.* New York: Random House, 1985.

"Basie Makes Chi Debut—Fields Flops in N.Y. 'Satchmo's' Book Reveals Boastful Artist," *Down Beat,* November 1936.

"Beers to Enlarge 3 Deuces in the Fall." *Down Beat,* July, 1935.

"Benson Losing Hold on Chicago." *Variety,* May 6, 1925, 49.

"Benson Losing Out in Chicago." *Variety,* April 8, 1925, 43.

"Benson No Longer Is Monopolizing Chi Music." *Variety,* July 6, 1925, 41.

Bergreen, Laurence. *Capone: The Man and the Era.* New York: Simon and Schuster, 1944.

———. *Louis Armstrong: An Extravagant Life.* New York: Broadway Books, 1997.

"Bert Kelly." *Variety,* December 30, 1921, 40.

"Biese Funeral Is to Be Held Here, Widow Awaited." *Chicago Tribune,* October 29, 1925.

"Blanket Raid Covers Chi Cafés with No Search Warrants Used." *Variety,* February 8, 1928, 55.

Blesh, Rudi. *Shining Trumpets.* New York: Da Capo, 1980.

Bogue, Merwyn, and Gladys Bogue Reilly. *Ish Kabibble.* Baton Rouge: Louisiana State University Press, 1989.

Bond, Jean. "Park Queen Perishes in Fire." *Chicago Tribune,* December 6, 1959.

———. "Wreckers Quiet Merry Gardens." *Chicago Tribune,* March 9, 1961.

*Book of Chicagoans: A Biographical Dictionary of Leading Living Men and Women of the City of Chicago.* Chicago: A. N. Marquis, 1917.

Bowman, Jim. "The Fast Life and Hard Times of Chicago's Arcadia Ballroom." *Chicago Tribune,* Sunday Magazine, September 25, 1983, 7.

———. "Joe E. Lewis: A Nightclub Funnyman Three Mob Hit Men Couldn't Silence." *Chicago Tribune,* Sunday Magazine, April 22, 1964, 6.

———. "When Ernie Byfield [*sic*] Played Genial Host to Society's Elite." *Chicago Tribune,* Sunday Magazine, November 11, 1984.

"Bright Spots around Town." *Chicago Daily News,* July 10, 1926.

Brotman, Barbara. "Last Dance Is Over for the Melody Mill." *Chicago Tribune,* May 1, 1984, sec. 2, pp. 1, 4.

Brunn, H. O. *Story of the Original Dixieland Jazz Band.* London: Sidgwick and Jackson, 1961.

Burns, Edward. "U.S. Padlocks Colosimo's for Dry Violations." *Chicago Tribune,* February 20, 1926.

"Business from Fair Helps Stevens Hotel Pay Off Back Taxes." *Chicago Tribune,* August 4, 1933.

"The Cabaret." *Variety,* December 30, 1921, 40.

"Cabaret Bills." *Variety,* January 21, 1916, 8; June 9, 1926, 46; August 18, 1926, 38; April 11, 1928, 56; May 23, 1928, 64; May 30, 1928, 56.

"Cabaret Life as It Exists in City Today." *Chicago Herald,* January 23, 1916, 1.

"Cabaret Reviews, Moulin Rouge." *Variety,* February 25, 1925, 34.

"Cabarets." *Variety,* November 5, 1915, 8; November 12, 1915, 7; January 7, 1916, 13; October 20, 1916, 18; November 24, 1916, 16; December 1, 1916, 8; January 5, 1917, 13; April 5, 1918, 10;

"Cabarets, Friar's Inn." *Variety,* September 23, 1921, 8.

Cahan, Richard, and Mark Jacobs. "Fair Ladies." *Chicago,* May 1996, 72–75, 111.

Caine, Dan. "Blue Note Memories." *Chicago Reader,* August 18, 1989, 1, 22–40.

Calloway, Cab, and Bryant Rollins. *Of Minnie the Moocher and Me.* New York: Thomas Y. Crowell, 1976.

Cappo, Joe. "Villa Venice's Years of Glory Die in Flames." *Chicago Daily News,* ca. March 1967.

Carroll, Margaret. "An Eye on Your." *Chicago Tribune,* May 19, 1980, sec. 3, p. 5.

Castle, Irene, and Bob and Wanda Duncan. *Castles in the Air.* Garden City, N.Y.: Doubleday, 1958.

"Century of Progress, 1934, Conditions in Chicago, Ill." Juvenile Protective Association, Chicago, Ill., file 89, Special Collections, University of Illinois at Chicago Library.

Chase, Al. "Army a Model Housekeeper in Chicago Hotels." *Chicago Tribune,* July 16, 1943, sec. H, p. 2.

———. "Famed Uptown Nightspot of 'Dry Era' Sold." *Chicago Tribune,* undated, ca. 1941.

———. "Mike Fritzel Leases Former Chez Pierre Café." *Chicago Tribune,* October 18, 1932.

———. "Plan $150,000 Chinese Café on the Rialto." *Chicago Tribune,* November 1, 1930.

———. "World's Famous Midway Gardens to be Reopened." *Chicago Tribune,* September 4, 1921.

"Cherniavsky Warms Refrigerator Room; 'Bowery Nights' Has Crowd in Uproar." *Down Beat,* February 1935, 1.

"Chicago Band Briefs." *Down Beat,* April 15, 1944; April 1, 1945, 4; November 15, 1945; March 11, 1946, 4.

*Chicago Central Business and Office Building Directory.* Chicago: Winters Publishing Company, 1917.

"Chicago Dance Hall Pays $3,000 for Band." *Variety,* December 1, 1922, 1, 4.

*Chicago Directory, 1923.* Chicago: R. L. Polk, 1923.

"Chicago Leads with Most Radio Stations." *Variety,* August 25, 1926, 52.

"Chicago Orchestra News." *Billboard.* November 7, 1925, 22.

"Chicago's Music Corp. Going after Local Biz." *Variety,* April 29, 1925, 39.

"Chi Eatery Adopts Dance Policy." *Variety,* August 25, 1926, 52.

"Chi Hotel Builds Jungle for Krupa's Wild Rhythm." *Down Beat,* March 1939, 29.

Chilton, John. *Stomp Off, Let's Go: The Story of Bob Crosby's Bob Cats and Big Band.* London: Jazz Book Service, 1983.

Choice, Harriet. "'Music Americana' Homeless." *Chicago Tribune,* February 25, 1972.

Christenberry, Robert. "The Hotel Manager Buys a Band." *Billboard,* November 26, 1939, 20.

Christiansen, Richard. "There's No Business Like Tony's Business." *Chicago Tribune,* June 4, 1995, sec. 13, p. 2.

"Close Marigold Gardens Doors; Bow to Dry Era." *Chicago Tribune,* November 24, 1923.

"Clyde Lucas Booked for Longer Stay at Terrace Garden." *Down Beat,* July 1934, 1.

Cohn, Art. *The Joker Is Wild: The Story of Joe E. Lewis.* New York: Random House, 1956.

"College Inn." *Variety,* February 8, 1928, 55.

"College Inn, Chi." *Variety,* March 31, 1926, 47.

"College Inn Starts Fifth Decade." *Down Beat,* June 1, 1943, 4.

"College Inn to End 38-Year Run July 5; Blames Cabaret Tax." *Chicago Tribune,* June 22, 1948.

Coller, Derek. "Frank Snyder." *Mississippi Rag,* April 1982, 7–8.

———. "More on Jack Pettis." *Mississippi Rag,* April 1993, 24–25.

Collins, Charles. "French Follies Represent Best Shows of Type." *Chicago Tribune,* June 9, 1934.

"Commercialized Prostitution in Morton Grove, Niles, Niles Center and Tessville, Illinois, May 1929." Juvenile Protective Association, Folder 100, Special Collections, Library, University of Illinois at Chicago.

Conn, C. G., Ltd. *Musical Truth* 13, no. 32 (April 1923).

"Coon-Sanders Original Nighthawks Orchestra." *College Radio,* December 1968.

Cressy, Paul. *The Taxi Dance Hall: A Sociological Study in Commercialized Recreation and City Life.* Chicago: University of Chicago Press, 1932.

"The Critics in the Dog House: 'Louis Panico.'" *Down Beat,* March 1938, 11.

Crowder, Henry. Letter to Dave Peyton, *Chicago Defender,* August 20, 1927.

Crowder, Henry, and Hugo Speck. *As Wonderful as All That.* Navarro, Calif.: Wild Tree Press, 1987.

*Current Biography, 1967.* New York: H. W. Wilson, 1967.

Cushman, Aaron. "Chicago's Chez Led the Way for Bands in the Loop Nighteries." *Down Beat,* March 22, 1953, 45.

Cutler, Irving. *Chicago: Metropolis of the Mid-Continent.* 3rd ed. Dubuque, Iowa: Kendall/Hunt, 1982.

Dance, Stanley. *The World of Earl Hines.* New York: Scribner's, 1977.

"Dance Hall Invades No. Side Society." *Chicago Sunday Tribune,* October 30, 1910, sec. 9, p. 3.

"Dancers Bid Farewell to Aragon." *Chicago Daily News,* February 8, 1964, 1, 3.

Dante, Mike. "From Big Time to Happiness." *After Beat,* January 1971, 7, 18, 19. First published in *San Diego Union,* October 23, 1970.

Daunoras, Lynn. "Willowbrook Founder-Owner to Celebrate His 91st Birthday." *Brookfield (Ill.) Enterprise,* January 25, 1967, sec. 2, p. 9.

"David A. Solovy." Obituary. *Chicago Tribune,* September 25, 1985, sec. 2, p. 7.

Dawn, Charlie. "Griff Williams, Raye and Naldi Lead New Empire Room Revue." *Chicago Herald-American,* September 6, 1941.

Death Records. Chicago Federation of Musicians, Local 10-208, AFM. Special Collections, Music Information Center, Chicago Public Library.

Dedmon, Emmett. *Fabulous Chicago.* New York: Random House, 1953.

"The Dells." *Variety,* June 9, 1926, 44.

DeLong, Thomas A. *Pops: Paul Whiteman, King of Jazz.* Piscataway, N.J.: New Century, 1983.

DeMaris, Ovid. *Captive City.* New York: Lyle Stuart, 1969.

DeMichael, Don. *Red Norvo.* Liner notes. Giants of Jazz Series Recording. Alexandria, Va.: Time-Life Records, 1980.

"Desertion of Chicago's 'Loop' Traced to Dance Places." *Variety,* June 9, 1922, 21.

"Did Rhythm Kings Borrow Ideas from Negroes?" *Down Beat,* September 1936, 6–7.

"Don't Know Whether Spitalny In or Out, Scheuing Says 'In.'" *Variety,* February 18, 1931, 69.

Douglas, Susan J. *Listening In: Radio and the Imagination.* New York: Random House, 1999.

Drury, John. *Dining in Chicago.* New York: John Day, 1931.

Duis, Perry. *The Saloon: Public Drinking in Chicago and Boston, 1880–1920.* Urbana: University of Illinois Press, 1983.

"Duration Contract for Williams at Empire Room." *Chicago Herald-American,* December 5, 1942, 11.

Eberly, Philip K. *Music in the Air.* New York: Hastings House, 1982.

Ebisch, Robert. "Whatever Happened to the Green Mill Gardens?" *Chicago Reader,* October 29, 1982, 1–2, 20, 22, 24.

"Edgar A. Benson." Obituary. *New York Times,* June 27, 1946.

Edmiston, Fred W. *The Coon-Sanders Nighthawks.* Jefferson, N.C.: McFarland, 2003.

"Ellington Band for Stevens in Chicago Soon." *Down Beat,* November 1, 1943, 1.

Enstad, Robert. "Sherman House Demolition to Start." *Chicago Tribune,* March 21, 1980, sec. 5, p. 1.

Erenberg, Lewis A. "Ain't We Got Fun." *Chicago History,* Winter 1985–86, 4–21.

"Ernie Young's fla. Revue." *Variety,* March 4, 1925, 45.

Evans, James F. *"Prairie Farmer" and WLS.* Urbana: University of Illinois Press, 1969.

"Fan-Dancing Queen Sally Rand Is Dead." *Chicago Sun-Times,* September 1, 1979, 6.

"Find Night Club Girls Cheating on State Dole." *Chicago Tribune,* May 10, 1940.

Fink, John. *WGN: A Pictorial History.* Chicago: WGN, 1961.

"Fire Destroys the Dells; Arson Is Suspected." *Chicago Tribune,* August 1, 1929.

"Fire Levels Ballroom; Routs 100 Families." *Chicago Tribune,* September 10, 1972, sec. 1, p. 3.

Firestone, Ross. *Swing, Swing, Swing.* New York: Norton, 1993.

Fitzpatrick, Thomas. "Morrison Hotel to Ring Down Curtain on Gaudy Era." *Chicago Tribune,* November 8, 1964.

"Five Years Ago in the Orchestra World—Echoes of the Past." *Orchestra World,* April 1921, 4.

Forbes, Genevieve. "Marigold Room Is Dowager of City's Cabarets." *Chicago Tribune,* July 11, 1922.

"Four from Gary Killed as Train Strikes Auto." *Chicago Tribune,* September 27, 1940.

"The Four Most Valuable Parcels of Land." *Chicago Tribune,* May 18, 1980.

"4,000 People of Chi Greet Ash at Farewell Dinner." *Variety,* May 9, 1928.

"Fran Coughlin, Noted Radio Writer, Dies." *Chicago Tribune,* no date, ca. 1969.

"Friar's." Variety, December 29, 1926, 37.

"Friar's Inn." *Billboard,* November 21, 1925, 22.

"'Friar's Inn Orch' and 'New Orleans Rhythm Kings.'" *Down Beat,* October 1936, 8.

"Frolics (Chicago)." *Variety,* June 2, 1926. 45.

Fuller, Ernest. "Wirtz Acquires Eitel Bismarck Hotel Stock." *Chicago Tribune,* January 10, 1956.

Gapp, Paul. "'80s Amenities Meet '20s Glitz in Hilton." *Chicago Tribune,* April 13, 1986, sec. 13, p. 32.

"Garber Pays $47,000 to Get Out of Contract." *Down Beat,* March 1936, 6.

Gault, Lon A. *Ballroom Echoes.* Glen Ellyn, Ill.: Andrew Corbet Press, 1989.

———. "Dancing and Gayly [*sic*] Romancing to the Music at the Melody Mill." *Dancing U.S.A.,* July–September 1983, 6–7.

Gavin, James M. "1st National Buys Control of Morrison." *Chicago Tribune,* March 28, 1963, sec. F, p. 7.

Ghrist, John Russell. *Valley Voices.* West Dundee, Ill.: JRG Communications, 1992.

"Girl Wounded by Robbers in Crowded Café." *Chicago Tribune,* December 21, 1931.

Gold, Anita. "Check in on a Bit of Chicagoana." *Chicago Tribune,* January 13, 1976, sec. 11, p. 9.

Gonzalez, Veronica. "Owner of Ivanhoe Theater, Restaurant." *Chicago Tribune,* February 12, 2002, sec. 2, p. 9.

"Grabbing a Breath of Air." *Down Beat,* July 15, 1941, 28.

"Granada." *Variety,* June 9, 1926, 46.

"Granada." *Variety,* April 11, 1928, 56.

"Granada Café Destroyed by $100,000 fire." *Chicago Tribune,* January 18, 1934.

"Grand Terrace Café Closed; To Open Again in September." *Chicago Defender,* March 16, 1935, 8.

Greb, Richard. "Edgewater Ends Reign as Queen of Chicago's North Side." *Arizona Republic,* June 7, 1970, sec. K, p. 12.

Greene, Victor R. "Friendly Entertainers: Dance Band Leaders and Singers in the Depression, 1929–1935." *Prospects: An Annual of American Cultural Studies* 20, 181–207.

Gunther, Mark. *The House That Roone Built.* New York: Little Brown, 1994.

"Hal Kemp." *Orchestra World,* August 1934, 8.

Hall, Ben M. *The Best Remaining Seats—The Golden Age of the Movie Palace.* New York: Da Capo, 1975.

Handley, John. "The Next Magnificent Mile(s)." *Chicago Tribune,* June 10, 2001, sec. N, pp. 1, 5.

"Hand's Death Shows Sacrifice." *Chicago Tribune,* October 20, 1916.

Harris, Pat. "Chicago Band Briefs." *Down Beat,* March 25, 1949.

"Harvey Roll Lengthy." *Orchestra World,* April 1931, 15.

Hayner, Don, and Tom McNamee. *The Stadium.* Chicago: Performance Media, 1993.

Heise, Kenan. *Chaos, Creativity, and Culture: A Sampling of Chicago in the Twentieth Century.* Salt Lake City: Gibbs-Smith, 1998.

Hentoff, Nat, and Albert McCarthy, eds. *Jazz.* New York: Grove Press, 1959.

"Here and There." *Variety,* February 17, 1926, 46.

Herman, Woody. "Why I Own Discery: Big Fish, Little Pond." *Down Beat,* April 22, 1953, 19-S.

Herrmann, Andrew. "Blackhawk Goes, but Memories Stay." *Chicago Sun-Times,* July 22, 1984, 4.

Hoefer, George. "How Radio Helped to Build Big Bands." *Down Beat,* April 20, 1955, 14–15, 52, 53.

Holbrook, Dick. "Mister Jazz Himself." Parts 1 and 2. *Storyville,* April–May 1976: 135–51; February–March 1977: 95–109.

"Hotel Mgrs. Adopt 'There'll Be Some Changes Made' as Theme Song." *Down Beat,* August 1936.

House That Jack Built, documents 510755 ML, 5478100 et al., Cook County Recorder's Office, Chicago, Ill.

"Hundreds Pay Final Tributes to Johnny Hand." *Chicago Tribune,* October 22, 1916.

Ibata, David. "Renovated Hilton: Eye on History." *Chicago Tribune,* November 4, 1985, sec. 4, p. 3.

"Ike Bloom's Deauville Popular in Chicago." *Variety,* February 25, 1925, 34.

"Isham Jones." *Variety,* March 18, 1925, 45.

Jackman, Arthur. "Old Memories to Fall with the Trianon." *Chicago Tribune,* January 2, 1927, sec. 2B, p. 12.

"James DeLisa; Owned Nightclub." Obituary. *Chicago Sun-Times,* June 17, 1985.

"Jimmy Blade Rites Planned; Musician." Obituary. *Chicago Tribune,* August 21, 1974.

"Joe Kayser and His Boys a Tremendous Success." *Merry Garden News,* November 1928, 1.

Johnson, Curt. *Wicked City: Chicago from Kenna to Capone.* Highland Park, Ill.: December Press, 1994.

Johnson, Dennis A. "Those Happy-Go-Lucky Sounds of Coon-Sanders Nighthawks." *Mississippi Rag,* January 1974, 9.

Jones, Max, and John Chilton. *The Louis Armstrong Story.* Boston: Little-Brown, 1991.

Kart, Larry. "Singer Polly Podewell—a Jewel for $3." *Chicago Tribune,* March 23, 1980, sec. 6, p. 24.

"Karzas Fired Band That Couldn't Play Waltzes; His Death Mourned." *Down Beat,* June 15, 1940.

"Kassel in Bismarck." *Orchestra World,* April 1931, 19.

Katz, Joel B. "Return Engagement for Stage Shows." *Chicago Scene,* March 29, 1962, 13–15.

Kayser, Joe. "Birth of the One-Nighter." *Billboard,* November 26, 1938, 18–19.

Kenney, William Howland. *Chicago Jazz: A Cultural History, 1904–1930.* New York: Oxford University Press, 1993.

Kettering, Ralph T. "Last Call for Landmarks." Letter to the editor. *Chicago Tribune,* December 27, 1945.

"Key Band Spots." *Down Beat,* March 15, 1944, 14.

"King to End 9-Year Reign at Aragon; Knapp Follows." *Down Beat,* August 1935.

Kinkle, Roger D. *The Complete Encyclopedia of Popular Music and Jazz 1900–1950.* 4 vols. New Rochelle, N.Y.: Arlington House, 1974.

Kinsley, Philip. "Stevens Paints Rosy Business Vision for Jury." *Chicago Tribune,* October 13, 1933.

Klatzko, Bernard. "Johnny Dodds, Clarinet in Blue." *78 Quarterly* (no. 10): 77–99.

"Knapp and His 'Band of Tomorrow' in Denver." *Down Beat,* November 1935.

"Knapp Crashes to Death in Own Plane." *Down Beat,* August 1936, 1.

Kobler, John. *The Life and World of Al Capone.* New York: Putnam, 1971.

Kogan, Herman. "Dreamland Fades but Memories of Dance Hall Linger On." *Chicago Sun-Times,* December 9, 1951, sec. 2, p. 2.

Kramer, Karl. "Jelly Roll in Chicago (1927)," Part 1. *Second Line,* January–February 1961, 1, 3, 5, 6.

———. "Jelly Roll in Chicago (1927)," Part 2. *Second Line,* March–April 1961, 19–22.

———. Unpublished history of the Music Corporation of America. John Steiner Collection, Chicago Jazz Archive, University of Chicago.

Kruty, Paul. *Frank Lloyd Wright and Midway Gardens.* Urbana: University of Illinois Press, 1998.

———. "Pleasure Garden on the Midway." *Chicago History,* Fall–Winter 1987–88, 10–24.

"Kyser Signs Contract for Lucky Strike Program." *Down Beat,* February 1938, 2.

Lait, Jack. "Chicago by Night." *Variety,* October 6, 1926, 32.

———. "The Night Life of the World, Chicago." Part 7. *Variety,* October 7, 1925, 5, 60.

Lait, Jack, and Lee Mortimer. *Chicago Confidential.* New York: Crown, 1950.

Langer, Adam. "Edgewater Beach Memories." *Chicago Reader,* November 10, 1989, sec. 1, pp. 1, 14, 16, 18, 20, 22, 24, 26, 28, 30, 32–34.

"Last Waltz at Aragon." *Business Week,* February 15, 1964, 30–31.

"Leader 50% of Band, Says Op." *Down Beat,* May 19, 1950.

Leiter, Robert D. *The Musicians and Petrillo.* New York: Bookman Associates, 1953.

Leonard, Neil. *Jazz and the White Americans.* Chicago: University of Chicago Press, 1962.

Leonard, Will. "After 20 Years, Boulevard Room Ice Revues End." *Chicago Tribune,* December 1, 1968, sec. 5, p. 18.

———. "The Death of a Loop Hotel." *Chicago Tribune,* January 21, 1973, sec. 6, pp. 1, 3.

———. "The Drummer Was a Real Snake." *Chicago Tribune,* March 9, 1975, sec. 6, p. 12.

———. "Final Act at Empire Room." *Chicago Tribune,* January 20, 1976, sec. 3, p. 4.

———. "Fritz Retires—and an Era Ends." *Chicago Tribune,* February 1, 1970, Arts and Entertainment, 1–2.

———. "The Jazz and the Glory." *Chicago Tribune,* Sunday Magazine, December 15, 1974, pp. 42, 44, 47, 49.

———. "King-Sized Memories of Mangam's Glory Years." *Chicago Tribune,* March 21, 1978, sec. 6, p. 18.

———. "Lombardo Brings Back the Old Days." *Chicago Tribune,* April 11, 1975.

———. "New College Inn Opens in the Sherman Tuesday." *Chicago Tribune,* September 3, 1967, sec. 5, p. 7.

———. "Too Much Pomp at Pump Room." *Chicago Tribune,* May 4, 1951, sec. 3, p. 7.

———. "Tower Ticker." *Chicago Tribune,* May 4, 1951, sec. 3, p. 7; September 25, 1951, 21; October 3, 1951.

Lesner, Sam. "Requiem for the Empire Room." *Chicago Daily News,* December 13–14, 1975, Panorama section, p. 5.

Lewin, Edward Paul. "Music Is First at 1934 Century of Progress." *Down Beat,* July 1934, 1, 5.

"License Denied for Reopening of Colosimo's." *Chicago Tribune,* September 15, 1952, 4.

Lindsay, Richard. *Chicago Ragtime.* South Bend, Ind.: Icarus Press, 1985.

"Lishon Has Smart Band at Club Royal." *Down Beat,* February 1935.

"Local Group Buys Drake Hotel." *Chicago Tribune,* June 16, 1979, sec. 2, p. 6.

Lomax, Alan. *Mr. Jelly Lord.* 3rd ed. Berkeley: University of California Press, 1971.

Lombardo, Guy, and Jack Altschul. *Auld Acquaintance.* Garden City, N.Y.: Doubleday, 1975.

"Lombardo's $150,000 Dates." *Variety,* January 21, 1931, 67.

"Long Hours but Kicks A-Plenty at Friar's Inn." *Down Beat,* April 8, 1946, 4.

Longstreet, Stephen. *Chicago.* New York: David McKay, 1973.

Lord, Ann. "Around Chicago with Ann Lord." *Orchestra World,* April 1931, 6.

Lyden, Jacki, and Chet Jakus. *Landmarks and Legends of Uptown.* Chicago: by the authors, 1975.

"Lymon in Chicago." *Variety,* February 18, 1925, 36.

"Marigold Ends Career as Café; Turns to Dance." *Chicago Tribune,* December 10, 1923.

"The Marigold Follies." *Variety,* December 15, 1916, 18.

Mastro, Frank. "57 TV Stations to Carry Bouts from Marigold." *Chicago Tribune,* May 2, 1954.

"MCA Guarantees $50,000 a Year to Columbia." *Down Beat,* undated, 1941.

"MCA Notes." *Billboard,* November 14, 1925, 22.

"MCA's N.Y. Offices and Music College." *Variety,* June 30, 1926, 41.

"MCA's Office in NYC." *Variety,* November 24, 1926, 52.

McCarthy, Albert. *The Dance Band Era.* Radnor, Pa.: Chilton, 1971.

McDougal, Dennis. *The Last Mogul.* New York: Crown, 1998.

"McVickers Theater." *Variety,* August 18, 1926, 44.

Melcher, A. H. "At the World's Fair." *Orchestra World,* August 1934, 12.

Mezzrow, Milton "Mezz," and Bernard Wolfe. *Really the Blues.* New York: Random House, 1946.

"Mike Fritzel, 75, Nightclub Owner, Dies." *Chicago Tribune,* September 29, 1956.

Miller, Paul Eduard, ed. *Esquire's 1946 Jazz Book.* New York: A. S. Barnes, 1946.

Mills, E. C. "Leaders and Publishers." *Variety,* October 1, 1924, 28.

Moldea, Dan. *Dark Victory.* New York: Viking Penguin, 1986.

Montgomery, Mike. "'New' Jelly Roll Morton Piano Roll Turns Up after Seventy-five Years." *Mississippi Rag,* September 1999, 14–15.

*Morton Grove, 1895–1995.* Morton Grove, Ill.: Morton Grove Centennial Commission, 1995.

"The Most Popular Attractions." *Variety,* January 5, 1917, 13.

Murray, B. J. "Dance Hall versus Ballroom." *Orchestra World,* April 1931, 20.

Murray, George. *The Legacy of Al Capone.* New York: Putnam's, 1975.

"Musical Musings." *Billboard,* November 8, 1924, 37.

"Musicians Balk on Strike." *Chicago Defender,* September 11, 1926.

"Mystery Girl." *Chicago Herald,* January 24, 1916, 1.

Nagelberg, Alvin. "Brundage Sells 96% Holding in LaSalle Hotel for $10 Million." *Chicago Tribune,* November 6, 1970.

Naylor, David. *American Picture Palaces: The Architecture of Fantasy.* New York: Van Nostrand Reinhold, 1981.

"New Bands 'Take Off' in the Windy City." *Down Beat,* April 1937.

"News about Town." *Tom Brown Topics,* December 1927, 1.

"New Silver Forest Room Has 'It.'" *Down Beat,* June 1936.

"1939, the Year for Live Talent" (advertisement). *Billboard,* December 3, 1938.

"No Incendiary Clues in Granada Café Fire." *Chicago Tribune,* January 20, 1934.

"No Jam in Chicago without O.K. Sez Petrillo." *Down Beat,* May 1938, 24.

Nome, Robert. "The Race and Music." *Chicago Defender,* January 29, 1916, reprinted from *Musical Courier,* n.d., n.p.

Nye, Russell B. "Saturday Night at the Paradise Ballroom, or Dance Halls in the Twenties." *Journal of Pop Culture* 7 (Summer 1973): 14–16, 19.

"Old Arcadia Hall Leased by Elevated Lines." *Chicago Tribune,* August 1, 1933.

"Old Rainbo Garden Will Get New Look." *Chicago Tribune,* September 29, 1957.

"$1-a-Shot Gin Sale Profits Told by Potson." *Chicago Tribune,* April 7, 1948.

"$120–$150 Weekly 2-Year Scale Tops N.Y. Pay." *Variety,* April 8, 1931, 67.

"$1,000,000 Dance Hall Takes Dancing out of Fad Class." *Variety,* December 15, 1922, 9.

"Orchestras Will Play over Ballroom Circuit by March." *Billboard,* November 22, 1924, 20.

"Patricola." *Variety,* January 12, 1917, 7.

"Paul Ash at McVickers, Playing on Stage and Pit." *Variety,* May 6, 1925, 50.

"Paul Ash Back to Bid Good-By to Old Friends." *Chicago Tribune,* January 23, 1930.

"The Paul Ash Record." *Variety,* May 9, 1928.

"Paul Ash, 67, Theater Band Pioneer, Dies." *Chicago Tribune,* July 14, 1958.

"Paul Ash's Record." *Chicago Tribune,* March 25, 1934.

"Paul Ash to Do His Stuff for WGN Fans." *Chicago Tribune,* May 9, 1928.

"Paul Biese, 38, Dies Suddenly after Operation." *Chicago Tribune,* October 28, 1925.

"The Pershing Palace." *Variety,* April 22, 1925, 38.

Petrillo, James C. "Dance Biz Needs New Blood." *Down Beat,* April 22, 1953, 3.

Peyton, David. "The Musical Bunch." *Chicago Defender,* March 1, 1924; December 4, 1926; May 7, 1927; May 14, 1927; January 21, 1928; September 22, 1928; May 4, 1929.

Pollack, Ben. "Ten Years of Good Bands and Bad Breaks." *Down Beat,* October 1936, 2.

"Quigley-Benson Tieup." *Variety,* January 25, 1925, 33.

"Rainbo Clicks with a Swing-Name Ork Policy." *Down Beat,* March 25, 1946.

"Rainbo Closed; 11 More Cafés Face Padlocks." *Chicago Tribune,* May 4, 1928.

"Rainbo Garden Sold, Will Be Reopened." *Chicago Tribune,* November 21, 1928.

Ramsey, Frederic, Jr., and Charles Edward Smith, eds. *Jazzmen.* New York: Harcourt Brace, 1939.

"Records." *Down Beat,* June 29, 1955, 20.

"Red Saunders Garrick's Star." *Down Beat,* April 8, 1946, 12.

Reich, Howard. "Grand Hotel." *Chicago Tribune,* July 3, 1994, sec. 13, p. 13.

"Rendezvous." *Variety,* March 4, 1925, 45.

*Riverview News,* 1919–21. Chicago Historical Society.

"Roadhouse Survey of Cook County, Illinois, July–August 1929." Juvenile Protective Association, folder 106, Special Collections, Library, University of Illinois at Chicago.

Rode, Glenn G. "The Concert Band in Chicago from 1893 to 1985." Master's thesis, Northeastern Illinois University, 1985.

Rose, Frank. *The Agency.* New York: HarperCollins, 1995.

"Routes Department." *Billboard,* November 8, 1924, 70.

Rust, Brian A. L. *The American Dance Band Discography, 1917–1942.* 2 vols. New Rochelle, N.Y.: Arlington House, 1975.

———. *Jazz Records, 1897–1942.* 2 vols. Middlesex, Eng., 1961.

"Sally Rand Dies at 75; Leaves Many Fans Behind." *Chicago Tribune,* September 1, 1979.

Sann, Paul. *The Lawless Decade.* New York: Crown, 1957.

Sawyers, June. "The Night Chicago Suffered Its Worst Hotel Disaster." *Chicago Tribune,* Sunday Magazine, May 31, 1987, p. 7.

———. "Whooping It Up, for a Price, with 'Texas' Guinan." *Chicago Tribune,* Sunday Magazine, January 29, 1989, 7.

Schaden, Chuck. *WBBM Radio—Yesterday and Today.* Chicago: WBBM News Radio, 1988.

Schulz, Barbara C. and Charles. "Carving a Community from the Prairie." *Northbrook: The Fabric of Our History.* Northbrook, Ill.: Northbrook Historical Society, 2001.

Schumach, Murray. "Hollywood's Music Mogul." *New York Times,* July 21, 1963, sec. X, p. 5.

Scott, Anika M. "Pride of Wheeling Gets New Life." *Chicago Tribune,* November 25, 1998, sec. 2, p. 7.

Secon, Paul. "Remotes Good Programming? Original Plugs 'Intrigue' Nets." *Billboard,* December 22, 1945, 13, 20, 22.

"Second Rhythm Concert Delights Local 'Cats' and '400.'" *Down Beat,* April 1936, 1.

Sengstock, Charles A., Jr. *Jazz Music in Chicago's Early South-Side Theaters.* Northbrook, Ill.: Canterbury Press of Northbrook, 2000.

Shapiro, Nat, and Nat Hentoff, eds. *Hear Me Talkin' to Ya.* New York: Rinehart, 1955.

Shaughnessy, Mary Alice. *Les Paul.* New York: Morrow, 1993.

Simon, George T. *The Big Bands.* New York: Macmillan, 1967.

Sippel, Johnny. "Music Affected by New Tax Measure." *Down Beat,* May 1, 1944, 1, 3.

"16,000 Beer Flats in Chicago Grab Customers from Cafés." *Variety,* May 9, 1928, 1, 37.

Starr, Louis M. "45 Years of Night Life and Mike Fritzel Still Has a Yen to Be a Farmer." *Chicago Tribune,* June 8, 1947.

Stearns, M. W. "The History of Swing—Friar's Inn Orchestra and New Orleans Rhythm Kings." *Down Beat,* October 1936, 8.

"Stuff Smith's Band Suffers $4,000 Loss." *Down Beat,* January 15, 1940, 1, 5.

Sudhalter, Richard M. *Lost Chords: White Musicians and Their Contribution to Jazz, 1915–1945.* New York: Oxford University Press, 1999.

Sudhalter, Richard M., and Philip R. Evans. *Bix: Man and Legend.* New Rochelle, N.Y.: Arlington House, 1974.

"Swing Fans Flock to Hear Frank Snyder." *Down Beat,* August 1936, 7.

"Swing Music Will Continue at the Congress Hotel—Ellington Booked." *Down Beat,* May 1936.

"Taylor Lands Chi Place." *Variety,* April 8, 1925, 43.

"Taylor Tried; Benson Got In." *Variety,* April 22, 1925, 37.

"10% of Everything." *Time,* March 17, 1958, 97–99.

"'That's the Man. There's Where I Saw Him!' Muggsy Spanier Breaks 27-Year Silence on Factor Kidnap." *Chicago's American,* February 16, 1960.

"They Play Good Ol' 2-Beat Jazz." *Down Beat,* June 1936.

"30% Law Modified." *Orchestra World,* August 1934, 3.

Thompson, John. "Potson Parole Recalls Reign at Colosimo's." *Chicago Tribune,* October 17, 1950.

Todd, Arthur J., William F. Byron, and Howard L. Viernow. *Chicago Recreation Survey, 1937.* Chicago: Chicago Recreation Committee and Northwestern University, 1937.

"Town Club." *Variety,* August 25, 1926, 54.

Tracy, Jack. "Chicago Musicians, Ops Resent Five-Day Week." Chicago Band Briefs. *Down Beat,* February 9, 1951.

———. "Ops Stunned by Local 10 Five-Day Week Order." Chicago Band Briefs. *Down Beat,* January 12, 1951.

Travis, Dempsey. *An Autobiography of Black Jazz.* Chicago: Urban Research Institute, 1983.

"12 Cafés Face U.S. Padlocks; Owners Term Tactics of Dry Raiders Unfair." *Chicago Tribune,* February 6, 1928, 1.

"23 Years—1934–1957: A Roundup." *Down Beat,* June 27, 1957, 13–14, 36.

"250 Café Artists—200 Musicians Losing Jobs by Chi's Padlocking." *Variety,* May 16, 1928.

U.S. Bureau of the Census. *Fourteenth Census (1920) of the United States.* Illinois, Cook County, Enumeration District 1476, sheet 9, line 59.

U.S. Department of Commerce. *Historical Statistics of the United States, Colonial Times to 1970.* Part 2. Washington: U.S. Department of Commerce, Bureau of the Census, 1975.

"U.S. Puts Lock on Rendezvous, Jeffery Tavern." *Chicago Tribune,* March 14, 1928.

Van Vorst, Paige. "The Chicago Bosses." *Mississippi Rag,* November 1998, 40.

"Veloz and Yolanda Annex 'Spike' Hamilton Ork." *Down Beat,* May 1936, 10.

"Veloz and Yolanda Use Shep fields Orchestra." *Down Beat,* June 1935.

Walker, Leo. *Great Dance Bands.* Berkeley, Calif.: Howell-North Books, 1964.

Wendt, Lloyd, and Herman Kogan. *Lords of the Levee.* New York: Bobbs-Merrill, 1943.

"Where the Bands Are Playing." *Down Beat,* December 15, 1939, 31; November 15, 1942, 22.

Whyatt, Bert. *Lonesome Road.* New Orleans: Jazzology Press, 1995.

Wiedrich, Robert. "Colorful Arena Once Site of Beer Garden." *Chicago Tribune,* April 26, 1964.

Williams, Martin. *King Oliver.* New York: A. S. Barnes, 1961.

Wittels, David G. "Star-Spangled Octopus." Part 1. *Saturday Evening Post,* August 10, 1946, 9–11, 44, 47, 49.

Wolters, Larry. "Radio Station News." *Chicago Tribune,* November 6, 1938.

"Wong: Restaurateur Wanted Mall along Argyle." *Chicago Tribune,* July 6, 2001, 1, 7.

Wood, Morrison. "A Half Century of the Culinary Arts in Chicago." *Chicago History,* Spring 1972, 22–23.

"Year's Padlock Is Put on Door of Club Ansonia." *Chicago Tribune,* May 25, 1928.

# Index

CHARLES A. SENGSTOCK JR. is a longtime researcher and writer on jazz, blues, and Chicago dance bands and music. After an early career in radio and television broadcasting, during which time he worked at WGN-Radio and Television in Chicago, he spent the next four decades in the public relations field. He was with Motorola, Inc., for nearly three decades, where his last position was Director of Corporate Public Relations, North America.

## Music in American Life

Traveling the High Way Home: Ralph Stanley and the World of Traditional
Bluegrass Music   *John Wright*

Carl Ruggles: Composer, Painter, and Storyteller   *Marilyn Ziffrin*

Never without a Song: The Years and Songs of Jennie Devlin, 1865–1952
*Katharine D. Newman*

The Hank Snow Story   *Hank Snow, with Jack Ownbey and Bob Burris*

Milton Brown and the Founding of Western Swing   *Cary Ginell, with special
assistance from Roy Lee Brown*

Santiago de Murcia's "Códice Saldívar No. 4": A Treasury of Secular Guitar Music
from Baroque Mexico   *Craig H. Russell*

The Sound of the Dove: Singing in Appalachian Primitive Baptist Churches
*Beverly Bush Patterson*

Heartland Excursions: Ethnomusicological Reflections on Schools of Music
*Bruno Nettl*

Doowop: The Chicago Scene   *Robert Pruter*

Blue Rhythms: Six Lives in Rhythm and Blues   *Chip Deffaa*

Shoshone Ghost Dance Religion: Poetry Songs and Great Basin Context
*Judith Vander*

Go Cat Go! Rockabilly Music and Its Makers   *Craig Morrison*

'Twas Only an Irishman's Dream: The Image of Ireland and the Irish in American
Popular Song Lyrics, 1800–1920   *William H. A. Williams*

Democracy at the Opera: Music, Theater, and Culture in New York City, 1815–60
*Karen Ahlquist*

Fred Waring and the Pennsylvanians   *Virginia Waring*

Woody, Cisco, and Me: Seamen Three in the Merchant Marine   *Jim Longhi*

Behind the Burnt Cork Mask: Early Blackface Minstrelsy and Antebellum
American Popular Culture   *William J. Mahar*

Going to Cincinnati: A History of the Blues in the Queen City   *Steven C. Tracy*

Pistol Packin' Mama: Aunt Molly Jackson and the Politics of Folksong
*Shelly Romalis*

Sixties Rock: Garage, Psychedelic, and Other Satisfactions   *Michael Hicks*

The Late Great Johnny Ace and the Transition from R&B to Rock 'n' Roll
*James M. Salem*

Tito Puente and the Making of Latin Music   *Steven Loza*

Juilliard: A History   *Andrea Olmstead*

Understanding Charles Seeger, Pioneer in American Musicology   *Edited by
Bell Yung and Helen Rees*

Mountains of Music: West Virginia Traditional Music from* Goldenseal   *Edited by
John Lilly*

Alice Tully: An Intimate Portrait   *Albert Fuller*

A Blues Life   *Henry Townsend, as told to Bill Greensmith*

Long Steel Rail: The Railroad in American Folksong (2d ed.)   *Norm Cohen*

The Golden Age of Gospel   *Text by Horace Clarence Boyer; photography by
Lloyd Yearwood*

Aaron Copland: The Life and Work of an Uncommon Man   *Howard Pollack*

Louis Moreau Gottschalk   *S. Frederick Starr*

Race, Rock, and Elvis   *Michael T. Bertrand*
Theremin: Ether Music and Espionage   *Albert Glinsky*
Poetry and Violence: The Ballad Tradition of Mexico's Costa Chica
    *John H. McDowell*
The Bill Monroe Reader   *Edited by Tom Ewing*
Music in Lubavitcher Life   *Ellen Koskoff*
Zarzuela: Spanish Operetta, American Stage   *Janet L. Sturman*
Bluegrass Odyssey: A Documentary in Pictures and Words, 1966–86
    *Carl Fleischhauer and Neil V. Rosenberg*
That Old-Time Rock & Roll: A Chronicle of an Era, 1954–63   *Richard Aquila*
Labor's Troubadour   *Joe Glazer*
American Opera   *Elise K. Kirk*
Don't Get above Your Raisin': Country Music and the Southern
    Working Class   *Bill C. Malone*
John Alden Carpenter: A Chicago Composer   *Howard Pollack*
Heartbeat of the People: Music and Dance of the Northern Pow-wow
    *Tara Browner*
My Lord, What a Morning: An Autobiography   *Marian Anderson*
Marian Anderson: A Singer's Journey   *Allan Keiler*
Charles Ives Remembered: An Oral History   *Vivian Perlis*
Henry Cowell, Bohemian   *Michael Hicks*
Rap Music and Street Consciousness   *Cheryl L. Keyes*
Louis Prima   *Garry Boulard*
Marian McPartland's Jazz World: All in Good Time   *Marian McPartland*
Robert Johnson: Lost and Found   *Barry Lee Pearson and Bill McCulloch*
Bound for America: Three British Composers   *Nicholas Temperley*
Lost Sounds: Blacks and the Birth of the Recording Industry, 1890–1919
    *Tim Brooks*
Burn, Baby! BURN! The Autobiography of Magnificent Montague
    *Magnificent Montague with Bob Baker*
Way Up North in Dixie: A Black Family's Claim to the Confederate Anthem
    *Howard L. Sacks and Judith Rose Sacks*
The Bluegrass Reader   *Edited by Thomas Goldsmith*
Colin McPhee: Composer in Two Worlds   *Carol J. Oja*
Robert Johnson, Mythmaking, and Contemporary American Culture
    *Patricia R. Schroeder*
Composing a World: Lou Harrison, Musical Wayfarer *Leta E. Miller and
    Fredric Lieberman*
Fritz Reiner, Maestro and Martinet   *Kenneth Morgan*
That Toddlin' Town: Chicago's White Dance Bands and Orchestras, 1900–1950
    Charles A. Sengstock Jr.

The University of Illinois Press
is a founding member of the
Association of American University Presses.

---

Composed in 10/13 New Caledonia
with Helvetica Neue display
by Jim Proefrock
at the University of Illinois Press
Designed by Paula Newcomb
Manufactured by Thomson-Shore, Inc.

University of Illinois Press
1325 South Oak Street
Champaign, IL 61820–6903
www.press.uillinois.edu